A Penchant for Prejudice

Dearest Glenn,
You have been a
wonder... It has
been a pleasure
getting to
know you.
Best to you always

A Penchant for Prejudice

Unraveling Bias in Judicial Decision Making

LINDA G. MILLS

Ann Arbor

THE UNIVERSITY OF MICHIGAN PRESS

2002   2001   2000   1999   4   3   2   1

A CIP catalog record for this book is available from the British Library.

Library of Congress Cataloging-in-Publication Data

Mills, Linda G.
    A penchant for prejudice : unraveling bias in judicial decision
making / Linda G. Mills.
        p.   cm.
    Includes bibliographical references and index.
    ISBN 0-472-10950-2 (acid-free paper)
    1. Social security—Law and legislation—United States.   2.
Disability evaluation—Law and legislation—United States.   3.
Social security courts—United States.   4. Judicial review of
administrative acts—United States.   5. Judicial discretion—United
States.   6. United States. Social Security Administration—Trials,
litigation, etc.   I. Title.
KF3650.5 .M55   1999
344.73'023—dc21   99-6024
                                                                CIP

Corde creditur ad iustitiam
she who believes in the heart will do justice

For Peter

Contents

Preface

From as far back as I can remember, I could feel people's pain. When my grandfather spoke of his escape from Nazi Germany, I didn't feel the excitement but the sadness. When my mother described how relieved she was, at 14, to arrive safely in London, I felt her loss beyond words. And when Granny Mills celebrated the life of her husband, I felt the devastation of his death that eventually destroyed her. I hid this pain in my tummy. Needless to say, my childhood was riddled with stomachache.

The first year I represented claimants at Social Security disability hearings, I was always sick. The same pain that plagued my childhood overshadowed my advocacy effort. Even when I won, my stomach ached. I was ashamed when Diana Sampson[*] revealed a childhood history of sexual abuse to a judge who objected to the time it took to tell her story. I couldn't help but feel Versie Hawkins's humiliation when she tried to explain why she felt suicidal when she received a denial letter from Social Security. And I was hurt when Dave Smith's intolerance for his own impotence was met with a judge's impatience. But most of all, I felt the pain of the two worlds colliding—judge and claimant—and the difficulty posed to me as go-between. I suppose that I have written this book to purge myself of these feelings and to place the pain where it belongs.

My contact or connection with clients was much deeper than might be expected of even a public-interest attorney. I started a community agency in a small, predominantly African-American city, Richmond, California, in Versie Hawkins's name. Mrs. Hawkins's reputation and support guaranteed my legitimacy and the Hawkins Center's success—people in Rich-

---

[*]All client names have been changed to protect their identities, except Versie Hawkins.

mond wanted and needed a place to be heard and were desperate for the legal assistance most white lawyers refused to give them.

I swore confidentiality when I spoke with clients about their experience with judges they only whispered were racist but believed deep down resented them, humiliated them, denied claims because those who brought them were other than white. I promised these clients that if they told me how they felt, if they told me what they thought, I would not tell. They were scared of losing their appeals or the benefits they had fought so hard to win. The point of this book is to do those conversations justice.

I got to know the judges both professionally and personally. I attended hearings with them—I knew their idiosyncracies, their likes and dislikes. I met their every whim. Short of breaking the law, I would do almost anything to win my clients' cases.

My most direct—and in some respects most revealing—experience with judges, though, was when I was invited in 1993 to design and participate in diversity training for administrative law judges (ALJs), an opportunity that followed on the heels of allegations from the General Accounting Office that Social Security's judges might be biased. The judges' feelings about certain applicants, impressions of certain neighborhoods and stereotypes about certain groups—most of which the ALJs never realized were biases—was the impetus for this book. However, the judges' particular secrets remain unrevealed.

So many people have influenced me and this work over a period of years. In the early stages of this project, I had the input and support of my cohort of Pew Fellows at the Heller School at Brandeis University, including Rochelle Rollins, Gwyn Barley, Jean McGuire, Stephen Wright, and Brian Gibbs. A very special thanks to Gwyn, Jean, and Rochelle for their love during my ordeal. Barbara Herbert, an honorary member of the Pew clan, was also a critical presence.

Thanks to Deborah Stone who helped inspire the project, and who cared deeply about the enterprise. Deborah was very instrumental in helping me get the National Science Foundation Dissertation Award that made this research possible. Martha Minow was central to the undertaking. She knew the meaning of *corde creditur ad iustitiam,* and she took the time to help me explore its contours. Shulamit Reinharz was an angel, her astute insight helped refine my critical analysis. Rosemary French and Marie Contreras of the Benchmark Institute worked with me on the Justice and Diversity Training. The precious time we spent together helped shape my views on judicial bias and on the training of judges.

Craig Snyder read and edited every page and got me through a hundred major tremors and aftershocks. Finding the watch serves as a metaphor for what went right. I also thank Rio and Shadow for their part in helping me sleep through the ordeal.

Friends who never directly touched the manuscript but who have influenced me in unquantifiable ways include Tatiana Flessas, Susan Greenwald, Sandy Horwich, Michael Fullerton, and Chris af Jochnick. Marty Schiffenbauer worked many late hours on the manuscript and contributed to its original form. Kelly Dunn was always there when I needed him. Dolly Saengswang, Christina Turcic, and Ed Cohen made taking off time from echoing green foundation possible.

Colleagues who have been supportive in multiple ways include David Caudill, Marianne Constable, Colleen Friend, Carole Goldberg, Laura Gomez, Joel Handler, Zeke Hasenfeld, Stuart Kirk, Harry Kitano, Duncan Lindsey, Jim Lubben, Dana McPhall, James Rubin, and Stan Wallack. Cindy Kamen was also invaluable when she did the herculian task of identifying relevant cases. I reserve in my heart a very special place for Karyl Kinsey, who understood what I was trying to do.

UCLA social work and law students and staff have also been wonderful. Phuong Hoang, Emily Maxwell, and Kimberly Yang are directly responsible for the details involved in putting this book together. Tamara Nestle checked and double-checked cites—she is nothing short of a saint. In addition, the UCLA Law Library staff has been invaluable in responding to my numerous requests. The National Organization of Social Security Claimants' Representatives is also deserving of appreciation. They provided both answers to my questions and advocacy to the claimants with whom this book is concerned.

My parents, who soothed my aching stomach, inspired and loved me. Their generosity modeled the spirit of giving for which I hope this book is remembered. I also thank Adele, Marissa, Paul, Sheri, Jim, Cara, Rita, Jack, Lee, and Stan for their tolerance and support and for putting up with my mishigas.

Chuck Myers at the University of Michigan Press was the kind of editor an author searches a lifetime to find. He was gentle and reassuring, committed and persistent. He understood me, and he was a friend.

Linda Durston's lessons in academic writing went beyond words, surpassing what employment, friendship, or love could expect. She made starting and finishing possible, and she was willing to do anything. I am indebted to her for life.

Ironically, while Peter Goodrich was, in some ways, least involved in the day-to-day nightmare of writing this book, he was most influential in its overall form and content. His presence in my life fuels my imagination and nurtures my perfectionism. While I cannot pinpoint exactly what effect he has had on the book, I can say that he is at the center of it, as he is with everything. Ronnie Goodrich naps while I write this preface. Sleeping or awake, he is the heart beating, he is the justice.

The work, most of all, is a gift to the claimants' whose cases I reviewed and to the countless conversations I have had with clients whom I represented. Versie Hawkins's experience with the Social Security Administration was the most poignant, and I thank her for her courage to share it with me.

Bias is not only particular to judges. My thanks to the judges who became friends in hopes that we can remain friends. The book is not personal—my thoughts of you as wonderful and kind beings remain unaltered by my findings and impressions of the hearing and decision-making practices of ALJs.

Finally, I blame no one but myself for the errors in this book or the attacks I am sure to take on its behalf.

Linda G. Mills
New York, New York

Introduction: A Penchant for Prejudice

My endeavor to understand judges began in 1984, when I presented my first case, a Social Security disability claim, heard by an administrative law judge (ALJ) at the Office of Hearings and Appeals (OHA). I remember wondering if he would be critical or pleasant, if he would care whether I wore pants or a skirt, or if he would know how inexperienced I was.

This judge was typical of the judges before whom I appeared over the course of the next 10 years: he was white, middle class, and at times bristly and impatient. His face was strong and deliberate, and he was opinionated. He was intimidating. Depending on his mood or the case I presented, he was pleasant or disagreeable. On one occasion, while using the OHA copy machine, he forgot to collect his copies. I became privy to a selection from an erotic novel he was writing. From that day forth, I assumed he preferred skirts.

Thus began my obsession with judges. What lies underneath the robes? What is the face behind the mask of a legal persona? Who are they really?

What is unique about practicing Social Security disability law is that you repeatedly appear before the same judges. You get to know them. You attend lunches with them and even occasionally meetings. You know the issues they tolerate, the claims they reject. You learn to know just how much you can get away with and what you cannot sneak past them. You become a master strategist, building a case based on whether the judge before whom you are scheduled to appear believes that depression is disabling or if he rejects, for example, all claims that suggest that childhood sexual abuse causes disabling illness in adulthood.

So when I began to design a study to examine Social Security judicial decision-making practices, I began with a history, a biography. I began with an advantage.

The two Social Security disability programs, Disability Insurance (DI) and Supplemental Security Income (SSI), are basic staples of the American welfare state. These two programs benefit applicants who prove they are physically or mentally unable to work for medical reasons that can be expected to last a year or result in death (42 U.S.C. § 423 (d); 42 U.S.C. § 1382 (c)(3)(B)). DI replaces income and covers medical costs for workers who become disabled after contributing substantially to Social Security. SSI provides cash assistance and, in most states, medical coverage to Americans who become disabled regardless of their work history (U.S. House 1994).

These two programs are what people rely on if they become too sick to work. Both rich and poor need and use these safety nets. Social Security disability applicants include a diverse cross-section of Americans: the parents of judges, the children of the rich and famous, and the otherwise faceless poor. As might be expected, a disproportionate number of poor women and people of color apply for these benefits (GAO 1992). The bulk of applicants, however, are working people, people who, after years of on-the-job physical and emotional strain, become incapable of meeting the demands of full-time employment.

Together, DI and SSI annually provide seven million people with a total of more than $60 billion in cash benefits (GAO 1997). In 1996, approximately 2.5 million Americans applied for disability benefits (GAO 1997), and approximately 1,100 Social Security administrative law judges (Balkus 1998) heard the appeals of nearly 500,000 applicants whose claims had twice previously been denied (GAO 1997).

The Social Security system is no different from any other American juridical process: it involves large monetary awards—often exceeding the money damages awarded in civil court (one disability pension can amount to $500,000 over a person's lifetime)—and judges who believe that they are fair and impartial adjudicators.

Given the monetary implication of an award of benefits and the administrative burden of deciding so many claims, the U.S. Social Security Administration (SSA) has not been beyond trying to pressure its employees in general, and its judges in particular, to decide claims more quickly and to deny the claims they hear. These pressures are exacerbated by the mandate that the ALJs play three distinct and conflicting roles in the adjudicatory process.

Judges are under constant pressure from the SSA to process an increasing number of cases. In 1974, ALJs received a total of 122,000 cases, whereas in 1996, ALJs received nearly 500,000 claims. In 1980, it took ALJs approximately 159 days to hear and decide a case, whereas in 1996, it took an estimated 350 days (NOSSCR 1997).

In addition, judges are subtly and, at times, not so subtly pressured to keep their award levels to a minimum (*Association of Administrative Law Judges, Inc. v. Heckler*, 594 F. Supp. 1132, 1141 (D.D.C. 1984). Although ALJs have fought for and supposedly enjoy judicial independence, they are nevertheless employed by an agency that is often on the brink of bankruptcy (Kollmann 1997). ALJs are concerned that SSA wants to undermine their independence and that they are subtly pressured to deny claims (Tolchin 1989; Pear 1997).[1]

Social Security disability hearings are nonadversarial; Social Security attorneys do not oppose an applicant's claim for disability benefits. As a result, a judge is under pressure to play multiple, conflicting roles at the hearing. That is, ALJs must be prosecutor for Social Security, defense counsel for claimants (whether or not they are represented), and adjudicator. As one judge anonymously commented, "As long as ALJs continue to swim through the warm jello of the 'three hat' fiction, we will have bad results."[2]

While these institutional influences may provide some explanation for why judges routinely violate rules, it cannot in any way explain or excuse the stereotyping I and other researchers have detected in the system.

About six years ago, I was invited to design a training on bias for Social Security ALJs. The training series, titled "Justice and Diversity," was initiated by those members of Congress who became concerned that the findings of a 1992 U.S. General Accounting Office (GAO) study suggested that Social Security judges systematically discriminated against African-American applicants. When, in the training, we confronted the judges with statistically significant evidence of their biased decision-making patterns, they not surprisingly became defensive, so much so that they sabotaged the consciousness-raising exercises that were offered. One senior judge read the newspaper while a diverse group of experienced trainers, myself included, presented material on the judges' propensity to stereotype. When pressed, these resistant judges claimed that once ordained as judges, they were able to transcend the prejudices to which all men and women fall prey. They believed that no matter what they said or did, they could hide behind the disinterested veil of judicial impartiality.

I pondered the judges' defense as I recalled my experience as a public-interest lawyer representing the applicants about whom these judges had claimed their impartiality. After attending hundreds of Social Security hearings, it was my experience (and that of my clients) that a claimant's ethnicity and poverty, addiction and illiteracy, depression and obesity were all too often judged less deserving than those claimants whose circumstances more closely resembled those of the judges who adjudicate the claims. Haunted by the divide between my impression of the Social Security hearing process and the ALJs' perceptions, I was driven to explore the problem of bias more systematically.

To determine whether my experience applied to more than just a few judges in one locale, I decided to scrutinize transcripts of Social Security hearings in which Social Security ALJs denied claimants' benefits. Only one set of records relevant to the Social Security disability decision-making process is, however, open to public review. These records are the ALJ hearing transcripts and decisions of Social Security claims that were appealed to federal court after having been denied at four levels within the system (initial evaluation, reconsideration, face-to-face hearings before an ALJ, and appeals to the Appeals Council). These transcripts and decisions constitute the only hard evidence available with which to study how bias may influence the way disability decision-making rules are applied and represent only a very small sample of the cases heard by Social Security ALJs nationwide.[3]

I selected three cities—Boston, Chicago, and San Francisco—on which to focus my research because these cities were revealed in the 1992 GAO race-bias study to be representative of the differential treatment by Social Security ALJs of African-American and Caucasian applicants. In total, I examined 67 hearing transcripts and decisions for uniformity and affectivity and reviewed more than 2,500 pages of materials. The cases involved a total of 38 judges, 36 of whom were male. Although no specific information is available on the racial and ethnic makeup of the judges whose cases I reviewed, statistics from 1992 revealed that nearly 90 percent of the 856 ALJs were white men (Office of the Chief Administrative Law Judge, personal communication, March 1992) and their average age was 63 (Stephen Kennedy, personal communication, November 1992).[4]

With the hearing transcripts and decisions in hand, I developed a two-step method for analyzing ALJ compliance with key rules. Toward this end, I developed a checklist that enabled me first to identify hearing and decision-making rule violations and second to analyze qualitatively the context and implications of these violations.

I undertook such microresearch because I was interested in learning more about how the dynamic of bias manifests in the day-to-day life of the American judicial system. I was eager to learn more about the intersecting layers of both negative and positive bias as they express themselves in a system committed to following rules that are inherently flexible, as they relate to both the evidence that is presented to adjudicators and the people who present that evidence. And I was particularly interested in learning how, in everyday interactions between judge and claimant, adjudicator and subject, the legal system, in political lawyering terms, is intolerant and judgmental of the diversity the system invites. I came to the research with a working hypothesis that judges often disregard rules, particularly when and if it suits their predilections and prejudices, and I thought this a useful unit of analysis for learning more about these critical dynamics.

What I found when I undertook this research was that no transcript was without rule violations. I also found that these violations consistently suggested that judges failed to positively accommodate claimants' special needs and that the ALJs negatively stereotyped the claimants most deserving of the attention the law mandated.

Specifically, I found that the rules themselves were often biased and that despite the presumed objectivity of the physicians who generate and interpret the medical evidence on which the system relies, they too may be gender and race biased. Indeed, I found that the literature tracing the Social Security disability decision-making process revealed a documented history that suggested prejudice at every level of the system. In the hearing transcripts and decisions I scrutinized from my own sample of cases, judges all too often failed to give a proper introduction to the hearing process despite a mandate to do so. Furthermore, the ALJs systematically failed to comply with rules governing the handling of unrepresented claimants, to assist claimants in obtaining necessary evidence and testimony, to follow rules related to a claimant's decision to adhere to prescribed treatment, and to make appropriate credibility determinations. These judges, as previous researchers had found, rendered both the uniform and affective dimensions of their judicial duties empty formalities.

Judges also failed, despite an affirmative duty, to engage and accommodate the historically oppressed groups they were mandated by law to engage, including such claimants as those who were unrepresented, who suffered from mental impairments, and who were illiterate or unable to speak English. Judges failed to engage such claimants when exploring their right to counsel, eliciting evidence by leading testimony to the detriment of these groups, being unnecessarily judgmental and rude to them, not following up on important issues these claimants or their evidence raised, and implying that the perspective of such claimants was wrong and/or should be ignored.

I found, too, that the hearing transcripts and decisions suggested that these judges stereotyped certain claimants, especially members of racial and ethnic minorities, women, those alleging mental impairments, people who are obese, and persons with educational or linguistic limitations. Recipients of welfare and workers' compensation benefits were also the subject of numerous prejudicial assumptions by judges.

In reflecting on the findings of my research and on the supporting documentation provided by other scholars, I am convinced that an important reason judges fail to accommodate and engage claimants is that the ALJs lack the ability or tools to do so. Similarly, I believe that the reason they stereotype claimants is that they lack insight which would help them reveal their prejudices. Too often, it seems, judges perceive that their appointment imbues them with an ethos of impartiality. That is, once assuming office, they forever reject or deny the possibility that their personal character or experience affects their ability to judge. Given these mostly unquestioned assumptions, judges lack the critical mind-set and/or emotional structure to recognize, acknowledge, and address the onslaught of stereotypical images that are bound unconsciously to prevent them from accommodating and engaging, and from reflecting on those images when processing and deciding claims.

The necessity of such reflection and the development of a method that helps judges recognize and acknowledge their prejudices are urgent tasks. I argue in this book that such a critical method, sensitive to the affective and interactive dimensions of judging, would make judges applying rules and interviewing claimants bound to acknowledge prejudicial beliefs and to address and evaluate the inadmissible and unconscious features of the cases they hear.

This proposition supports and goes beyond the general premise advanced by legal realists, and more recently by critical and feminist legal scholars, that judges, as human beings, cannot entirely disengage emotionally from the legal proceedings they judge. I contend, rather, that the modernist legal notion of impartiality blinds judges to the subtle ways in which subjectivity, in the form of stereotyping, unconscious predilection, or prejudice, necessarily enters into their decision-making process. I argue that a mandate forcing judges to make a deliberate effort to expose their biases is necessary to address the prejudice I and other researchers have

detected. Only in this way, by acknowledging the affective and unconscious dimensions of judges' responses to concrete situations and specific
claimants, is it possible to make some critical use of judges' prejudice. To
deny the existence of prejudice under the legalistic guise of impartiality, or
to denounce it as an evil that cannot somehow be expunged, simply renders it unconscious and its effect more virulent and pernicious. I argue,
and there is social-psychological research to support my position, that
acknowledgment of prejudices is the first step to analyzing and critically
utilizing them.

My thesis, however, goes beyond the need for self-reflexivity and the
unraveling of judicial biases. The Social Security system, like most—if not
all—legal institutions in the United States, is interesting and worthy of
reflection insofar as it is part of a system of justice that ideally hears and
responds to individual claimants and provides them with substantively
just decisions. In the denied claims reviewed for this study, I found that
judges had little or no trouble criticizing the claimants appearing before
them. However, these ALJs were entirely incapable of expressing any
affirmative feeling toward the claimants who, by law or mandate, were
entitled to such positive treatment. This negativity was repeatedly demonstrated in the judges' inability to provide the legal or judicial support necessary to collect relevant evidence when adjudicating a claim made by an
unrepresented person. The judges further illustrated this point when taking testimony, particularly that of claimants who were handicapped by
illiteracy, limited education, poor English-language skills, mental impairments, or institutionalized sexism or racism.

Together, the themes of affectivity and duty, critical self-reflection and
client narrative, traverse the three primary arguments in this book. Chapter 1 argues that prevailing notions of impartiality, particularly among
members of the judiciary, are inadequate because they deceive judges and
the public at large—they perpetuate the myth that emotion, in the form of
bias, does not enter the hearing and decision-making process. The previous studies discussed in chapter 3 and the hearing transcripts and decisions
scrutinized in chapters 4, 5, and 6 provide evidence that unconscious and
unspoken dynamics of prejudice—that is, negative emotion—influence the
hearing narratives and decision discourses, at least in my sample of cases.
The definitional and theoretical literature on bias and affectivity discussed
in chapter 1, the procedural history of Social Security decision making in
chapter 2, and the empirical evidence in chapters 4, 5, and 6 reveal that the
myth of detached decision making is actually only one of two conflicting

ideals. On the one hand, the system proclaims a commitment to impartiality, the idea that everyone deserves uniform treatment regardless of the adjudicator hearing the individual claim. On the other hand, the system mandates that judges take the time and make the effort to engage individual claimants. This book reveals that in the Social Security context there are regulations and accompanying case law that direct judges to accommodate and engage the needs of special claimants, including such vulnerable groups as claimants who are unrepresented and people who are illiterate. This requirement demands judges to feel—to discriminate positively on behalf of claimants who require special treatment.

Although the system proclaims an emotional distance through the ideal of impartiality (chapter 1), it is in practice riddled with negative emotion in the form of prejudice, most prominently in the form of stereotyping (chapter 6). Not only do the judges in my sample prove incapable of achieving impartiality in decision making—indeed, have outright biases against some claimants—but this negative emotion impedes their expression of positive emotion in the form of accommodation or engagement (chapter 5). Ironically, my evidence reveals that the same claimants who are not accommodated are also those who are stereotyped.

I conclude from this evidence that judicial case narratives and judgments are necessarily influenced by unconscious bias and that, in consequence, the ideal of impartiality, as it is currently conceptualized, will never be realized and indeed is self-defeating. The conventional nature of impartiality in effect forces the judges to deny their biases and so precludes them from ever addressing the influence of prejudices or stereotypes on judgment. They are forced to pretend, to act as if they have no feelings, experiences, or biases. The critique of this notion is developed most deliberately through my proposal for mandating judges to become aware of their positive and negative emotional involvement in cases through self-reflection and training (chapter 7).

The second dominant theme in the book builds on the first. Here I deconstruct the doctrine— both the policies and the rules on which Social Security decision making are based—to uncover its prejudicial underpinnings (chapter 3). In addition, I critically examine the hearing transcripts and decisions, or case material. In this undertaking (chapters 4, 5, and 6), I give the claimant a voice beyond the text; I make the effort to understand how claimants would feel had they been given the space and support to express themselves. Simultaneously, I hear the judges: their spoken and unspoken predilections and prejudices, their reason, and the emotions that inform it. Since the rules as well as the texts are flat, merely words on a page, my task in the evidentiary chapters is to make the rules, the hearing, and its accompanying decision three dimensional; the challenge is to reveal the face of Social Security doctrine and decision making. Like a psychotherapist, I interpret and uncover hidden or unconscious material—the story behind the story. However, this is no easy task, as narratives are often opaque, it is unclear what they really mean or how they are to be interpreted. In this regard, I attempt to navigate my way through the dark night of the law's soul using not only the hearing transcripts and decisions themselves but the supporting federal court materials as well.

The third argument builds on the first two in that the theoretical problem and practical solution find themselves inextricably intertwined in how the concepts of impartiality and accommodation and the evidence of bias converge. In the book's conclusion, I argue that judges trained in a formalist legal tradition may be incapable of truly feeling their own prejudice (chapter 7). I raise a heretical question: Should lawyers be judges? This question must be addressed directly. If judges are otherwise incapable of realizing that judging is expression, not repression, emotional engagement, not detached distance, then policymakers should reconsider whether judges trained in law schools are appropriate adjudicators for a legal system that demands sensitivity, not disdain, engagement, not distance, relation, not estrangement. A passionate and engaged decision-making process, I suggest, will enable adjudicators—whether lawyers or therapists—to ensure that they are conscious of the ways they stereotype claimants and of the ways they must compensate emotionally to ensure that they accommodate appropriately and effectively engage claimants. In the conclusion, I build on such psychoanalytic methods as conscious self-reflection and countertransference (a technique for unraveling how interactions evoke reactions) to present a model for training judges in the affectivity of decision making.

Most directly, chapter 1 presents historical and social psychological evidence of the tension between impartiality and bias and the inevitability that stereotyping will enter the decision-making process. I also draw on critiques of formalism from critical and feminist scholars to reveal how objectivity and hence impartiality are contingent on the normative assumptions that underlie them. This analysis helps illuminate the connection between bias and accommodation and the significance of injecting affectivity into the decision-making process.

In chapter 2, I review the rules that are designed to lend the Social

Security disability decision-making process legitimacy and objectivity. In chapter 3, I reveal how the rules themselves may be biased and trace the history of studies on Social Security decision making, which suggests that the system is riddled with prejudice.

Chapters 4, 5, and 6 present my findings from my quantitative and qualitative analysis. Chapter 4 documents how judges violate particular rules. Chapter 5 reveals how they fail to accommodate claimants despite a mandate to do so, and chapter 6 presents evidence of stereotyping detected in the transcripts. In chapter 7, I present my policy recommendations and suggest directions for judicial selection, training, and practice.

This book provides the material and impetus for exploring a new definition of judicial impartiality and for formulating an innovative method for adjudicating claims. This method realistically incorporates the negative and positive features of the stereotyping that inevitably affects the process of decision making when resolving the claims of disaffected applicants who are so easily stereotyped. The cornerstone of such an approach, I argue, is a self-reflective method in which judges would have the tools not only to resolve the facts in any given dispute and to apply the law but also to be conscious of their propensity to stereotype negatively and positively. Judging, I argue, requires the judge to learn to engage claimants to afford them the nonessentialized justice they deserve. Without such an affective approach, my evidence and other studies reveal that the Social Security system will continue to inflict unconscious stereotypes on innocent people who are otherwise powerless to counteract the vicissitudes of life that bring them to these legal tribunals.

CHAPTER 1

Unraveling Bias

To formulate a more precise understanding of exactly how bias may be operating in the Social Security disability decision-making process, and to uncover more fully how judges find it difficult to carry out their affirmative duty to accommodate and appropriately engage claimants, it is useful first to reflect on the current doctrinal conception of impartiality. I begin with an account of the doctrinal analysis of impartiality and then draw from critical legal studies, feminist jurisprudence, and critical race theory to deconstruct the formalism that underlies impartiality. Through these lenses, I analyze the limitations of the dichotomy between impartiality and bias. I also do this work in the context of the social-psychological literature, which suggests that the suppression of bias may actually contribute to its reproduction. This presentation of the supporting literature forms the backbone for advancing both my theory that the repression that necessarily accompanies impartiality contributes to bias and my empirical findings, which this account supports. Finally, I reconsider the definition of bias and its relationship to impartiality in light of judges' apparently conflicting duties to accommodate and engage claimants in the hearing process.

Judicial Impartiality: Doctrinal Context for the Term *Bias* and Its Contemporary Application

The ideal of judicial impartiality is embedded in the U.S. Constitution (*Ward v. Village of Monroeville*, 409 U.S. 57, 61–62 (1972)) and extends not only to state and federal court judges but to administrative proceedings as well (*Hummel v. Heckler*, 736 F.2d 91, 93–94 (3d Cir. 1984)). Judicial impartiality is a basic requirement of a fair tribunal and due process. The U.S. Supreme Court has defined *fairness* as an "absence of actual

11

bias" (*In re Murchison,* 349 U.S. 133, 136 (1955)). According to prevailing doctrinal conceptions, to apply the standard of judicial impartiality, judges must eliminate either "hostile feeling or spirit of ill will" or "undue friendship or favoritism" toward any litigant whose case they hear (46 *American Jurisprudence* 2d § 167).

The Social Security Act embodies a standard of impartiality (42 U.S.C. § 405 (b) (1); 42 U.S.C. 1383 (c) (1)), as does the definitive Social Security Administration's OHA policy and rule book, *Hallex: Hearings and Appeals Litigation Law Manual* (hereafter, *Hallex*): ALJs "must inquire fully into all matters at issue and conduct the administrative hearing in a fair and impartial manner" (SSA 1992, I-2-601).[1] Indeed, key Social Security personnel have explicitly affirmed their commitment to impartiality in disability decision making. For example, as stipulated in the *Federal Register,* the associate commissioner of hearings and appeals "is responsible for maintaining a hearings and appeals system which is impartial and supports the tenets of fairness and equal treatment under the law" (53 Fed. Reg. 29779 (8 August 1988)). The Social Security commissioner's response to the 1992 GAO report on the treatment of racial differences in disability decision making reiterates this commitment: "It is paramount that the Social Security Administration ensure that all people seeking assistance are afforded the fairness and equity that is so imperative to the soundness of the American system of government" (King 1992, 3).

Just as judicial impartiality has authoritatively been characterized as the absence of judicial bias, judicial bias has come to be defined as the opposite of judicial impartiality. Judicial bias, then, involves positively or negatively prejudiced "feelings or spirit" toward the claimants in the cases being heard. It involves, in other words, precisely the kinds of feelings that judges are obligated by the ideal of judicial impartiality to expunge from their reasoning and decisions (46 *American Jurisprudence* 2d § 147).

American Jurisprudence goes yet a step further in refining how judicial bias is currently formulated. It defines the word *bias* as the "leaning of the mind or an inclination toward one person or another" (§167). *Prejudice* is a "prejudgment or forming of an opinion without sufficient knowledge or examination" (§167). The Supreme Court has gone further to stipulate when this mental attitude disqualifies a judge from hearing a given case: "The alleged bias and prejudice to be disqualifying must stem from an extrajudicial source and result in an opinion on the merits on some basis other than what the judge learned from his participation in the case" (*United States v. Grinnell Corp.,* 384 U.S. 563, 583 (1966); see also *Berger v. U.S.* 255 U.S. 22, 31 (1921) and *Liteky et al. v. U.S.* 510 U.S. 540 (1994)).

The doctrinal conception of bias is based on an opposition between bias and impartiality, a rejection of one for the other. Yet my findings and the studies that preceded them indicate that in practice, bias is a consistent dimension of what is considered "impartial" decision making. My results reveal that impartiality in the narrow scientific sense, in which doctrine has used it, is itself a form of bias and that a historically and contextually sensitive definition of bias, taking account of the communities and cultures that come to be judged in the legal system, must overcome the modern dualistic notion of impartiality as the exclusion of bias to respond to the fluid and fluctuating needs of the diversity of applicants and the judges who adjudicate their claims. Indeed, my findings reveal that to exclude bias is to engender prejudice in the form of what I will term repressed and therefore unconscious determinations of judgment.

While judicial impartiality is well recognized and much applauded by all levels of the legal system, there has always been debate on if and how judges should expunge bias, their positive or negative prior feelings, from legal proceedings (Minow 1995). My findings clearly indicate that the ALJs in the cases I reviewed consistently failed to eradicate such feelings and that infractions of the stipulated rules for impartial decision making are endemic to the system.

A case example illustrates this point. Miss Plain was, at the time she appeared before this ALJ, a 52-year-old woman with three years of formal education and no recent work history (87-5258, IL). She had last worked in 1966 as a nurse's aid. In that capacity, she would "clean up . . . the old patients . . . change them and clean them up." Miss Plain was disabled due to obesity, thrombophlebitis of the right leg, mild to moderate high blood pressure with heart enlargement, degenerative joint disease of the spine, osteoarthritis in the knees and ankles, and tension headaches. Miss Plain was illiterate and could write nothing more than her name.

Miss Plain was a homemaker. Since disability is defined as being unable to engage in paid employment, nothing in the rules prevents judges from finding a homemaker eligible for disability benefits. Indeed, the rules are sympathetic to those applicants who have not recently engaged in competitive employment. Embedded in these rules is the assumption (or bias) that people who have been unemployed for long periods of time often lack the necessary skills to compete in the job market. In addition, the rules recognize that such limitations as illiteracy prevent applicants from engaging in a panoply of employment opportunities.

Miss Plain's case reveals the ways a judge's bias creeps into the hearing process. Despite Miss Plain's testimony of her illiteracy and 30-year gap in employment, the judge suggests in the hearing, and subsequently in the decision, that she was not disabled and that she could work. The judge actually suggests, at one point in the hearing, that Miss Plain could get a job as a receptionist even though she could not read and write. This response to Miss Plain runs so contrary to the rules and to the judges' mandate to adjudicate claims fairly that any reflective account of the process of judgment must address the question of what motivated this judge to be so unreflective, to be so negatively predisposed to this case.

An initial answer can be suggested by turning to research in social psychology. One recent study has examined this question by means of an experimental design that explored the degree to which preexisting stereotypes ("category-based, subjective expectancies") determined the willingness of a judging subject to seek individuating information before making a decision (Trope and Thompson 1997). Trope and Thompson found that when negatively stereotyped people are asked questions, they are asked fewer questions, and the questions are asked in a way that tends to elicit confirmation of the stereotype rather than information that would individuate the subject or challenge negative stereotyping. In sharp contrast, questions to positively stereotyped people are more symmetric and therefore likely to elicit responses that would either confirm or disconfirm a particular stereotype. Trope and Thompson found that to disconfirm a stereotype, a relatively large amount of information was necessary to reach a conclusion attentive to individuals and their responses. Their study participants were willing to base their judgments on a relatively small amount of individuating information when the target was negatively stereotyped: "In essence, our participants gave stereotyped targets relatively few opportunities to express their personal views on the issues at hand" (240).

Trope and Thompson's study suggests that a judges' formula for approaching this and other cases involving people who are easily stereotyped, such as African-American women like Miss Plain, may be influenced by their unconscious tendency to search only for a confirmation of the stereotype rather than for a more complete picture of the overall ability to function. Had the judge taken the time to gather the information necessary to move beyond his stereotype of Miss Plain, he would have more fully discussed with her what realistic employment options existed. Such questions might have included: What are a typical day's activities? How much lifting can you do? How much sitting can you do? From the answers to these questions, the judge could have developed a list of skills, if any, from which he could extrapolate realistic jobs she might have done.

To reflect on Miss Plain's case and on her circumstances, to engage her rather than to respond with a predisposed negativity, is the ideal we should strive to achieve in judicial practice.

Miss Plain was eventually vindicated by the federal court that reversed the judge's denial of her benefits on the grounds that he ignored Miss Plain's illiteracy. As for the race and gender implications of this case, my theory, which is supported by the social-psychological literature, is that ALJs in the Social Security system may all too easily be influenced by the stereotyping that is driven underground by the ethos of impartiality.

Miss Plain's case supports the contention that it is necessary to become aware of the ways in which racial, gender, or other indistinguishable prejudices are embedded in people's cores and illuminate those hidden forms by scrutinizing the ways they appear in routine interrogations of claimants. To do so, it is useful to explore further the role that emotional detachment or objectivity, the staple fare of legal education and of the professional myth of the rule of law, play in contributing to the judges' propensity to stereotype.

Acknowledging Emotion

Despite the apparently self-evident bias that my study reveals, most judges will, no doubt, unwittingly adhere to the implausible belief that impartiality demands a neutral and detached decision maker and, more particularly, one who is in no way guided by emotion (46 *American Jurisprudence* 2d § 147). Such a view could be explained in terms of the self-interest of decision makers or the ideology of judicial sanctity. But it could also at a more fundamental level reflect an inherent flaw in the conception of decision making, which contemporary doctrine inherits largely unreflectively from its nineteenth-century forebears. This conception is predicated on the classical liberal view that law should remain outside of society and should judge disputes from a position that somehow transcends the political conflicts of everyday life.

The classical liberal view depicted law as the governance of rules rather than of men. The position of judgment was defined by a tradition of sovereign arbitration in which the judge passed on or disinterestedly "declared" a law that existed external to and independently of him and of the subject to be judged. In its late-nineteenth-century formulation, law was a science of rules, and judgment was the deductive enterprise of subsuming particular facts under general norms. In the hands of Langdell and his followers, the science of law, and more particularly of legal education, was that of abstracting the fundamental doctrines and principles of law from exemplary cases and then applying them in a neutral and objective manner to the task of systematizing the substantive legal disciplines (Goodrich 1986).

This formalist and Olympian view of law was neither uncontested at the time of its elaboration nor universally adhered to as perceptions of the role of law in society gradually began to change. Practitioners such as Justice Benjamin Cardozo, for example, recognized that the deductive model of legal decision making was, at the least, superficial, in that "[d]eep below consciousness are other forces, the likes and the dislikes, the predilections and the prejudices, the complex of instincts and emotions and habits and convictions, which make the man, whether he be litigant or judge" (1921, 167).

Justice William Brennan similarly rejected the prevailing myth that a judge's personal values are irrelevant to the decision-making process, acknowledging the important role that qualities other than reason must play in the judicial process. "In ignoring these qualities, the judiciary has deprived itself of the nourishment essential to a healthy and vital rationality" (1988, 9). Such essentially psychological sensitivity to the biography, elite status, privilege, and concomitant sensibility of those who judge was one of several defining themes in the work of legal realists and has also been important in contemporary critiques of gender and race bias in the legal system as a whole.

My argument elaborates and refines the position developed by Justice Cardozo and the legal realists. It also augments and radicalizes their awareness of the social context of legal rules by suggesting unequivocally that the scientific ideal of impartiality is inappropriate to legal decision making. Legal realists certainly augmented the factors that should be taken into account in assessing the grounds of decision. They argued, for example, that in addition to logic, "[s]ocial context, the facts of the case, judges' ideologies, and professional consensus critically influence individual judgments and patterns of decisions over time" (Singer 1988, 470). Implicit in this view, as Joseph Singer has argued, is the assumption first that legal rules are often "vague" and "ambiguous" and are therefore subject to broad interpretation: "reasonable persons could disagree about what these concepts meant" (1988, 470). Second, legal realists assumed that a holding in a case can always be interpreted in at least two ways: "it could be read broadly to establish a general rule applicable to a wide range of situations, or it could be read narrowly to apply only to the specific facts of the case" (Singer 1988, 470). And finally, given the ambiguity of the law and the numerous interpretations to which cases are subject, the realists argue that jurists could always seek "competing and contradictory rules" to decide any given case (Singer 1988, 470).

Where legal realism argues that discretion is an inevitable feature of the indeterminacy of rules and therefore that the process of decision making cannot be understood without taking account of the individual biases, social ideologies, or institutional or cultural predilections of judges, it was nevertheless the goal of realism to bring decision making as close to impartiality as was possible: "The focussing of conscious attack on discovering the factors thus far unpredictable, in good part with a view to their control" (Llewellyn 1962, 61). Indeed, as Llewellyn argues, "Close study of particular unpredictables may lessen unpredictability" (1962, 61). At root, legal realism criticized legal science for not being scientific enough. Later work associated with critical legal studies, feminist jurisprudence, and critical race theory has moved toward a more radical position. Knowledge is culturally and politically embedded, and even science has been shown to have proceeded historically within the constraints of gender and race bias.

The concept of a science of law is the product of the legal academy, and in this regard it makes sense to trace the problem of impartial judging back to law school training and more particularly to the scholarly model of legal reason. Critical legal studies grew out of a leftist political critique of law and attempted to further the legal realist project by making explicit the extent to which the classical conception of an objective system of legal rules perpetuated the interests of economic elites and promoted class-based privilege. This theme of inequality and of the legal perpetuation of privilege is central to Roberto Unger's famous 1983 book, *The Critical Legal Studies Movement.*

In Unger's at times eloquent and at times opaque account, the legal academy still trains a priesthood, a sacral profession of law. Maintenance of the necessary faith in law depends on the inculcation of a faith in the scientific rationality of law. Legal formalism dominates in the law school and preaches a deductive logic of law that not only promises veneration of the system but also requires the existential adoption of a position of obedience to the hierarchy that such a system implies (Kennedy 1992). The formalism of the legal academy serves to train a profession that is in principle protected—by science, by logic, by reason—from the social and political realities of the subjects that the judge must eventually manipulate the rules of law to judge.

Other critiques endeavored systematically to prove the inevitability of the political character of legal decision making by evidencing the linguistic indeterminacy of the normative order. Thus, in an influential piece on the metaphysics of American law, Gary Peller (1985) demonstrates that legal language and specifically a system of precedent based on reasoning by analogy, by likeness, could not help but force judges to resort to value choices in deciding which application of a rule to enforce. Jack Balkin (1987) similarly resorted to Continental philosophy to evidence the extent to which contemporary linguistic thought requires that the indeterminacy of legal texts and hence the value choices of their interpreters determine textual outcomes. Feminist and critical race scholarship have specifically addressed this substantive and experiential challenge to the formalist's faith in rules.

Feminist jurisprudence has contributed to the critique of objectivity and, by extension, impartiality by arguing that legal rules simply reflect the inegalitarian social reality of a masculine—or, more technically, homo-social—legal institutional order (Naffine 1990). More specifically, feminist legal scholars have argued, as I do, that the rules, the case law, and the judges who interpret them adjudicate from a point of view, from their experience as social beings embedded in a gendered political and economic culture. These points of view, which are based in male privilege, blind adjudicators to their partiality, while the doctrine of impartiality protects the blind from seeing. As Martha Minow has cogently argued, impartiality prevents observers of the legal system from noticing "the coincidence between the viewpoints of the majority and what is commonly understood to be objective or unbiased" (1990, 60).

Numerous feminist authors have advanced the argument that neutrality and objectivity hide the oppressive quality of legal decision making. To take a synoptic example, Ann Scales (1986) argues that male legal norms are often coded as neutral. She illuminates this historical fact by presenting numerous case examples. In one celebrated 1872 Supreme Court opinion (*Bradwell v. The State* 83 U.S. 130), Justice Bradley in a concurring opinion held that the Fourteenth Amendment's privileges and immunities clause did not entitle Myra Bradwell, a woman, to membership in the bar:

> The constitution of the family organization, which is founded in the divine ordinance, as well as in the nature of things, indicates the domestic sphere as that which properly belongs to the domain and functions of womanhood. . . . The paramount destiny and mission of

woman are to fulfil the noble and benign offices of wife and mother. This is the law of the Creator. And the rules of civil society must be adapted to the general constitution of things. (141–42)

These and other case examples of judges who are so obviously directly influenced by their perspective of class and gender privilege and denial trace a history of bias in judicial decision making that exists well beyond the Social Security context. That history also traces an inevitable danger that accompanies a fixed, homosocial law, a legal system that fails to take account of the affectivity that translates oppression to violence. As Robert Cover has so eloquently described, "The relationship between legal interpretation and the infliction of pain remains operative even in the most routine of legal acts" (1986, 1607). This is evidenced throughout my study, as case example after case example uncovers an abuse claimants are forced to endure at the hands of the "impartial" judge. Rectifying the violent underpinnings of the so-called neutral or impartial legal system is no easy task.

Scales (1986), like other feminists, myself included, argues for a relational concept of law. This relational notion moves beyond abstract legal-rights jurisprudence and its objectifying practices and embeds feminist legal practice in the everyday experience of people's lives. In this regard, law is emotionally engaged; it responds not to the fixed and distant male norms to which doctrine has historically adhered but rather to the fluid needs and interests of the lives of people who are touched by law (Mills 1996). This relational approach is evidenced throughout this book, as I hold judges accountable to the mandate that they engage and accommodate the claimants who appear before them.

Pivotal to the arguments advanced by critical legal scholars and by feminists is the method of training received by lawyers and, hence, judges. L. Amede Obiora (1996) traces the history of legal education beginning with Harvard Law School and explores how the earlier formalist framework became the cornerstone for the homosocial training of lawyers. The science of legal education and its presupposition of the neutrality and objectivity of law insulated legal scholars, practitioners, and judges from the complexity of human relations. Emotion was seen as outside the realm of legal reasoning, as divorced from the practice of men and of law. This analysis of the homosociality of law is central to the feminist argument which claims that gender dynamics in the legal academy reflect biased dynamics in society as a whole (Guinier, Fine, and Balin 1997). Studies consistently reveal that women students must tolerate stereotypical images of themselves, sexist language, and other negative characterizations in the classroom and that male students witness tacit approval for it (Frug 1992; Lahey 1991; Banks 1990). Male professors either perpetrate this biased behavior or participate in it through their silence (Krauskopf 1994). It is not surprising, then, that people trained in these law schools, in this language, and in these methods would reflect and embody these images once ordained as judges.

The experience of oppression and the approval for certain biased values in law school are not limited to women students. Students of color and, by extension, faculty and other members of the profession who are of color experience the domination and alienation that they have learned to expect from the culture at large. Critical race theory provides the intellectual landscape in which these vexing problems have been explored conceptually. In critical race theory, postmodernism converges with radical politics to create a movement by legal scholars that reinterprets legal philosophy and practice and decenters legal conventions in light of these critiques.

For example, Derrick Bell (1995), one of the movement's leaders, observes that abstract legal principles such as *equality* harm African Americans and perpetuate their marginalization. "Racism provides a basis for a judge to select one available premise rather than another when incompatible claims arise" (302). Bell and critical race theory more generally recognize and seek to publicize the violence inflicted on people of color through the myth of legal neutrality and abstract law.

As numerous examples exist in feminist jurisprudence of gender-based judicial bias, so too is critical race theory rich with instances of judicial action that denies racism in the guise of objectivity. In one of the most famous examples, Bell (1995) deconstructs the violence evident in the *Regents of the University of California v. Bakke* (438 U.S. 265 (1978)) decision by arguing that the U.S. Supreme Court, in holding that it was illegal to discriminate against whites in favor of historically disadvantaged groups, took what looked like a racially neutral position by ignoring the rampant disparity between blacks and whites, especially with regard to their access into higher education. Bell argues that the Court was able to hide its racist intent by relying on abstract concepts such as *equality* to mask the real history of black oppression. For critical race theory, like legal feminism, *equality, objectivity,* and *impartiality* are veils for protecting the privilege of the white male elite. It is from this privileged history that the points of view of judges are finally revealed.

Patricia Williams (1995) traces the dynamics that give rise to such sub-textual racism to elementary school education. According to Williams, one white first-grade teacher in Pennsylvania asked two black students to pretend to be slaves during a discussion on the topic and displayed these pupils to the class to illustrate how their experience might have felt. The girl, the teacher explained, would have been sold for $10 as a housecleaner; the boy was used to demonstrate how slaves were flogged. Williams interprets this thoughtless lesson as a reenactment of a power dynamic "in which some people get to imagine oppression, and others spend their lives having their bodies put through its most grotesque motions" (26). What Williams is most concerned about, as am I, are the ways in which this kind of education reinforces among the dominant group, the belief that they have become sensitive to oppression. This disguise helps the dominant group avoid a deeper reflection on racism and their role in perpetuating it and reinforces the unspoken silence in which these dynamics become inextricably intertwined.

If law school marks the beginning of the judge's professional life, it is useful to explore how racial dynamics in the legal academy may be contributing to judge's points of view. Linda Greene's (1997) essay on her experience as a black law teacher reveals a similar dynamic to that witnessed for women more generally, but also exposes its distinctly racialized dimensions. Greene describes the marginalization black women law professors experience in the academy both from their students and from their colleagues. Tokenism, as she sees it, represents only a symbolic equality and blurs the racism and sexism that underpins the appointment of women of color in the legal academy. She argues that the reluctance of white men to welcome black women into their law faculties stems from the resistance of members of the academy to relinquishing their power. These efforts by the dominant group are disguised by what has been called a color-blind meritocracy (Kennedy 1995), which is no more than code for racial privilege and white isolationism. The danger is that the white students who ultimately become judges witness these dynamics in law school and obtain, in new and powerful forms, unconscious approval for negative raced and gendered texts and subtexts.

The interpretations advanced by critical legal studies, feminist jurisprudence, and critical race theory traverse with the theme of law and emotion presented in this book. Formalism and the objectivist model of judgment that it proposes are detached from emotion and from the real experiences of people. Critical and feminist approaches unravel that myth and situate judges squarely in the sexist and racist paradigms from which they judge.

Ironically, while the legal system has been reluctant, even unwilling, to recognize that impartiality is only an ideal, the system has nevertheless been cognizant of the need to have an engaged judiciary. The system has come to rely on the judge's awareness of difference to ensure that the important goal of an accommodating justice is embraced. Far from being an undesirable or alien element of the legal decision-making process, bias in the sense of attachment or affection, culture or context, is an intrinsic dimension of judging (Brennan 1988; Minow 1995). Justice has always required that the judge pay attention to the singularities of litigant or claimant, evidence or plea, and that the judge listen to the unique and individual characteristics, to see the face of the person who appears before the law. To ignore this reality would simply be to repress bias and to deny the emotive dimensions of the art of judging.

As has been claimed cogently by Martha Minow and Elizabeth Spelman (1988), it is quite simply futile to ignore emotion. They argue that the consequence of ignoring emotion is a severe injustice that results from the failure to recognize or perceive the details of the case. In Minow and Spelman's view, to repress emotion is in effect to expunge or exclude a highly significant dimension of the dispute that the judge is supposedly in office to hear. Their article ends laudably with a call for judicial decisions to be based on a combination of emotion and reason in the belief that doing so will lead to compassionate and more predictable justice. The authors' argument and the criteria they suggest for the incorporation of emotion into the justification of decision making imply but do not expressly dictate the abandonment of the doctrinal conception of impartiality. My argument wholly vindicates their position but also suggests that it is necessary to rethink radically the dualisms of bias and impartiality as well as of reason and emotion. For administrative law judges to act justly and to judge fairly does not require impartiality to the exclusion of bias. It requires, rather, a sensitivity to personal biases and a recognition of fears, blindnesses, and desires, however indirectly they seem at first sight to affect the perception of the claimant or the ability to recognize the context of the claim.

As philosophers and psychologists have increasingly begun to doubt the ability of the human mind to separate reason from emotion, so too have legal scholars, myself included, realized the futility of perpetuating the myth that judges or lawyers can make such distinctions (Zipursky 1990; Mills 1996). Rejecting the notion that a judge must cease to be human or else be impermissibly prejudiced, I and others acknowledge emotion's role in the judicial process and argue that judges always bring their own perspectives and experiences to the cases they hear (Minow 1995; Resnik 1988).

I believe that we must move beyond approaches that merely or negatively acknowledge emotion's effects on decision making and instead affirmatively integrate and reflect on emotion's role in the judicial decision-making process, a method I have come to call Affective Lawyering (Mills 1996) or Affective Advocacy (Mills 1998).

Rejecting the prevailing notion of impartiality that mandates that adjudicators should be neutral and detached, my argument suggests, on the contrary, that the only way to avoid negative stereotyping and the failure of judges to engage and protect claimants is to mandate that judges show their affectivity by publicly exposing their likes and dislikes, prejudices and predilections, and affirmatively integrating them into their hearing and decision-making practices. This issue is explored in more depth in chapter 7, where I present a method for mandating judges to confront their biases.

By *affectivity* I refer to the emotion, feeling, predilection, and most relevantly the penchant for prejudice that judges have been trained to hide. By *affective approaches* I mean the experience everyone feels in meeting someone new, judging them, and categorizing and stereotyping them. Whether or not people are conscious of these judgments or thoughts, the social-psychological literature suggests that they are inevitably there (von Hippel, Sekaquaptewa, and Vargas 1995). This affectivity takes the form of both positive and negative emotion. Most importantly, if it is revealed as it should be, as emotion that colors judgment, it is then up to the judge to reject the irrelevant criteria and to be sure that relevant factors are considered in the face of that honesty. This kind of reflection actually holds promise for addressing the insidious bias, described in chapter 3, to which the system has been victim since its inception.

Social psychologists have long recognized the difficulty of divorcing emotion from judgment, impartiality from bias. Patricia Devine's groundbreaking work on the mechanics of prejudice is relevant to my critique of prevailing juridical practice. Her studies have analyzed stereotypes and prejudices, particularly whether people can or want to control their biases. In her most famous study (1989), Devine used three research designs to test automatic and controlled processes involved in prejudice. Her study which focused on African-Americans, assumed that both high- and low-prejudiced people are equally knowledgeable about cultural stereotypes based on the assumption that people are commonly socialized. In addition, she assumed that stereotypes are automatically activated when in the presence of an African-American and that both low- and high-prejudiced people cannot escape the activation of the stereotype. Finally, she assumed that high- and low-prejudiced people differ with respect to their personal beliefs about African-Americans. High-prejudiced people are likely to have beliefs similar to the cultural stereotype, whereas low-prejudiced people have decided that the stereotype is an inappropriate basis on which to judge a person. This new thought structure, or way of processing and rejecting negative stereotypes, does not, according to Devine's theory, supplant the older belief system and therefore is only activated when there is an intentional inhibition of the old belief system.

Using this model, Devine sought to test her hypotheses. Study 1 of her three-part research design examined whether high-prejudiced people (where personal beliefs overlap substantially with cultural stereotypes) and low-prejudiced people (where cultural stereotypes have been rejected as criteria for evaluation) are equally knowledgeable of cultural stereotypes. Devine found that stereotypes (in this case, about African-Americans) are automatically activated in both high- and low-prejudiced people. In study 2, Devine tested the degree to which high- and low-prejudiced people can control their automatically activated stereotype. She found that when subjects were unable consciously to monitor the activation of stereotypes, both high- and low-prejudiced people are equally biased. Study 3 examined what happens when high- and low-prejudiced people can consciously direct their prejudice. She found that when given the opportunity to control their negative stereotyping, low-prejudiced subjects could inhibit the stereotypical thoughts and could replace them with thoughts reflecting the rejection of the stereotype.

Devine's research is significant to my work for several reasons. First, it is relevant because she found that even low-prejudiced people, who pride themselves on their nonracist beliefs, were as knowledgeable about cultural stereotypes as those people who were considered highly prejudiced. This is important because it suggests that prejudicial beliefs exist in our psyches, in our unconscious. This is confirmed in study 2, where Devine revealed that even low-prejudiced people were unable to control the entry of stereotypes into their thinking when the influence involved a process they could not control. Study subjects were not given time to reflect on their responses, which allowed Devine to test automatic or unconscious response. She found that if subjects were prevented from consciously monitoring the activation of their stereotypes, both high- and low-prejudiced subjects had "prejudice-like" responses. Her conclusion from the first two studies was that both high- and low-prejudiced people hold stereotypes that support prejudiced responses. These findings imply that if judges, even those with low prejudices, are actively discouraged from reflecting on their stereotypes (insofar as they have been convinced that impartiality protects them from those beliefs), they too are likely to be held captive to those stereotypes. As Devine describes it, "Thus, even for subjects who honestly report having no negative prejudices against Blacks, activation of stereotypes can have automatic effects that if not consciously monitored produce effects that resemble prejudiced responses" (1989, 12).

In study 3, Devine found that when forced to contemplate their prejudice, low-prejudiced people were able to replace the negative stereotyping information with thoughts that expressed nonprejudiced values. High-prejudiced people, conversely, were willing to ascribe prejudicial traits to the group at large. Devine concluded that "controlled processes can inhibit the effects of automatic processing when the implications of such processing compete with goals to establish or maintain a non prejudiced identity" (1989, 15). This finding underscores the importance of developing a method for judges to reflect on their biases and for making gender, race, and other stereotypes conscious through deliberate and direct efforts.

Other researchers have further refined Devine's work. Macare et al. (1994) suggest that efforts to suppress stereotypes may actually heighten their accessibility and influence. Even Devine (1989) suggested that prejudice could be reduced by inhibiting stereotypical thought. Macare et al. suggest that to the contrary, there are costs associated with the act of suppression. When perceivers attempt to suppress their prejudicial thoughts, "unwanted stereotypic thoughts were shown to return and impact on [the] perceivers' treatment of a stereotyped target" (1994, 815). These findings have important implications for my policy suggestion that judges should be mandated to reflect on their penchant for prejudice and my proposal for training judges, both of which are addressed more fully in chapter 7.

In sum, I argue that judicial impartiality, as it is currently constructed, mandates the absence of even a reflection on bias or emotion and hence creates an institutional ethos that promotes stereotyping and a deliberate denial of the affective dimensions of judging. I propose a new definition of *impartiality* that attends to bias as a necessary ingredient in the attempt to achieve justice and judgment. My argument begins with judges' formalist and detached training in the legal academy and proposes changes appropriate to the recognition of the particularized emotional as well as factual complexity that each case presents. I argue that it is precisely the affectivity of judgment that creates the process of accommodation, one that is aware of and does not deny how unconscious forces prevent judges from realizing the ideal of justice that the classical conception of impartiality so desperately and so ineffectively endeavored to achieve.

Tempted as judges—even realist judges—are to pretend that their office itself is imbued with the objectivity necessary to judge fairly, this book supports the conclusion that in so doing, judges are remiss in their responsibility to adjudicate in a consistent, measured, and particularized manner. As my evidence will reveal, not only are the facts of any given case necessary and relevant for judicial consideration, as is the law, but equally important are the unspoken, unspeakable, emotional features of the claimants and claims presented and the feelings generated in relation to them. While judges believe they have the benefit of neutrality and detachment, the previous studies outlined in chapter 3 as well as the evidence described in subsequent chapters confirm that judges are mired in biography, in stereotypes reflecting the dominant culture's judgment of good and evil, deserving and undeserving, worthy and worthless. To rework the modern notion of impartiality is to recognize that there is no detached observer and that no judges can escape the affective parameters of their role. I argue that an understanding of the prejudice that is inevitably bound up in judgment will allow the law to recollect the forms of engagement and accommodation on which a judge depends to do substantive justice.

In the next chapter I set out in detail the rules that govern the Social Security disability decision-making process, including the five most essential mechanisms designed to distinguish the deserving from the undeserving. In addition, I present supporting materials that underpin my contention that Social Security judges must accommodate and engage the claimants who appear before them.

CHAPTER 2

Mandate for a Uniform and Affective Justice

The underlying assumption of the Social Security disability programs is that they can be administered fairly and equitably. Fairness and equity are arrived at through a uniformity in disability decision making, which is further enhanced by a series of doctrinal protections, all of which are also designed to protect the federal coffers from illegitimate claims. Often, as the evidence of prejudice in the system will reveal in subsequent chapters, these goals conflict as judges scramble to compromise these objectives through the decision-making process.

To ensure that the disability programs are fair in allocating benefits, Social Security devised several substantive and procedural mechanisms to adjudicate the claims of each American who applies. Of these mechanisms, the following five are considered essential to ensuring uniformity: (a) the listings of impairments that form a standard measure of disabilities; (b) a requirement that disabling conditions be verified by objective medical evidence; (c) the medical-vocational guidelines, or "Grid," that consider vocational factors; (d) a five-step sequential evaluation process that dictates the order in which decisions are made; and (e) an appeals procedure that grants dissatisfied applicants a hearing before an impartial administrative law judge.

In this chapter, I describe how these mechanisms form a part of Social Security's commitment to impartiality and to distinguishing the deserving from the undeserving. More importantly, however, this chapter provides necessary background for my developing thesis that Social Security's attempts to make decision making impartial through the use of these mechanisms has failed because these rules not only are themselves biased but also are often disregarded by the adjudicators mandated to adhere to them. Moreover, in practice, these rules all too often conflict with those

27

mandates that direct judges to affirmatively accommodate and engage claimants in the hearing process. This conflict manifests most dramatically in the narratives of the denied cases presented in chapters 4, 5, and 6, which document the ALJs' consistent predilection to criticize claimants or be biased and never or rarely to positively accommodate or engage the claimants who appear before them.

The Listings of Impairments

The listings of impairments (the "listings") are lists of medical criteria against which every applicant's medical condition is compared (20 C.F.R. 404, subpt. P, app. 1). The listings describe more than 100 medical conditions by their symptoms, signs, and laboratory findings. For each condition, the listings also establish levels of severity that can usually be presumed to result in an inability to work.

The listings attempt to standardize the disability application process because they measure each recognized condition by the same criteria. In two very straightforward examples, applicants who are mentally retarded will be judged "disabled" according to the listings if their IQ is 59 or less (20 C.F.R. 404, subpt. P, app. 1, 12.05 B), and claimants who have one foot and one hand amputated will also be judged "disabled" under the listings (20 C.F.R. 404, subpt. P, app. 1, 1.09 C).

Symptoms reflecting the applicants' own perceptions of their impairment carry little or no weight unless supported by visible signs or laboratory findings that are considered "objective medical evidence" (42 U.S.C. § 423 (d) (5) (A)). If the claimant's medical condition is the same, similar to, or worse than the description in the listings, the claimant automatically is determined to be disabled.

The requirement that adjudicators make disability decisions based on "objective medical evidence" is among the most important safeguards afforded to disability claimants. Underlying this requirement is the assumption that if disability decisions are based on objective medical evidence, the adjudicator's possible biases with regard to issues such as a claimant's illness, race, or gender will be prevented from penetrating the process.

If claimants' conditions do not meet the listings, they are judged on additional criteria, including age, education, and previous work experience, as described in detail later in this chapter.

The Requirement That Disabling Conditions Be Verified
by Objective Medical Evidence

To recognize a condition as disabling, the Social Security system requires that the symptoms be verified by "objective medical evidence"—that is, by visible signs or laboratory findings made by physicians (42 U.S.C. 423 (d) (5) (A)). This requirement is considered central to ensuring that the application process is fair and unbiased and that it disqualifies all but the truly deserving. The objectivity of medical evidence, however, naturally depends on the physicians who generate, interpret, and explain it.

Four types of physicians play critical roles in the disability decision-making process: the applicant's treating physician, consultative examiners (CEs), disability determination services (DDS) physicians, and medical experts (MEs). The applicants' own physicians are the most influential of these groups because Social Security regulations grant controlling weight to the opinions of treating physicians as long as they are well supported by clinical and laboratory findings and not inconsistent with other evidence in the record (Social Security Rulings 1996 96-2P). Treating physicians, or personal physicians, provide disability adjudicators such as judges with clinical impressions and diagnoses in the form of photocopied medical records and specially prepared medical reports.

CEs are paid by a state agency to examine an applicant (usually only once) and to provide medical findings and reports only when applicants cannot afford a treating physician or when treating physicians refuse to cooperate or are deemed unqualified (20 C.F.R. 404.1517). When a claimant is required to visit a CE, the doctor will both examine and interview the applicant and give a medical impression according to that single meeting.

In every case, at least one physician from the DDS, a state agency that helps make disability determinations for the federal government, evaluates the applicant's medical file at the first two stages of the application process to make findings of fact about the medical evidence and what additional tests are needed (20 C.F.R. 404.1527 (f) (1)). The DDS assesses the medical records and reports to determine the eligibility of the claimant for benefits. Unlike CEs, DDS physicians have no direct contact with the applicant.

Finally, MEs advise ALJs in cases where judges require assistance in interpreting medical evidence at the hearing. The MEs never examine the claimant but make their assessments based on their review of the medical records and their impressions of the claimant's testimony at the hearing. Typically, MEs attend claimants' hearings and decide whether applicants meet or equal a listing and how their medical impairment limits their ability to perform job-related activities (20 C.F.R. 404.1527 (f) (2)).

In sum, physicians help satisfy the requirement that disabling conditions be verified by "objective" medical evidence. This mechanism, therefore, assumes both that medical evidence is objective and that the people generating that evidence are unbiased in the methods applied when ordering and evaluating clinical tests.

The "Grid"

The medical-vocational guidelines, commonly referred to as the "Grid," are a standardized set of rules from the Code of Federal Regulations that are laid out in grid format. These factors become relevant in a disability claim when an applicant's condition does not meet or equal the listings. Adjudicators are required to render disability decisions based on the Grid's recommendation (20 C.F.R. 404, subpt. P, app. 2). In cases in which an impairment restricts an applicant's physical capabilities, disability adjudicators rely on the Grid roughly as follows. Adjudicators take into account the applicants' remaining physical capabilities—that is, their "residual functional capacity," along with other factors including age, education, and previous work experience—and refer to the Grid for a standardized determination of what employment possibilities still exist. For example, according to the Grid, a physically disabled 55-year-old woman with an eleventh-grade education and previous experience as a retail salesperson would be found "not disabled" if she had residual functional capacity—that is, she still retained the ability to perform telephone sales sitting at a desk (20 C.F.R. 404, subpt. P, app. 2, 201.03). The Grid is therefore facially neutral and hence objective insofar as it standardizes decision making by plugging applicants into a predetermined decision-making formula.

The Five-Step Sequential Evaluation Process

The five-step sequential evaluation process, the fourth mechanism designed to increase objectivity and promote uniformity in disability decision making, requires adjudicators to evaluate each disability claim in a prescribed order. Adjudicators must follow the five-step sequence throughout the application and appeals process.

The process for determining each disability claim begins with the DDS, the state agency hired by the federal government to evaluate the medical grounds of the claim and to supplement them as needed. The federal government contracts this function out to state agencies so that initial and reconsideration-stage medical workups and evaluations are made in the claimant's home state. This delegation makes sense because state-run agencies have stronger institutional ties to the professionals and local agencies needed to process and adjudicate claims.

A DDS evaluation is carried out by a team of examiners that includes a physician who is well-versed in the rules (20 C.F.R. 404.1527 (f) (1)). As noted, DDS evaluators base their decisions exclusively on medical and related records and reports; they have no face-to-face interviews with applicants. As the first step of the sequential evaluation process, DDS adjudicators establish whether applicants are working. Work is defined as involving "significant physical or mental activities" and is done "for pay or profit" (20 C.F.R. 404.1572 (a), (b)). If claimants are working, benefits are denied. If claimants are not working, their cases proceed to step two in the sequential evaluation process.

In step two, evaluators determine whether the claimants' impairments are "severe." An impairment is considered severe when it significantly affects a person's ability to work. If the claimants' impairments are considered nonsevere, the claim is denied; if they are found to be severe, the claims proceed to step three.

In step three, evaluators consider whether the applicants' medical problems meet or equal the conditions defined in the listings of impairments. If the condition matches or exceeds the listings requirement, the claimant automatically qualifies for benefits. If the condition is closely related but not identical to the definition in the listings, the DDS adjudicators determine whether the impairment is "close enough" to the listings. If they assess the documented condition as "close enough," the claimants are found disabled on the theory that their conditions "equal" the description in the listings (Social Security Rulings 1986, 86-8). If the applicants' conditions are assessed as less severe or are not included in the listings, evaluators proceed to step four.

At step four, a claim is denied if evaluators conclude that the applicants' conditions do not prevent them from doing work they did in the past. If the applicants are found incapable of performing their past work, evaluators move to step five.

In this final step, adjudicators assess the claimant's "residual functional capacity"—that is, whether the alleged medical condition affects the claimant's ability to perform activities common to many kinds of work, including sitting, standing, walking, lifting, carrying, pushing, and pulling (Social Security Rulings 1983, 83-10). To make this assessment, adjudicators also consider the applicant's age, education, and work experience (Social Security Rulings 1983, 83-10). Taking all these factors into account, evaluators decide whether the applicant is physically or mentally capable of doing any full-time work in the national economy. If the impairment is physical, the Grid is applied to make that final decision; otherwise, the adjudicator evaluates the claim in light of the physical and mental impairments alleged. If claimants are found capable of working, their disability claims are denied. If they are found incapable, their claims are approved.

In sum, this five step-process further standardizes decision making by ensuring that each applicant's case is given the same procedural and substantive treatment.

The Appeals Process

The final mechanism designed to ensure applicants a fair and uniform determination is an appeals procedure that grants dissatisfied applicants a hearing before an ALJ. It is useful to characterize the hearing process in the context of the overall application procedure.

Eligibility for disability benefits begins with an application that is initially processed by a claims representative at a Social Security district office. Social Security claims representatives do not themselves make substantive disability determinations. Rather, they help applicants fill out necessary forms, forward all the relevant paperwork to the DDS for a decision, and process approved claims.

If the application is denied, the applicant has recourse to various levels of appeal. The first of these, called a reconsideration, allows the applicant to submit additional medical or other related evidence to a team of DDS examiners but does not usually include a face-to-face interview (20 C.F.R. 404.913).[1] The chances of a favorable decision at the reconsideration stage are relatively low. Of the 2.5 million Americans whose initial applications were reviewed in 1993, approximately 60 percent were denied benefits (U.S. House 1994, 57). That same year, only 48 percent of those whose initial applications were denied applied for a reconsideration, and 86 percent of them were again denied benefits (U.S. House 1994, 57).

More recently, Social Security has attempted to improve and streamline the application process. The SSA's "Reengineering" or "Disability Redesign" Plan proposes to reduce the length of the application procedure in half and to make decisions between adjudicators more consistent (GAO 1997; NOSSCR 1998). Although this plan is moving forward, it will be several more years before it can be fully implemented and the benefits, whatever they will actually be, can be realized.[2] Some minor changes, however, have already been detected. In 1996, 2.4 million applications were received, with a denial rate of 69 percent, compared to the 60 percent rate 3 years earlier. Fifty percent of denied applicants requested a reconsideration, and 87 percent of them were denied reconsideration (GAO 1997). If these numbers suggest a trend, Social Security's reengineering effort should render fewer applicants eligible for benefits overall. As discussed later, those that are eligible are more likely to be found disabled at the initial or reconsideration stages.

At the second appeal, applicants are guaranteed a face-to-face hearing before an ALJ. Indeed, the hearing transcripts and decisions that form the basis of my work are taken from this stage of the decision-making process. As federal adjudicators, judges are explicitly directed by the U.S. Code to be fair and impartial, and they are required to comply with the listings, to base decisions on objective medical evidence, to employ the Grid, and to follow the five-step sequential evaluation process (42 U.S.C. § 405 (b) (1)). The ALJs are also mandated to serve not only as judges but also as "prosecutors" for Social Security (no agency representative, other than the judge, who is supposedly "independent," is present at the hearing). If the claimant is unrepresented, the judge is also charged with helping the claimant manage the hearing or otherwise to act as a kind of "defense" counsel.

In addition to these safeguards, ALJs are required to follow a number of other procedural and substantive rules and regulations. This second stage is probably the system's most important protection for applicants (Taibi 1990). In fact, as detailed later, ALJs award benefits to more applicants than do initial and reconsideration evaluators.

Among the several important procedures judges are bound to follow is the hearing notification process, which is regulated by *Hallex: Hearings,*

Appeals and Litigation Law Manual. Hearing notices inform claimants of the time and place of the hearing and whether an expert will be present. The notice, which is usually in English but is also available in Spanish, informs applicants that the hearing is informal and that they have a right to representation.[3] Usually, the notice includes a list of legal-services agencies and other organizations available to represent claimants on their cases. In the first quarter of 1997, 58.9 percent of claimants appearing before Social Security ALJs were represented by an attorney (SSA 1996–97). Of the favorable decisions awarded in 1997, 58.6 percent of claimants were represented, while 39.3 percent of the favorable decisions were issued to claimants who were unrepresented (SSA 1998).

Hearing conduct and procedure are also regulated by *Hallex*. In general, claimants arrive at the OHA with their attorneys or representatives half an hour before the scheduled hearing time. This period enables claimants to review, usually for the first time, their medical records, which have now been placed in a folder called an exhibit file.

When the hearing is about to begin, a hearing assistant (someone who helps the ALJ with the hearing proceedings) calls claimants and their attorneys (if applicable) into the hearing room. When claimants enter the hearing room, most judges are already seated. Judges sit at a large, raised, wooden desk and generally wear a judge's robe (although *Hallex* does not require judges to do so).

Once the proceedings begin, *Hallex* requires judges to introduce themselves to claimants and to present an opening statement that explains the following: (a) the manner in which the hearing will proceed, (b) the procedural history of the case (that the case was previously processed by DDS adjudicators and when), and (c) the issues that the judge will resolve (i.e., a claim for DI or SSI) (SSA 1992, I-2-650; I-2-652). Usually within the opening statement, judges describe how the hearing process will proceed— that is, that they will take the claimants' testimony by asking questions and by providing the attorneys the opportunity to ask questions.

If the claimant is not represented by an attorney, the judge "must secure on the record an unrepresented claimant's acknowledgment of the right to representation and affirmation of the claimant's decision to proceed without a representative" (SSA 1992, I-2-652). Although Social Security judges are not mandated to provide representation, as in criminal cases, obtaining what is called the "acknowledgment and waiver" of the Social Security claimant's right to an attorney is still key given its practical significance. This mandate extends even further. Should the claimant not be represented, the judge has an affirmative duty, described more fully in chapters 4 and 5, to assist the claimant through the hearing process. This constitutes the second instance, in addition to the opening statement, in which judges are affirmatively mandated to make the claimant's journey through the hearing process as emotionally hospitable as possible.

Next, the ALJ administers an oath to the claimant and any witnesses present at the hearing, including vocational and/or medical experts (SSA 1992, I-2-654). Following the oath, the judge must determine from the attorney or claimant whether the exhibits have been examined and whether there are any objections to the records contained in the exhibit folder (SSA 1992, I-2-658). When such objections are raised, they are usually against a particular medical report or record prepared by a physician who never or only briefly examined the claimant.

The primary purpose of the hearing is to give claimants an opportunity to present their cases before an ALJ and to prove that they suffer from physical or mental impairments that are severe enough to prevent them from working. In addition, the hearing gives the judge an opportunity to evaluate claimants face to face, to question claimants about their impairments, to resolve ambiguities between the medical evidence and the claimants' complaints, and most importantly to evaluate the claimants' credibility with regard to symptoms that are hard to verify with objective evidence, such as pain and fatigue (Social Security Rulings 1996, 96-7p). These credibility determinations are regulated both by agency policy in the form of rulings and by federal common law, which has evolved to help standardize the way judges evaluate subjective concerns, such as: Is the applicant's pain disabling? Do the applicants' impairments really prevent them from working six to eight hours a day? Finally, ALJs are in many cases mandated to use the hearing to determine whether they should order further medical examinations or tests to consider impairments not fully developed in the record. For example, it is not uncommon for a mental impairment to go undeveloped in the record until an ALJ meets the claimant and orders an evaluation or for a claimant's heart condition to be considered nonsevere until testimony reveals otherwise. This too represents the judge's affirmative duty to develop the claimants' cases and to ensure that the evidence in the exhibit files adequately reflects the extent and nature of the impairments.

There is no standardized length of time for a hearing, although they usually last from 30 to 45 minutes. Some are as short as 10 minutes, and some last as long as 90 minutes. Sometimes a hearing takes longer because judges have medical or vocational experts who assist them with the cases' technical aspects.

Following the hearing, judges wait for any additional evidence to be submitted and then write decisions, supporting their findings with "their reasons for the decision," "based on evidence offered at the hearing or otherwise included in the record" (20 C.F.R. 404.953). *Hallex* rules explicitly govern how a decision should be prepared: they direct the ALJ to "avoid using emotionally charged words, pejorative terms, and personal judgments or opinions, even if the harmful language appears in evidence or testimony" (SSA 1992, I-2-835A1). In essence, *Hallex* mandates that judges respect claimants and balance the interests of eliciting testimony against the aggression that all too often manifests in judicial proceedings involving people who are distinctly less advantaged than the adjudicators hearing their claims.

ALJs grant the highest rate of awards of any adjudicators in the Social Security disability system. Of the applicants denied benefits at reconsideration in 1993, 54 percent requested a hearing. Of the more than 240,000 cases heard by ALJs that year, 68 percent were ruled eligible for disability benefits (U.S. House 1994, 57). One of the most dramatic changes detected from SSA's efforts to redesign the decision-making process has been in ALJ award rates. Studies reveal that since redesign was implemented, OHA allowance rates have dropped 11 percent (NOSSCR 1998).[4]

If denied benefits at the hearing stage, claimants may appeal their cases at four more levels: the Appeals Council, an administrative appeals branch of the SSA located in Washington, D.C.; U.S. District Court; U.S. Circuit Court; and finally the U.S. Supreme Court. Approximately 60,000 cases are considered by the Appeals Council each year. In 1993, the majority of these appeals—70 percent—resulted in a denial of benefits. Of the cases denied at the Appeals Council, 10 percent were appealed to U.S. District Court (U.S. House 1994, 57). At district court, judges review cases to be sure the ALJ had substantial evidence on which to deny the claim. District courts can deny or grant cases or order remands—that is, send cases back to ALJs either for further evidentiary development or for additional hearing proceedings. If a case is denied at district court, an applicant can appeal to U.S. Circuit Court. Approximately 8 percent of cases are appealed to circuit court. Very few cases are appealed to the Supreme Court.

Although, in theory, these substantive and procedural mechanisms are designed to ensure that DDS adjudicators and ALJs are bound by similar rules and procedures, there is evidence presented in the next chapter and in several studies described therein that suggests both that the mechanisms themselves may be inherently biased and that disability decision makers are often inconsistent, inaccurate, and even prejudicial in their practices. It is important first to describe what other procedures accompany and complement these uniform measures to better understand how the disability decision-making process has become riddled with contradictory and conflicting mandates.

Mandate for an Affective Justice

The adjudication of disability claims, like most judicial procedures in the United States, addresses the ultimate goal of making fair and impartial decisions by using two principal, often conflicting, approaches: on the one hand, it employs techniques such as objectivity or emotional distance, cross-examination, and uniformity; on the other hand, it mandates that judges accommodate and engage claimants, identify and distinguish differences, and ensure that all participants receive the individual treatment they deserve. In this regard, the process is simultaneously withholding and giving, rule bound and engaging, preoccupied with treating everyone the same yet recognizing and treating differences as the circumstances might demand.

Whereas the first section of this chapter focused almost exclusively on procedural and substantive mechanisms that make the disability decision-making process uniform, this section describes those rules and procedures that mandate that judges tailor their proceedings to claimants' particular needs, needs that often require judges to identify special traits of claimants needing individualized treatment. The conflict lies in the fact that the uniformity rules dictate that judges apply the rules similarly to similar applicants (to put aside biases), whereas the rules described in this section specifically require judges to distinguish claimants according to certain unique traits and to provide a hearing process that takes those differences into account.

As chapter 3 will demonstrate and the evidence already presented has intimated, the Social Security system as a whole and ALJs in particular have a well-documented history of identifying particular characteristics of claimants to disadvantage them—that is, to bias the decision-making process against them. Chapter 5 will show that in the denied cases reviewed, judges were resistant to using identifying characteristics in any positive sense, to accommodate the special needs of less advantaged claimants or to engage them in the otherwise uniform and bureaucratized process of disability decision making.

Before describing in some detail the mechanisms of accommodation and engagement, it is important to note that these procedures, all embedded in doctrine in one form or another, are no less important than the so-called uniform mechanisms described in the previous section.[5] The only difference is that these mechanisms require judges to affirmatively accommodate or engage claimants and/or their evidence. Painfully, the judges in my small sample fail on all scores—they are capable neither of uniformly applying rules to render fair decisions (of putting aside their biases) or of meeting their affirmative duty to accommodate or engage claimants through the hearing process (of using the differences deemed relevant in the decision-making process to protect those claimants who by law are entitled to that protection).

Doctrinal Foundation for an Affective Justice

The U.S. Supreme Court has held that an ALJ has the ultimate responsibility for ensuring that every claimant has a full and fair hearing (*Richardson v. Perales,* 402 U.S. 389 (1971)). Social Security case law likewise requires the ALJ to "scrupulously and conscientiously probe into, inquire of, and explore for all the relevant facts . . ." (*Hennig v. Gardner* 276 F. Supp. 622, 624 (N.D. Tex. 1967); *Gold v. Secretary of Health, Education and Welfare,* 463 F.2d 38, 43 (2d Cir. 1972)).[6] This mandate holds whether or not a claimant is represented by counsel but particularly if a claimant has "ill health" or an "inability to speak English well" (*Gold v. Secretary of Health, Education and Welfare,* 463 F.2d 38, 43 (2d Cir. 1972)).[7]

To develop their records fully, all Social Security disability applicants require some accommodation or assistance because they are all either physically or mentally ill. However, several claimants have needs that case law identifies as requiring special accommodation or that other research strongly suggests requires such accommodation.[8] In this regard, unrepresented claimants, people who are illiterate, applicants with a limited education, applicants with mental impairments (including addictions), and applicants who do not speak English well have all been legally recognized as requiring special accommodation.

Under certain circumstances, socioeconomic status also presents needs that require special accommodation. For example, when claimants cannot afford to obtain medical records or reports needed to validate their claims, an ALJ has an affirmative duty to obtain relevant records and reports (20 C.F.R. 404.950(d); 20 C.F.R. 416.1450(d)).

The mandate to accommodate claimants with special needs is derived from the broad requirement that judges "scrupulously" and "conscientiously" probe the issues, ensuring a full development of the record.[9] Accommodation requires judges to make an affirmative effort to ensure that claimants' special needs are addressed. Such accommodation differs depending on the special need of the claimant. Briefly, minimum accommodation for people who are unrepresented and illiterate, lack an education, or have difficulty reading English requires judges to inquire whether the claimants can read or comprehend the exhibit file on which the disability decision largely rests. Accommodation of claimants who are illiterate, lack an education, have difficulty reading English, or have a mental impairment—regardless of whether they are represented—requires judges to be patient, understanding, and especially inquisitive to ensure that all the facts in the case are uncovered given the particular difficulty such claimants may have in articulating their problems. The failure-to-accommodate requirement stems from the mandate that "[a]ll Americans seeking assistance from their Government must know that the principles of fundamental fairness and equity will be afforded them regardless of race, sex or national origin" (Labaton 1992).

In sum, legal safeguards designed to accommodate and engage such claimants as the unrepresented, the illiterate, the uneducated, those suffering from mental impairments, and those who do not speak English well are deeply embedded in legal doctrine and in constitutional law. In theory, these safeguards are designed to ensure that claimants who are at an inherent disadvantage due to their differences from the majority culture in general and ALJs in particular are treated with the special care they require to negotiate an otherwise uniform system that allegedly treats everyone as competent and capable of presenting their case.

In the next chapter I explore whether the rules themselves are susceptible to bias and examine the record of physicians who generate and interpret medical evidence for the system. In addition, I review the studies that predate my research and provide foundational material for exploring ALJ decision-making practices in more depth.

CHAPTER 3

Uniformity and Affectivity:
A Record of Failure

Previous studies of the Social Security system, and of the physicians and adjudicators who are integral to it, support my unfolding thesis that uniformity and its companion, affectivity, have never been realized in an institution riddled with substantiated problems. Researchers have identified significant biases in both the procedural and substantive dimensions of disability adjudication, in the rules and in the adjudicators who apply them, and in the system's overall decision-making outcomes.

Biases Detected in Social Security's
Decision-Making Process

Chapter 2 explained that physicians provide the foundation for the disability decision-making process: they generate, interpret and explain the medical evidence on which the system relies. Despite the presumed objectivity of the evidence physicians provide, research has shown that both diagnostic and treatment decisions reflect gender and race bias. For example, studies indicate that women are not treated for heart disease as aggressively as are men. A 1991 study demonstrated that doctors referred fewer women than men for cardiac catheterization, despite the fact that women reported more debilitating symptoms resulting from their experience of angina than those reported by men who were referred for the procedure (Steingart et al. 1991). Another 1991 study revealed that women are less likely than men to undergo angiography, angioplasty, or coronary surgery when admitted to the hospital with a diagnosis of heart disease or chest pain (Ayanian and Epstein 1991). A study of black women reveals that regardless of income and region they receive less mammography than white women, even when there is evidence that they visit their primary care physicians at similar rates (Burns et al. 1996). This finding may explain why black women with breast cancer have a decreased 5-year survival rate when compared to white women.

Other research confirms that African-American patients in general are disadvantaged. A 1993 study demonstrated that white men are more likely than black men to undergo invasive cardiac procedures even when financial incentives are absent (Whittle et al. 1993). These results were confirmed in a 1994 study at the Department of Veteran Affairs, which revealed that rates of cardiac catheterization were significantly higher for white patients when compared to black patients (Mirvis et al. 1994). In addition, white patients were more likely to receive surgery. This study also found that patients with vulvular disease, like coronary artery disease, experienced similar rates of racial bias in treatment. While racial differences varied in part based on region and facility, the researchers concluded that differences in resource utilization persisted even when economic factors were minimized. If, as these studies suggest, treating physicians are less likely to perform diagnostic tests on some groups, white women and African-American applicants are less likely to have corroborating evidence of disability. This problem is further exacerbated by the claimants' ability to pay for tests and related reports documenting their health care problems in disability claims. In a study by Blendon et al. (1995), 32 percent of African-American adults report they had problems paying health-related bills (including bills for physicians, hospitals, and prescription drugs) compared with 17 percent of whites.

In other instances, physicians may erroneously assume that female patients are disabled psychologically when in fact they are physically impaired. Several studies show that based solely on their gender, men and women are assessed differently with regard to psychological illness (Unger and Crawford 1992). A 1991 study of primary-care physicians found that "doctors classified as disturbed a larger proportion of nondisturbed women than nondisturbed men" (Redman et al. 1991, 527). In a 1983 study, physicians who were presented with identical men's and women's case-history vignettes on average judged the female patients as "more emotional" than the male patients (Colameco, Becker, and Simpson 1983).

In 1992, the Ninth Circuit Gender Bias Task Force surveyed claimant representatives, most of whom were attorneys, to determine whether they believed that the gender of the applicant influenced the testimony of medical experts at Social Security disability hearings. Thirty-nine percent of the male representatives and 98 percent of the female representatives believed that the gender of the claimant did have an impact on medical experts (U.S. Court of Appeals [Ninth Circuit] 1992, 99). These findings suggest that as long as the Social Security disability system relies on exclusively medical evidence, the desired impartiality of the process may be corrupted by the biases of the physicians who generate and interpret that evidence.

The use of the Grid is similarly problematic. While the Grid is gender neutral on its face, its application can be gender biased. The Grid advantages individuals with no previous work history or with a strenuous work history (20 C.F.R. 404, subpt. P, app. 2, 201.00 (d)). The former classification favors women who work in the home, while the latter favors men, particularly those who previously held unskilled or semiskilled heavier occupations. The Grid also disadvantages people who, having worked in lighter occupations, are more likely to have transferable skills that would render them not disabled. For example, the Grid disadvantages women who have held traditionally female jobs in the service industry, such as nurses, clerical workers, and teachers, and who therefore would be more likely to have skills that would transfer to sedentary jobs.

The listings of impairments set a standard of severity that must be met for decision makers to presume disability. The impairments listed are described in terms of symptoms, signs, and laboratory findings (20 C.F.R. 404, subpt. P, app. 2, 201.00 (d)). Since the claimant's symptoms tend to be of little determinative value, adjudicators rely heavily on signs and findings, which are often based on results of biomedical research.

Women routinely have been excluded from biomedical research, and, as a consequence, their symptoms and diseases are less likely to be included in the listings than are diseases and symptoms that predominantly affect men. Such is the case although ample evidence indicates that "heart disease, AIDS, depression, and numerous other ostensibly 'gender neutral' conditions are expressed differently in men and women" (Dresser 1992).

In addition, Social Security's listings of impairments exclude two diseases believed by members of the medical community to be predominant among women: multiple chemical sensitivities and chronic fatigue syndrome (CFS). Both these maladies have posed significant problems for ALJs who have been reluctant, and even unwilling, to recognize them as disabling.[1] Only very recently has SSA engaged in a dialogue with the Chronic Fatigue and Immune Dysfunction Syndrome (CFIDS) Association to draft a ruling for the proper evaluation of CFS in disability proceedings, a step which recognizes the inadequacies of current methods for adjudicating CFS claims and others like them (NOSSCR 1998).

When female manifestations of diseases or entire maladies are excluded from the listings, applicants with these problems are likely to be denied disability benefits, particularly at the initial stages of determination. When a woman's disability is not included in the listings, her claim must then be heard by an ALJ, who considers not only medical evidence but also the applicant's credibility with regard to her pain and other symptoms. The judge is the first evaluator to consider whether the claimant's statements about her ability to function, her pain, and her work limitations are credible. Chapter 4 explores this issue in depth by analyzing how judges' credibility determinations, at least in my small sample of cases, may be affected by normative and otherwise repressed assumptions. In the next section I explore more broadly how Social Security adjudicators and judges perform when making disability decisions.

Decision-Making Outcomes

Initial and Reconsideration Stages

Efforts to study the question of disparity between SSA decision-making rules and practices began with government-supported examinations of the initial and reconsideration stages of the process. Funded by the U.S. Department of Health, Education and Welfare (HEW), Saad Nagi's *Disability and Rehabilitation: Legal, Clinical, and Self-Concepts and Measurements* (1969) was one of the earliest studies to examine the issues of objectivity and fairness in SSA disability decision making. Nagi was particularly interested to learn how the disability standard applied by DDS decision makers differed from the standard applied by teams of clinical experts who were not trained in the rules. Nagi explored this issue and HEW funded his project because disability decisions should be based on objective clinical evidence. Hence, Nagi sought to test whether decision makers were actually carrying out the purposes of the Social Security Act governing disability determinations (6).

Thus, focusing on the first two stages of the process, Nagi compared the results to two groups of decision makers who reviewed the identical claims of approximately 2,500 claimants. On the one hand, teams of clinicians—each consisting of a social worker, a physician, a psychologist, an occupational therapist, and a vocational counselor who were not trained in the rules governing disability decisions—applied clinical expertise to determine eligibility for benefits. On the other hand, teams of adjudicators from state DDS offices who regularly made disability decisions applied Social Security criteria to the same sample of cases.

The results of Nagi's analysis revealed a significant rate of what he called "incongruencies." Reviewing the same medical evidence, clinical teams awarded benefits to more than 55 percent of the claims that DDS decision makers denied. The clinical teams found these applicants to be incapable of work activity outside the home or to be "totally unfit for [any] work," even work that could be done in the home (Nagi 1969, 94). (For purposes of Nagi's study, both these categories rendered people unable to do paid work and were thus equivalent to a DDS decision maker's approval of a claim.) While Social Security rules were supposedly founded on clinical evidence, Nagi's clinical teams thus drew conclusions that differed dramatically from those of DDS decision makers.

While the clinical teams would have awarded benefits to more than half of the claimants that the DDS teams denied, the incongruencies between the two teams were not uniform across the board. For example, the clinical teams would have awarded benefits in 76 percent of the cases involving psychological limitations, but DDS decision makers would have done so in just over 50 percent of such claims (Nagi 1969, 99). When it came to physical impairments, however, the two teams more closely agreed: DDS decision makers allowed benefits to almost 89 percent of the applicants that the clinical teams found to have severe physical limitations (Nagi 1969, 99).

Incongruencies were not Nagi's only important finding. When he looked closely to explain these discrepant findings, he noticed an interesting pattern with regard to gender. The DDS decision makers granted benefits to almost all the white male applicants that the clinical teams found to be disabled (65.2 percent and 68.6 percent, respectively) (Nagi 1969, 111). But the DDS teams granted benefits to far fewer white female applicants than the clinical teams did (46.7 percent versus 66 percent) (Nagi 1969, 111). Nagi attributes this discrepancy to DDS decision makers' preferences for physical impairments, previously described, and to the fact that white women were more likely than white men to allege mental limitations.

Interestingly, DDS decision makers and the clinical teams decided cases involving men and women of color similarly. DDS allowed benefits in 68.8 percent of the cases involving men of color; the clinical teams considered 70.5 percent of these same claimants unfit for work (Nagi 1969,

111). Similarly, DDS allowed benefits in 60.5 percent of cases involving female claimants of color, while the clinical teams granted benefits to 64.5 percent of these claimants (Nagi 1969, 111). Nagi attributes this congruence in clinical and DDS decisions involving people of color to certain factors: the lower educational levels of disability applicants of color, which led to a high allowance rate by DDS evaluators; and the tendency of applicants of color to allege physical rather than mental impairments, which almost always yielded higher award rates (Nagi 1969, 111–13).

Nagi's analysis of occupation-related findings, like his impairment-related findings, yielded some interesting implications related to gender, although he did not draw them out. While his investigation reveals no clear pattern of the effect of occupational history on disability decision making, it does suggest one very important point: unskilled laborers (mostly men) were allowed benefits more often than they were denied; however, clerical and sales workers (mostly women) were denied benefits more often than they were allowed (Nagi 1969, 122).[2] While these results might partially be explained by the vocational aspect of the disability equation (which tends to favor applicants who previously performed heavy as opposed to light work on the basis that their skills are less likely to transfer to lighter, more highly skilled jobs should they become too disabled to perform heavy work), Nagi neglected to analyze the obvious gender implications of these findings.

The examples discussed here indicating disparity between administrative and clinical standards represent some of Nagi's most startling findings. The administrative and legislative response to Nagi's work was to impose more stringent regulatory control over the process and to fund several other studies that investigated similar issues. As for its relevance to my work, Nagi's analysis sets a trend not only in subject matter but also in manner of treatment: Particularly with respect to his findings related to gender but also, to a lesser extent, to kinds of impairment and occupational history, Nagi discovered something that potentially suggests that Social Security decision makers are biased, although he did not develop this thesis. While Nagi and subsequent researchers note that the disparities they detect may suggest inequities in the decision-making process, he and the others do little or nothing to elucidate these factors, their underlying causes, and ultimate effects.

The GAO (1976) also conducted a study, considerably smaller than Nagi's, concerned with the uniformity of the decisions of initial and reconsideration adjudicators. Personnel from 10 DDS state agencies were asked to adjudicate a sample of 221 actual DI and SSI claims that had previously been decided at the initial and reconsideration levels. Each sample case was adjudicated by DDS examiners from at least two different states. The study showed a significant disagreement among the 10 states on the disposition of the 221 claims. The states completely agreed to approve or deny benefits on only 38 of the 221 claims (approximately 17 percent) (GAO 1976, 6). Even in this narrow margin of agreement on final decisions, the adjudicators often disagreed on the rationale behind their decisions.

In this study, as in others reviewed here, researchers were concerned with consistency in outcomes, not the presence and/or operation of bias or other factors of disparity in the process of decision making. As a result, the GAO interpreted its findings as evidence that the SSA had failed adequately to supervise state-level adjudicators and recommended, as a remedy, strengthening the federal-state administrative structure and enhancing training and information-disseminating activities.

In response to this GAO study, the Subcommittee on Social Security of the Senate Committee on Ways and Means studied the problem of inconsistencies at the initial and reconsideration stages (U.S. Senate 1978). Like the administrative response to Nagi's study, the committee determined that to remedy this problem of inconsistencies, more federal administrative control over DDS decision making was needed. Thus, still more legislation was proposed and eventually enacted to tackle the problem of inconsistency. This new legislation took the form of regulations describing the performance standards, administrative requirements, and procedures to be followed. Though the legislative hearing voiced much concern that decisions were not uniform, it entailed little or no discussion of possible patterns of bias against particular groups or kinds of disabilities. The committee rather focused almost entirely on restructuring the disability administration to strengthen Social Security's federal voice in the state-by-state decision-making process.

In a follow-up study to the 1976 GAO report that documented inconsistencies at the initial and reconsideration levels, HEW examined the consistency of initial disability decisions among and within the states (SSA 1981). As in the Nagi research and the 1976 GAO report, HEW's 1981 report was not as concerned with bias as with whether DDS decisions were inconsistent. The specific purpose of the study was to examine whether different states reviewing the same cases decided them similarly.

Trying to replicate the 1976 GAO study, the SSA's Office of Policy conceptualized the test in very much the same way as the GAO study. A total of 504 cases were randomly assigned to states, and determinations of DDS adjudicators in different states were compared. This study also revealed disagreement within and between states to be significant. There was roughly a one in eight chance that any adjudicators from any two states would agree on a given claim. There was about a one in six chance that two examiners from one state would agree. That HEW found an even lower rate of consistency in 1981 than GAO found in 1976 was surprising, especially considering the effort that had been made since Nagi's 1969 study to assure that the disability program was based on objective and uniform federal standards.

To explain the enormous variation they had found, HEW statistically analyzed three characteristics of claimants—impairment, age, and education—to determine whether these factors led to the disparities in the state decisions. Were adjudicators in some states, for example, more sympathetic to claims involving physical impairments than mental impairments or to older applicants rather than younger applicants? The HEW did not consider gender and race variables in their analysis.

HEW researchers found that factors they considered did not seem to explain the variations, although they cautioned that their findings may be explained by the small size of their study sample. Ultimately, though, HEW explained the glaring inconsistencies in and among the states that they discovered as follows: (1) a certain amount of disagreement in decisions is to be expected; (2) the results are limited to eight states and cannot be generalized to all states; and (3) the states were in flux given the recent implementation of the Grid. As in all previous instances, HEW investigations concluded that efforts to improve the structure should focus on uniform SSA guidelines and federal instructions for individual adjudicators. They ignored the possible influence of bias in the decision-making process. They also neglected to consider how factors other than age, education, or impairment may have influenced the process.

One of the most significant studies of disparity in the initial decision-making process was published by the GAO in 1994. Researchers were charged with examining gender differences in the 1988 claims of DI applicants. They found that women in older age groups received DI benefits at lower rates than did men. The GAO, explaining two-thirds of the disparity, suggested that there were logical reasons why older women received benefits at lower rates. More specifically, the report opined that women apply for benefits with less severe impairments and that women are more likely to work in occupations with lower allowance rates, regardless of gender. The GAO's explanations, however, should not go unquestioned. As I argued earlier in this chapter, what may appear to be less severe impairments may in fact be hidden forms of gender bias in medical diagnostic and treatment protocols. When women are offered fewer diagnostic tests or invasive procedures, the medical evidence is much more likely to render a claimant's impairment "less severe." Other forms of structural sexism may also explain why older women qualify less often for disability benefits based on their previous occupations. For example, the Social Security rules are more likely to grant benefits to men who have previously worked in strenuous occupations and to deny benefits to women who have skills that would transfer to sedentary jobs (Mills 1993).[3]

The ALJ Hearing Process

A related set of inquiries has focused on the ALJ hearing process, the third stage of the Social Security disability adjudication process, and the stage with which my study is concerned. The first of these examinations was conducted in 1973 by Robert Dixon. Dixon examined ALJ reversal-rate statistics; these statistics summarize the percentages of ALJs who granted benefits to claims that had previously been denied. Dixon sought to determine whether fairness, equality of treatment, and correctness were being achieved at ALJ hearings. Dixon's study revealed a high degree of variation among ALJs' reversal rates, not only within a given region but also within individual hearing offices. Dixon's overall findings reveal that some ALJs granted benefits in as few as 8 to 12 percent of the cases they heard, while others granted benefits in as many as 84 to 88 percent.

To explain this disparity, Dixon hypothesized that ALJ decisions rested "significantly on the personality of the examiner as well as the actual record" (1973, 135), yet he did not consider what those personality influences might be. Rather than tackle these issues, Dixon, like researchers before him, instead concluded that more substantive regulations on disability determinations should be promulgated to insure uniform guidance. He went so far as to suggest that his findings were so disturbing that Congress should consider abolishing the ALJ hearing process altogether.

In 1978 Mashaw et al. presented the results of a major study they undertook of the Social Security disability hearing process. Their primary concerns were (1) whether the Social Security disability system had the capacity to produce accurate and consistent decisions efficiently; and (2) whether the ALJ decision-making process could be redesigned to be both fair and cost-effective. Following an intensive investigation of four ALJ hearing offices that included interviews with judges and claimants; a statistical analysis of a random sample of disability hearing transcripts, evidence, and decisions; and observations of actual hearings, the authors made several important findings. Drawing on Dixon's finding that the variance among judges' awards of benefits ranged between 8 and 88 percent, the authors recognized a significant problem of inaccuracy in the ALJ decision-making process. They argued that this inaccuracy "is truly a product of subjective factors, probably relating primarily to the interpretive role of the ALJ rather than the investigative one" (Mashaw et al. 1978, 21). These conclusions were based on the premise that since cases are randomly assigned to judges and each judge should get a similar mix of cases, it is reasonable to expect that different judges, if impartial, should approve similar numbers of cases. While Mashaw and his colleagues followed previous researchers in recommending better specifications of standards and more training and conferences to improve accuracy and consistency among judges, the authors parted from earlier scholars in conceding that "these efforts will leave a substantial residuum of variance among the ALJ corps" (Mashaw et al. 1978, xxi–xxii).

From reviewing transcripts and observing hearings, Mashaw and his team gathered an important finding that helped to illuminate why they believed that ALJs' decisions may never be fully consistent. These researchers found, and the results from my small sample of cases confirm, that judges rarely gave adequate opening statements and often made insincere inquiries into the claimant's desire to be represented by counsel. Hence, judges frequently render such responsibilities an "empty formality" (Mashaw et al. 1978, 66). In other words, Mashaw's study, published nearly 20 years ago, detected evidence of the same pattern of disregard for the rules meant to ensure impartiality as I found in the hearing transcripts and decisions I reviewed. However, Mashaw et al. did not systematically analyze the hearing process for violations of rules, they did not systematically examine the violations they observed, and they did not attempt to explain the inaccuracies or inconsistencies they described as potential signs of bias. They seem rather to have regarded rule violations as an afterthought and did not consider their possible relation to the "subjective," "interpretive" factors that, as they saw it, rendered the ALJ hearing process variable and inaccurate. Thus, Mashaw and his colleagues concluded that the high levels of inconsistency they found are unavoidable; inconsistency must be tolerated, or aspects of the process must be abandoned altogether.

Overall Disability Decision-Making Process

Several studies have considered the issue of disparity in the overall decision-making process. In *Bureaucratic Justice* (1983), Jerry Mashaw's analysis further illuminates and attempts to resolve the myriad of dilemmas presented by the enormous Social Security bureaucratic decision-making process, which aspires both to be fair and impartial and to operate with dwindling resources and rising costs. Ultimately, Mashaw develops the conclusion he and his colleagues previously sketched (Mashaw et al. 1978) to recommend abolishing the current ALJ hearing process altogether. With this recommendation, he also suggests that the federal court appeals process and legislative oversight of Social Security rules and decisions likewise be curtailed. To examine a little more closely how he reaches that conclusion, it is useful to summarize his three models of justice, all of which he believes figure prominently in the disability process as it is currently organized.

Bureaucratic rationality. Bureaucratic rationality, the bureaucratic model SSA uses at the initial and reconsideration stages to make disability decisions, is concerned with distinguishing between true and false claims at the least possible cost: As a model for adjudicating claims that is both accurate and cost-effective, bureaucratic rationality seeks to "minimize the sum of error and other associated costs" (Mashaw 1983, 25). Mashaw regards bureaucratic rationality ideally as the sole or at least the predominant model to be used for disability decision making. Decisions made by this model, Mashaw argues, often differ with those generated by the other two models, professional treatment and moral judgment, because the basic values reflected in the models clash.

Professional treatment. The professional-treatment model brings professionals—physicians, vocational experts, counselors of all kinds—into the decision-making process to examine the needs of the claimant more or less holistically. Thus, according to Mashaw, the goal of the professional-treatment model is mostly to serve. When professionals become involved in the process, disability decision making becomes concerned with income support, medical care, vocational rehabilitation, and counseling—all needed to improve the claimants' well-being and perhaps self-sufficiency, but all at odds with the need to decide the greatest number of claims as consistently as possible at the lowest possible cost. Thus, since professionals are influenced by facts, intuition, and judgment and not necessarily accuracy and efficiency, the professional-treatment model clashes with the bureaucratic-rationality model and introduces inefficiency into the system.

Moral judgment. Mashaw's moral-judgment model refers to the decision-making processes Social Security ALJs use at the hearing level rather than the processes DDS adjudicators use at the initial and reconsideration levels. Moral judgment, according to Mashaw, approaches decision making as a clarification of values. At issue is whether the applicant "deserves" benefits. He further characterizes this model by "its promise of a full and equal opportunity to obtain one's entitlement" (Mashaw 1983, 31). While Mashaw recognizes that all three models are ultimately concerned with attaining the same goal—that is, factually correct decisions—he finds the moral-judgment model to be the least efficient means to this end, because its regulators, ALJs, by the nature of their task, have the greatest "error proneness and inefficiency" (Mashaw 1983, 41).

Mashaw is convinced that a bureaucratic model that allows an organization to govern itself with as little interference as possible from outside regulators is capable of achieving the goal of uniform decision making and even the public perception of fairness. According to Mashaw, outside regulators such as ALJs, federal judges, and legislators place constraints on the Social Security disability decision-making system that undermine the bureaucracy's ultimate goal, which is to distinguish efficiently between true and false claims. Thus, Mashaw believes that Social Security and bureaucracies like it should be permitted to operate on their own through what he calls internal law (that is, written instructions and interpretations, standard bureaucratic routines, and developmental and decisional practices). Toward this end, he expands Dixon's (1973) and his own previous (Mashaw et al. 1978) suggestion and explicitly recommends abolishing the current ALJ and federal court appeals process and curtailing legislative oversight. He would replace these agencies with what he calls a superbureau, an institution that would combine a "judicial chamber" with the functions of other federal agencies such as the GAO and the Justice Department's Office of Legal Counsel. Toward this end, such a superbureau would supervise the entire functioning of the bureaucracy and oversee instances of maladministration (Mashaw 1983, 226).

Mashaw's contention that Social Security's bureaucracy should be trusted to ensure fairness and equity without ALJ, federal court, or legislative oversight is incomprehensible. In my view, and based on all the previous research, more, not less, sensitivity and individualized attention needs to be incorporated into the disability decision-making process. As Justice William Brennan has suggested, such a bureaucracy should not be distant and detached but instead should embrace a passion that puts bureaucrats and line workers in touch with "the dreams and disappointments of those with whom they deal" (1988, 19). Mashaw's superbureau seems to embody none of these important concerns. Indeed his solution ignores the commitment made by Congress and the courts to provide a scrupulous and conscientious inquiry into each individual claim. Checks and balances provided by the system's current formulation are required to preserve and protect the juridical process from the stereotyping and indifference Mashaw and other researchers have detected.[4]

In *The Disabled State* (1984), Deborah Stone reveals the presence of an inherent contradiction within the Social Security disability program. Her analysis surpassed most previous efforts to explain disparity in the system and clearly established the need for studies of the possible influence of bias in the decision-making process. Concerned about the expansion of disability programs in the United States and abroad, Stone's analysis of the U.S. Social Security system exposes the political mechanisms the United States has used to resolve the difficult issues concerning the distribution of benefits to people with disabilities. In the process, she discovers that the goal of objectivity in disability decision making is inherently contradictory with the flexibility of the clinical standards, which rely on physicians' impressions, findings, and interpretations.

Stone argues persuasively that because clinical criteria cannot draw adequate boundaries between disability and ability to work, they cannot provide the objectivity the U.S. Social Security disability system seeks. She explains this shortcoming as follows:

> [C]linical tests can provide a measure of some phenomenon, but no single test can tell whether a person is "impaired" or "disabled" or still able to work. Someone has to decide what level of any measurement is indicative of an inability to function and how the information from different tests ought to be combined. (1984, 128)

Stone contends that even clinical "tests" that are supposedly objective are open to interpretation: Laboratory studies and X-rays show "alarming discrepancies," patients can manipulate some test results by making only partial effort, and physicians' interpretations of laboratory findings show "wide discrepancies" (1984, 129, 131). Given that the evidence underlying a disability claim is so easily manipulated and that the rules are not conducive to being objectively applied, Stone is convinced that the accuracy and consistency of decision makers is unlikely to improve with more rules or tougher SSA oversight.

Stone's interpretation of the contradiction embedded in a system that on the one hand strives for objectivity and on the other relies on highly subjective evidence does not directly address the issue of potential bias on the part of Social Security disability decision makers. Rather, like that of Dixon and Mashaw, Stone's analysis suggests that the problem of inaccuracy and imprecision in Social Security disability decision making is irremediable by stricter regulation and oversight and, as such, is probably a foregone conclusion. Stone, however, raises a concern relevant to the current study. Taking her idea just one or two steps further, it is arguable that because the clinical evidence on which the system relies is highly flexible and standards for applying that evidence are imprecisely defined, the system may, in this way, implicitly encourage decision makers to inject their personal views (and hence their biases) into the disability decision-making process. Institutional pressures on ALJs to decide cases quickly, to deny as many as possible, and to act as defense, prosecutor, and judge are three other means by which the system may encourage decision makers to inject personal views into the process. Although I refer to these institutional pressures in passing when analyzing my results, it has not been my primary focus.

Probably the single most important study undertaken so far on the issue of impartiality of Social Security decision makers is the 1992 GAO study of the impact of claimants' race on disability decision making. The principal objective of this research was to analyze the circumstances surrounding the lower proportion of allowances among black applicants relative to white applicants. Using quantitative methods, GAO researchers analyzed issues and decisions at the initial, reconsideration, and ALJ-hearing levels. The researchers reviewed claims filed in 1983, including approximately 700,000 cases involving white applicants and 245,000 cases involving black applicants.

The GAO found that demographic characteristics and impairments could largely explain the difference in allowance rates to black and white DI applicants (claimants with a work history) at the initial and reconsideration levels. Thus, the black allowance rate was lower than the white rate "primarily because Black applicants were concentrated in age groups and had impairments, such as hypertension, that had low allowance rates regardless of race" (GAO 1992, 4).

However, for SSI applicants (those without a work history) between the ages of 18 and 24, the racial difference was "largely *unexplained* by differences in education, sex, geographic location, percent urban population or impairment type" (5). Thirty-four percent of African Americans who applied were allowed benefits compared with 47 percent of Whites (GAO 1992, 5; emphasis added). The only explanation for the difference was race.

At the ALJ-appeals level, ALJs granted benefits to 55 percent of black DI applicants compared to 66 percent of white DI applicants. They granted benefits to 51 percent of black SSI applicants compared to 60 percent of white SSI applicants. "For the most part, GAO could not explain the racial difference [in ALJ decisions] by other factors, such as demographics or impairment type" (GAO 1992, 5). The researchers found that blacks living in the Chicago region who applied for DI benefits were 17 percent less likely than whites to receive benefits at the hearing level. Blacks living in the Chicago region who applied for SSI benefits were 10 percent less likely than whites to receive benefits when their cases were considered by ALJs. The Boston region revealed similar results. Blacks who applied for DI benefits were 14 percent less likely than whites to win their claims before ALJs. Black SSI applicants were 10 percent less likely than whites to receive benefits from ALJs. The San Francisco region results revealed a 12 percent difference for black DI applicants and a 7 percent difference for black SSI applicants when their cases were adjudicated by ALJs (43). Although the 1992 GAO study does quantitatively analyze the disability decision-making process for bias against black applicants, it does not consider why, how, and under what circumstances race plays a role or how other biases may potentially influence decision makers.

One other study examined the effects of gender in disability decision making. The preliminary and final reports of the Ninth Circuit Gender Bias Task Force (U.S. Court of Appeals [Ninth Circuit] 1992, 1993) further suggest that ALJ decision making may be biased. Using surveys of claimant representatives and focus groups of attorneys who specialize in representing applicants before ALJs, the task force documented instances in which women respondents believed that gender influenced judges. For example, the statistics generated by the task force study indicate that all of the female representatives who responded to the survey believed that the gender of their female claimants had some effect on how ALJs evaluated credibility: 32 percent of female representatives believed that ALJs in general attributed greater credibility to the testimony of men than women, and 80 percent of female respondents believed that male ALJs attributed less credibility to the testimony of women than men (U.S. Court of Appeals [Ninth Circuit] 1992, 99). The task force found that pain is one of the symptoms ALJs most commonly consider in assessing credibility. Since women are far more likely than men to claim disability because of chronic pain syndrome and since 75 percent of applicants with chronic pain syndrome are denied benefits, the task force concluded that these judges' decisions may reflect gender bias (U.S. Court of Appeals [Ninth Circuit] 1992, 93–104).

The male judges who responded to the study survey did not agree. All 83 male ALJ respondents reported that gender plays no role in disability decision making (U.S. Court of Appeals [Ninth Circuit] 1992, 99). In contrast, four of the seven female ALJs who responded reported that disparaging remarks about women occur "frequently" or "somewhat frequently" (99).

Although the Ninth Circuit Gender Bias Task Force explored the effects of gender in both the hearing process and its outcome, the investigators did not examine ALJ hearing transcripts and decisions to learn systematically how that bias may enter into the system and how it operates once there. Using these findings as a springboard, my study looks directly at ALJ hearing transcripts and decisions precisely to devise a means to investigate these issues.

Recent Studies of Decision Making

Recent efforts to study and improve decision making in disability claims have followed in the wake of the 1992 GAO race bias study. In March 1993, the Social Security Administration's Disability Hearings Quality Review Process (DHQRP) became fully operational. This unit developed and implemented a peer review method by which ALJs, acting as Reviewing Judges (RJs), analyze the decisions of their peers to "promote fair and accurate hearing decisions" (SSA 1997, 13). While the two DHQRP reports issued to date covering the periods 1992–93 and 1995–96 (SSA 1995, 1997) make no mention of the 1992 GAO race bias study, there is no doubt that the quality review process was prompted, in large measure, by the GAO's suggestion that there were racial disparities in the system (GAO 1997; Skoler 1994). The history is critical as the DHQRP's findings should be analyzed in light of SSA's motivation to improve their badly tarnished image.

Consistent with the SSA's history of systematically denying allegations of prejudice, neither of the two reports issued by the Office of Program and Integrity Reviews have examined the extent to which race or gender bias may be operating in the decision-making process. Indeed, the SSA's DHQRP has peer reviewed over 9,000 cases using a systematic method for evaluating ALJ decision making; not one question on the 18-page evaluation form studies the extent to which race or gender bias might be operating in the process. Nevertheless, SSA's findings merit attention, as these are the first studies to examine ALJ compliance with key rules.

The SSA DHQRP solicits ALJs to serve as RJs for a four-month period. The judges selected as RJs represent a cross section of experience and are selected from different regions. Since its inception, 108 ALJs have served as RJs, representing approximately 10 percent of the ALJ corps.[5]

SSA's findings focus on several issues that are relevant to determining whether judges comply with procedural or substantive safeguards. For example, the data collection form requires RJs to assess such matters as whether ALJs adequately inform claimants regarding their right to representation and whether ALJs obtain appropriate waivers of that right from claimants; whether ALJs meet their obligation to protect the claimant's rights; and whether ALJs provide an opening statement, identify witnesses, and obtain specific testimony (the specific rules governing these procedures are described in more detail in chapters 4, 5, and 6). In addition, the RJs are asked to determine whether the ultimate decision is supported by substantial evidence, the standard the Appeals Council uses when deciding whether the ALJ decision should be affirmed. If the RJs conclude that the decision was not supported by substantial evidence, RJs elaborate why based on a number of factors. Finally RJs are asked whether ALJs abused their discretion or made errors of law, both of which are standards for Appeals Council review and remand or reversal. The RJs are then asked to perform an "independent" review of the entire record to determine if they would have reached the same conclusion as ALJs making the respective decisions.

None of their findings are particularly startling. Overall, the RJs concluded that most hearing denials were supported by substantial evidence (82 percent for 1992–93 data and 92 percent for 1995–96 data) (SSA 1997). In 1992–93, RJs concluded that they would have made the opposite decision in only 4 percent of denied cases and in 1995–96, RJs concluded that they would have made the opposite decision in only 2 percent of denied cases. Similar data were generated for approved claims. RJs would have made the opposite decision in 5 and 6 percent of cases they reviewed in 1992–93 and 1995–96, respectively. In 1992–93, RJs believed that 14 percent of denied cases needed more documentation and by 1995–96, only 6 percent of denied cases needed more documentation.

During 1992–93, in 9 percent of the denied cases reviewed by RJs, there was an "abuse of discretion" and by 1995–96, only 5 percent of the denied cases involved an "abuse of discretion." In general, when abuse of discretion was detected, there were three primary explanations: expert medical or vocational testimony was either inadequate or misrepresented in the decision; appropriate procedures were not followed, such as ALJs did not send posthearing evidence to claimants or their representatives; or claimants were pressured to proceed without representatives.

Errors of law were more common. In 1992–93 cases, 19 percent of hearing denials contained errors of law and in 1995–96, 16 percent of hearing denials contained errors of law. Of those cases containing errors of law, RJs identified several areas in which ALJs made such errors, including but not limited to: credibility (20 percent for 1992–93 and 3 percent for 1995–96); procedural issues (12 percent for 1992–93 and 9 percent for 1995–96) and evidentiary issues (33 percent for 1992–93 and 34 percent for 1995–96).

Overall, RJs concluded that in 1995–96, ALJs protected claimants rights in 96 percent of the cases; in 1992–93, they found this protection evident in 95 percent of the cases. For 1995–96, 95 percent of denied claimants rights were protected whereas 89 percent of denied claimants rights were protected during the 1992–93 review.

In those cases in which RJs concluded that the denial of benefits was not supported by the evidence, RJs believed that ALJs failed to obtain such information as the impact of other symptoms or pain on the claimant, activities of daily living, the treating physician's opinion, and past relevant work (SSA 1997). In addition, the RJs found that in those denials where there was insufficient evidence to support the decision, claimant's evidence or testimony was lacking in 63 percent of the cases. As was detected in previous studies, it seems that the evaluation of mental impairments remained problematic for some ALJs. In the 1992–93 cases reviewed by RJs, only 78 percent of mental impairment denials were supported by substantial evidence; in 1995–96 cases, 86 percent of mental impairment denials were supported by substantial evidence.

The findings with regard to procedural issues are particulary interesting insofar as many of the SSA's inquiries mimic the areas of inquiry in this study. The RJs found that most judges administer the oath to both allowed and denied cases (97 percent in 1992–93 and 1995–96) and in 90 percent of denied cases, witnesses were introduced (1995–96 data only) (SSA 1997). RJs also found that in 1992–93, 26 percent of denied and awarded claimants did not receive an opening statement. By 1995–96, 18 percent of all claimants did not receive an opening statement. Data from 1995–96 revealed that ALJs are more likely to give opening statements in denied cases (15 percent of denied claimants did not receive opening statements while 21 percent of claimants who received favorable decisions were given an opening statement).

Questions relating to the interrogation of claimants revealed that RJs found some ALJs hearing and decision making practices to be lacking. Taken from the 1995–96 data, ALJs had the most difficulty with gathering evidence related to claimants medication and their adherence to medical treatment prescribed by a physician (78 percent), daily activities (81 percent), sources of current income (72 percent), and physical capabilities (72 percent) (SSA 1997). Similarly, these problems surfaced when questioning the experts present at the hearing. Again relying on 1995–96 data, the ALJs did not adequately address the ME's evaluation of pain and/or symptoms (adequately addressed in only 73 percent of denials), the ME's professional qualifications (adequately addressed in only 53 percent of denials), assessment of mental capacity (adequately addressed in only 60 percent of denials), and asking the ME if more claimant information is needed (adequately addressed in only 51 percent of denials). Similar problems were detected in the questioning of VEs.

In a review of the RJ data relating to unrepresented claimants' cases, it was found that in 1992–93, 77 percent of unrepresented claimants whose claims were denied were adequately informed of their right to representation. In 1995–96, 80 percent of unrepresented denied claimants were adequately informed of their right to representation. In addition, RJs found that 80 percent of those claimants whose cases were denied, using the 1992–93 data, were supported by substantial evidence, compared to 89 percent in 1995–96. The SSA found that the difference between represented and unrepresented claimants for 1995–96 was statistically significant (94 percent for represented claimants who were denied). This finding suggests that ALJs may be more inclined to provide stronger evidentiary decisions in cases involving claimants who were represented. This also suggests that claimants who are unrepresented may not only be deprived of adequate instructions regarding their right to be represented, but might also receive decisions that are not supported by substantial evidence. Statistically significant differences which disadvantaged unrepresented claimants were also detected with regard to errors of law.

Overall, these findings suggest that RJs believe that their fellow ALJs do a fair to excellent job when hearing cases and evaluating claims, especially with regard to denied applicants. In 1992–93, RJs concluded that they would make the same decision in 89 percent of the 1992–93 denied cases and in 94 percent of the 1995–96 denied cases. As for allowances, RJs would have made a different decision in 83 percent of the 1992–93 allowed cases and 72 percent of the 1995–96 allowed cases. Hence, at least according to RJs, ALJs are more often correct when they deny claims, than when they grant them.

The variations that RJs detected in these efforts motivated SSA to improve both the training and practices of ALJs. Indeed, SSA's most recent report (1997) finds "dramatic" improvement between the two study periods (1992–93 and 1995–96) with "ALJs improving significantly in many areas of case adjudication" (69). What is most stunning about these results however, is the absence of any attempt to explore whether prejudice persists in the ALJs outcomes.

In 1994, Dan Skoler, Associate Commissioner for OHA, described the development of the DHQRP peer review program and its relationship to detections of bias. This effort, he claimed, would "identify and explore factors in hearing-level claims that might contribute to the disparity dilemma" (19). Yet nothing in the SSA reports suggests that this peer review process was concerned with or ever considered the impact of bias on decision making. Indeed, even though race and gender data are available for the 9,000 cases reviewed for these two periods, no analysis of this data has been undertaken or published. While SSA analyzed the relevance of age and impairment on ALJ and RJ reviews, it neglected to analyze the data in light of other factors such as race or gender. As with previous studies, the SSA remains unwilling, in any meaningful way, to scrutinize ALJ decision making practices for bias.

One final recent study merits mention. In 1997, the GAO issued a report in which they compared initial and reconsideration decision making, to the awards and denials of ALJs. Twenty years on, the federal government is still trying to determine why disparities between these two sets of decision makers persist. Essentially, the GAO concludes that DDS examiners and ALJs differ over claimants ability to function: ALJs are much more likely than DDS examiners to conclude that claimants have severe limitations which prevent them from working. They attribute those differences to a number of policy and procedural factors, including but not limited to ALJ reliance on claimant testimony and the opinions of treating physicians. The GAO seems heartened by the downward shift in award rates by ALJs and the SSA's support for programs like DHQRP that monitor the decision-making practices of ALJs to ensure that their decisions comport with agency policy. This GAO study however, like previous studies, is not concerned with race or gender disparities in decision making, but rather with making decision making consistent between the two sets of decision makers. Implicit in the GAO report are two guiding assumptions. First, ALJs grant too many disability claims, especially when their decisions are compared to DDS examiners. Second, ALJs should be the decision maker of last resort; the GAO assumes that most claims should be decided by DDS examiners at the initial or reconsideration stages of the process. The GAO recognizes the long-standing problem in inconsistent decision making between DDS and OHA and concludes that confidence in the decision-making process and the costs associated with expensive ALJ appeals demands system reform. They recommend unification initiatives, similar to the redesign plan, to rectify the consistencies they detect.

Despite the disability system's procedural and substantive safeguards, the evidence presented here raises serious questions about the fairness of and thus the potential influence of bias in disability decision making. The mechanisms designed to ensure impartiality, including the listings, the Grid, and the five-step sequential evaluation process, may operate to standardize and mask bias rather than to eliminate it. Moreover, the findings of Nagi, the GAO, the SSA, Dixon, and Mashaw, and more recently of the DHQRP, which document incongruencies, inconsistencies, and inaccuracies, suggest that factors other than the stated guidelines influence decision makers, including ALJs, and that errors in determinations are detectable and prevalent. But no researcher examined how and at what point subjectivity or personal judgment may enter the hearing or decision-making process; none of these previous studies, that is, took the issue of impartiality head on. Nor did they propose any real options for addressing the disparities detected.

Deborah Stone's political analysis raises the question of how clinical standards permit bias to occur—a question that, to some extent, presupposes that bias is an inevitable feature of disability decision making. The 1992 GAO race study indicates that personal bias probably does influence the process, but it does not explain how that prejudice operates in practice. The reports of the Ninth Circuit Gender Bias Task Force provide a starting point for an analysis by suggesting that the gender of a claimant may affect such matters as how judges elicit evidence from women. The DHQRP reports (SSA 1995, 1997) tentatively suggest that even the peer review process has revealed some procedural and substantive irregularities in the system, despite its silence on the role of race or gender in the dynamic between judge and claimant.

In the next chapter I explore in greater detail the cases in my sample. My findings further suggest and illuminate exactly how judges fail to apply the rules uniformly and with the affectivity the system requires.

CHAPTER 4

Empty Formalities

In 1978 Mashaw et al. were disturbed by their finding that judges rarely gave adequate opening statements and often were insincere in their inquiries into the claimant's desire or need for representation. These formalities, which Mashaw et al. found "empty" involve a complex legal and emotional mandate on judges to insure both that the procedural requirements of a case are met (such as the right to an introduction, to be represented by counsel, and to obtain relevant medical evidence and testimony) and that these mechanisms are imbued with the passion necessary for the claimant to fully engage in the hearing process.

To formulate a more precise understanding of how uniformity fails to operate in any consistent manner in the Social Security disability decision-making process, at least in my sample of cases, I begin this chapter by presenting the method and design of my study of these formalities, or rules, including how I selected the 50 cases that comprise my sample and the salient characteristics of the claimants and judges I culled from the transcripts and decisions. I also present the procedural and substantive rules that comprised the focus of my investigation into whether judges adhered to their mandate to comply with the relevant rules and present my rationale for focusing on certain rules and not others. This chapter also summarizes why I chose to focus on judges' failure to comply with these rules and how their inability to accommodate or engage claimants and simultaneous tendency to stereotype them emerged as central themes in my research.

Description of Sample Cases

Origin and History of Cases

My findings are based on an analysis of 50 federal court cases that contain 67 ALJ hearing transcripts and decisions of Social Security claims that were denied throughout the disability-review process and eventually appealed to federal court. This sample includes all such Social Security disability federal court cases that closed in San Francisco and Boston in 1990 and half of such cases that closed in Chicago in 1990. Thus, I reviewed a total of 17 federal court cases from San Francisco, 10 cases from Boston, and 23 cases from Chicago (where I selected all odd-numbered cases).

I chose Chicago because the GAO (1992) found it to be the region in which African Americans experienced the greatest disadvantage. As previously noted, African Americans were 17 percent less likely than whites to receive DI benefits from ALJs in Chicago. I selected Boston and San Francisco because they also represented regions with high racial differences according to the GAO's findings (14 percent and 12 percent, respectively). (Kansas City and Philadelphia had racial differences as low as 5 and 6 percent, respectively.) I focused on Chicago, Boston, and San Francisco because I wanted to learn more about what the GAO had detected. By selecting cases from three regions, I hoped to ensure that my study did not reflect merely local phenomena.

By selecting claims that closed in 1990, I restricted my sample to cases that were heard by ALJs between 1985 and 1989, which allowed me to ensure a representative cross-section of judges and a reflection of more recent attitudes and beliefs.

Although all the cases I reviewed were denied by ALJs at the hearing level, several of them were approved at the federal court level. The district court awarded benefits outright in six of the fifty cases, without requiring claimants to reappear before an ALJ. District court or court of appeals judges remanded 26 of the cases to ALJs for further proceedings.[1] The district court judges ruled in favor of Social Security and upheld the ALJs' denial of benefits in only 14 cases. Two cases were dismissed and never pursued further. I have no final disposition for two other cases.

Boundaries of the Study

Also of methodological concern is the small number of cases I reviewed, 67 total, which amounted to approximately 2,500 pages of case transcripts. While the size limited the generalizability of the study, it had several positive features. Every research formulation is a partial picture, a snapshot. This study was deliberately designed to build on the large quantitative studies that preceded it and that were also deeply flawed. Although those studies provided a sense of what may be operating, they failed to reveal the process of decision making that led to the detected bias. The purpose of this study was not to supplant the work of other quantitative researchers but rather to understand how the bias they detected operates in everyday interactions.

The problem with looking only at cases appealed to federal district court is that these cases may not reflect the typical case denied by an ALJ. Most claimants denied at the hearing level do not appeal their cases to federal district court (while 87 percent of claimants appeal to the Appeals Council, only 10 percent appeal to federal district court). Given that federal court cases are the only Social Security files open to public review, these cases remained the only avenue I could pursue to learn more about how judges handled specific cases.

Characteristics of Claimants and Judges

The claimants of the cases I reviewed represented a broad mix of ethnic and linguistic backgrounds. Twenty of the claimants (twelve males and eight females) were African-American. Seventeen (nine males and eight females) were Caucasian. Thirteen claimants came from other racial or ethnic backgrounds: eight were Hispanic; two were Portuguese; one woman was Italian; one man was Greek; and one woman was Jordanian. The cases were almost evenly distributed between men and women: 26 claimants were male and 24 were female.[2]

I defined *illiteracy* as the inability to read English. Although Social Security defines *illiteracy* more broadly (the inability to read in any language), my analysis of whether judges violated the rules regarding their inquiry into illiteracy was interpreted more narrowly. Because I was not concerned with whether a claimant is capable of working (which is the SSA's primary concern) but rather with whether ALJs complied with rules relevant to inquiring into a claimant's ability to read, it was necessary to factor into my equation the effect of English illiteracy on people from other cultures who appeared before ALJs. I used the *illiteracy* designation most when I evaluated whether judges accommodated or engaged claimants or when or whether they stereotyped them. When I evaluated whether judges had properly complied with rules mandating them to elicit testimony about literacy, I naturally applied Social Security's broader standard.

Twenty of the fifty claimants, or 40 percent, were illiterate in English. Two Caucasian male claimants and seven African-Americans (five men and two women) were illiterate by this standard. All of the claimants who required the use of an interpreter were illiterate in English. Four of the Hispanic claimants (three males and one female) spoke English well enough not to require the use of an interpreter at the hearing. However, two of these four English-speaking Hispanic claimants (one man and one woman) were unable to read and, therefore, illiterate in English. In addition, four female Hispanic claimants spoke only Spanish and required interpreters at their ALJ hearings; these claimants were clearly considered to be illiterate for the purposes of this study. Of the two Portuguese applicants (one man and one woman) whose cases were reviewed for this study, the male spoke only Portuguese and required the use of an interpreter. The female Portuguese applicant spoke English but was not literate in it. The Italian and Jordanian women and the Greek man required interpreters at their hearings.

Compared to a national study of Social Security disability applicants who had been denied benefits, my sample included more women (49 percent compared to 37 percent), fewer Caucasians (42 percent compared to 67 percent), and more African-Americans (39 percent compared to 24 percent).[3] As for "other"[4] racial and ethnic minorities, my sample included 19.4 percent, whereas the national denied applicant pool contained only 9 percent. There were more women and minorities in my sample almost certainly because I selected cases from three large urban areas. Since both single women and minorities are more heavily represented in major American cities, it is understandable that they would also be more heavily represented in the disability applicant pool of such areas and, hence, in my sample. No comparative statistics were available on national applicants' literacy.

Since I did not seek to estimate the extent or magnitude of ALJ compliance with rules and procedures in the Social Security disability system but rather to learn more about the phenomena that previous researchers had detected, the fact that my pool did not reflect a sample of denied applicants nationwide did not present a methodological problem. My sample was big enough to detect a variety of these deviations and geographically disparate enough to ensure that I was not seeing the peculiar culture of one or two local hearing offices.

Prior to their appearance in district court, several claimants whose cases I reviewed received more than one hearing before an ALJ either because the first ALJ had ordered a second hearing to obtain additional testimony or because the federal court remanded the case, resulting in a second or, in some cases, a third hearing. One judge heard seven cases and another judge heard five. Five ALJs each heard three cases. Another 9 ALJs each heard two cases. The remaining 22 ALJs each heard one case. Hence, a total of 38 judges heard and/or decided the 67 hearing transcripts and decisions I reviewed. Further, in some of the federal court cases, hearing transcripts did not have accompanying decisions, and vice versa. I decided to examine every hearing and decision contained in each federal court case so that I could have more instances in which to understand the phenomena in which I was interested. This approach made sense since, again, I did not attempt to measure the extent or magnitude of any given phenomenon or the responsibility of any given judge.

Thirty-six male and two female judges generated the 67 hearing transcripts and/or decisions contained in these 50 federal court files. The transcripts and decisions contained no information on the racial or ethnic makeup of the judges.

Given Dixon's 1973 finding that ALJs' rates of approval vary from 8 to 88 percent, and given the possibility that such variation may still occur,[5] I wanted to verify whether the approval rates of the judges whose cases I reviewed were typical. Social Security stopped publishing award rates for individual ALJs in the 1980s. Therefore, I was only able to obtain averages on 16 of the 38 judges I reviewed. The award statistics I reviewed were from 1982, at which time judges, on average, granted 50 percent of the cases they heard. Of the 16 judges on whom I could obtain statistics, 8 granted between 40 and 60 percent of the cases they heard. Six judges granted more than 60 percent of the cases they heard, while two granted less than 40 percent of the cases they heard (36.4 percent and 26 percent, respectively). I concluded from these statistics that the judges whose cases I was reviewing were probably typical.

The Study Approach

Step one of the study approach involved examining the hearing transcripts and decisions to determine whether judges complied with certain key rules that are designed and implemented to govern how ALJs conduct hearings, evaluate evidence, and make decisions. My focus on rules in the first step enabled me to gauge whether judges were capable of satisfying the most obvious requirement or mandate in the system. To follow or not to follow the rules, I reasoned, is a beginning point for assessing the judges' competence at complying with uniformity. This reasoning is consistent with SSA's peer review approach (1995, 1997), which also tests ALJ compliance with the rules. My study however, took a more critical look at ALJ compliance by examining rule nonconformity element-by-element and by deconstructing the factors that might have influenced ALJ deviation. With regard to each set of rules, I highlight my quantitative results with qualitative data that describe the phenomena I uncover.

Rules with which I was particularly concerned included those that establish how ALJs introduce the hearing process, treat claimants' right to counsel, elicit their testimony, help claimants obtain evidence and apply the so-called treating-physician rule, analyze claimants' failure to comply with prescribed treatment, and evaluate credibility.

The opening statement establishes the tone, structure, and procedure of the entire hearing. Without it, claimants, whether represented or not, would be highly unlikely to understand how to participate in the process according to their best advantage (Durston and Mills 1996). Similarly, the means by which judges question applicants about their right to an attorney and especially their decision to forgo legal counsel involves a very fundamental right that may bear heavily on the outcomes of the cases.[6] Finally, the methods judges use to question applicants—that is, to elicit testimony—influence directly the kind and depth of answers. Misunderstandings are common because different people interpret the same question differently; it is critical to explore verbal interactions from different points of view.

The treating-physician rule, the rule governing an applicant's failure to comply with prescribed treatment, and the rules governing how judges make credibility determinations also warrant brief explanation. The treating-physician rule gives controlling weight to the opinion of the physician who treats the applicant rather than to a consultative physician who examines the claimant once for the purpose of determining eligibility for disability, assuming it is well supported by clinical and laboratory findings and it is not inconsistent with other evidence in the record. The rule is predicated on the assumption that treating physicians know patients best and therefore have the most accurate medical information on them. This rule, a long-standing feature of the disability program, requires judges to prioritize the evidence they evaluate and therefore functions as one of the mechanisms the SSA uses to standardize judges' decisions.[7]

The rule governing applicants' failure to comply with prescribed treatment is also critical to the fairness and impartiality of disability decisions. Holding that claimants whose medical conditions fall within the definition of disability may not be entitled to benefits if they fail to follow physicians' prescribed treatment that could improve their condition, this rule provides one of the only ways judges can deny medically qualified applicants. Since this rule is often used and since, when applied, it is used to deny claims, it seemed a likely place where judges might use their discretion.

The third substantive area I examined was credibility—the determination judges make regarding whether claimants' testimony and demeanor are believable. I chose to evaluate credibility because it involves the judges' discretion and personal judgment. Many prevalent disabling conditions, most notably pain, fatigue, and shortness of breath, are impossible to measure objectively; moreover, as Deborah Stone (1984) has persuasively contended, even seemingly objective clinical and laboratory tests are open to wide interpretation. Consequently, a judge's evaluation of the believability of a claimant's testimony regarding such subjective matters can be crucial to the outcome of the case. Given the Ninth Circuit Gender Bias Task Force's (1992, 1993) finding that several claimant representatives believed that judges evaluated women as less credible than men, and given the findings of other gender-bias studies and research, which revealed that female witnesses are less often believed than male witnesses (Swent 1996), it was particularly important to study how ALJs evaluate credibility.

To ensure that the rules I considered were fair and accurate test sites for identifying and measuring potential bias, I focused my research on rules and formalities common to many legal proceedings. All jurists, for example, make opening statements in courts of law; most judges must address a claimant's right to counsel; all judges must elicit and weigh testimony; and all make credibility determinations. While not all judges encounter the treating-physician rule or a rule that assesses a claimant's failure to follow prescribed treatment, all are required both to comply with a prioritization of evidence (as is the function of the treating-physician rule) and to make step-by-step analyses of the evidence (as is required by the rule governing an applicant's failure to follow prescribed treatment).

Hence, given that the SSA seeks to decide disability claims uniformly and that the rules here examined are common expressions of that ideal, it made sense to use ALJ noncompliance with the rules as a starting point—that is, as the first step for evaluating whether claimants are disadvantaged by ALJ hearing and decision-making practices. Step two of my method, which isolated specific instances in which ALJs violate rules for concomitant effects of ALJ inability to accommodate or engage claimants (described more fully in chapter 5), and/or to stereotype them (described more fully in chapter 6), presents a tentative assessment of why, how, and under what circumstances these rule violations may occur. The second step of my critical investigation, then, elaborated on and qualified the first.

The ALJs' Introduction and Opening Statement

As prescribed by *Hallex,* the Social Security disability hearing should begin with introductions, an opening statement, and other remarks and procedures (SSA 1992 I-2-650). Specifically, *Hallex* mandates that judges introduce themselves and any hearing office staff present in the hearing room, explain the reason the staff is present (i.e., to run the recording equipment and take notes), and identify and explain the role of any other people present (including interpreters, vocational experts, medical experts, and the claimant's friends or family members) (I-2-652). After the introductions, the hearing officially begins with an opening statement that explains "how the hearing will be conducted, the procedural history of the case, and the issues involved" (I-2-652).

Hallex leaves the exact content and format of the opening statement to the discretion of the ALJs; nevertheless, a strict interpretation of *Hallex* suggests that the opening statement should satisfy numerous specific requirements. It should be brief yet explain how the hearing will be conducted, including mentioning that ALJs will take claimants' testimony on questions about their age, education, work history, and impairment and that claimants will respond by giving testimony under oath. The mandate to explain the procedural history of the case is usually thought to require judges to reference the dates when the initial application, the reconsideration, and the request for hearing were filed and when the notice of hearing was sent. To explain the issues involved in the proceeding, judges mention whether the claim is for DI or SSI, what the sequential evaluation process is and how it will be applied to evaluate the case, and the reason, if applicable, that vocational and/or medical experts are present and how these professionals will be questioned. ALJs should inform claimants that the burden of proof initially rests on them in Social Security cases. Finally, ALJs must ask whether claimants have any questions about the hearing process.

Again, *Hallex* leaves the exact content and format of the opening statement to the discretion of ALJs. However, a sample opening statement provided by the central OHA (SSA 1993) illustrates how succinctly these conditions can be met:

The record in your case established that you filed an application for (SSI/SSDI) on (date). You were advised that your claim was denied on initial and reconsidered determination. On (date) you requested a hearing. A notice of hearing was sent to you and we are here pursuant to that notice. The general issue is whether you are entitled to a period of disability and disability benefits under the provisions of Title II of the Social Security Act (or to Supplemental Security Income under Title XVI of the Social Security Act). I will be taking evidence as to the severity and expected duration of your impairments and as to your age, education, and work experience. In preparing my decision, I will consider the following: First, whether you can be found under a disability solely on the basis of the medical evidence. If not, I will consider whether your impairments are severe and whether they prevent you from performing your past relevant work. If they are, I will next consider whether they are severe enough to prevent you from performing any work that exists in the national economy considering your age, education and work experience within the past 15 years. Do you have any questions as to the nature of these proceedings, the history of your case or the issues to be considered?

The introduction with which ALJs are legally mandated to open hearings is important. Such information as that mandated helps to ensure the reviewability of the hearing, should it be appealed to a higher court. Identification of medical and vocational experts is crucial because judges rely heavily on expert testimony and because unidentified participants obviously cannot be held accountable for their statements or other contributions. It is important that judges mention in their opening statements the procedural history of the case and the issues involved. Aside from facilitating review, this formality is necessary to ensure that all relevant participants know that each participant is aware at the time of the actual hearing that they are discussing the same and appropriate circumstances.

The judge's introductions and opening statements are important, however, not only for that potential future audience—the federal court judges who may eventually review the case. The introductions are also essential to ensure that all participants in the hearing—the judge, the claimant, the claimant's representatives, and any witnesses—are afforded the opportunity to realize their respective intentions and fulfill their particular responsibilities to the other people present whose contributions comprise the larger discourse (Durston and Mills 1996).

To make an opening that is clear and engaging to the claimant whose testimony the judge is about to hear requires the judge to recognize the claimant as actually present; such acknowledgment increases the likelihood that the judge will listen to the claimant. To the extent that the ALJ delivers an introduction that not only acknowledges the claimant but actually engages the claimant in a genuine community of minds, that judge satisfies the often-conflicting hearing requirements, which simultaneously makes the hearing uniform and engaged, impartial and unique for this particular claimant. It establishes the claimants as free to speak to the best of their ability. To the extent that judges fail to engage claimants, perhaps delivering the mandated introduction in a language and tone that would satisfy only reviewing courts, judges effectively disregard their mandates for both uniformity and affectivity. Such judges contribute to the "exclusion of dialogue in favor of monologue" (Goodrich 1986, 188). These claimants are never engaged as a being capable of having and telling stories.

Thus, ALJs' introductions are important for their effective participation in their role as judges. The statements are certainly also crucial for the claimants whose cases are being heard. For the most part, claimants are nervous when they sit down for their hearings. Few are familiar even with informal court procedure and fewer still have the training required to follow the language, details, and sequence of events that make up the disability hearing. Moreover, claimants are about to discuss issues ranging from impotence to anorexia. Finally, for most claimants, the stakes are very high. By the time they enter the hearing room, many claimants have waited two years or longer to have the issue of their future benefits decided. The combination of economic hardship since becoming disabled and unable to work, the suffering experienced from the disability, and the pain of having been denied benefits at the initial and reconsideration levels makes the hearing itself an extremely charged event. Effectively confronting anyone in those circumstances with a room full of strangers conversing in abstract language that appears to have no beginning, middle, and end no doubt is intimidating and even antagonizing. In no way could such a situation be expected to encourage the openness and presence of mind needed to act effectively and meet the burden of proof of the complex Social Security hearing process. Introductions of strangers, explanations of their roles, and a complete opening statement that establishes a genuine community of minds and explains to claimants what they can expect in the hearing can help lessen the intimidation they are likely to face and encourage them to participate as freely and effectively as they must to prevail.

Thus, the judge's introductions and larger opening statement are essential to ensure fairness in the process (Durston and Mills 1996). These opening remarks provide the only orientation into this highly complex hearing procedure that claimants, who are often largely, if not wholly, unschooled in the process, are legally entitled to receive. The opening statements are essential to instruct claimants on what to expect from the hearing and what is expected of them. At the same time, the introductions provide an assurance that judges acknowledge claimants and the special claimant-judge relationship.

Despite the tremendous importance of an effective introduction and all the rules in place to ensure that in every case judges make one, I found in my sample of cases that Social Security ALJs rarely fulfill this basic obligation. Of the 65 cases that required introductions (two cases involved claimants whose cases were continuing from previous hearing dates and therefore did not require an exordium), I found that judges did not introduce themselves 57 percent of the time (37 cases) and failed to introduce their staff 86 percent of the time (56 cases). The judges failed to explain why staff people were present in the hearing room in 74 percent of the cases (48). Similarly, judges introduced interpreters in only 10 of the 17 instances in which interpreters were involved. Although judges tended to do a better job of introducing experts (17 of the 19 experts were introduced), only 2 of 19 judges explained what role the experts would play.

Furthermore, judges in 18 of the 65 cases (28 percent) reviewed failed to give any opening statement at all, and another 44 percent (29) gave only an incomplete opening. Thus, judges in 47 out of 65 cases (72 percent) fell considerably short of their legal responsibility. Eleven of the thirty-four cases (32 percent) in which ALJs did not so inform applicants involved claimants who did not speak English. Social Security already has a poor reputation for communicating with claimants in languages other than English, and these violations appear only to perpetuate the non–English speakers' alienation from the process (U.S. Senate 1992).[8]

With respect to other rules, almost all judges failed to comply with the rule requiring them to summarize the procedural history of the case before them. Thus, 72 percent (47 out of 65 cases) failed to mention even the crucial detail of when the initial application was filed. Noncompliance with reference to other important dates was even higher. More than half of the judges (34 out of 65 cases, or 52 percent) failed to mention whether claimants had applied for DI or SSI, despite the legal requirement to do so. Failing to verify such information with the claimant can and does result in unnecessary administrative delay and appeals.

In 97 percent of the applicable 65 hearing transcripts (63 out of 65) studied, the judge failed to explain to the claimant that the SSA employs a sequential evaluation to make disability determinations, that the sequence involves five steps, and what those five steps are. Also in 63 out of the 65 cases, judges neglected to inform claimants that the burden of proof initially rests on them in Social Security cases. Even in the two cases in which judges complied with this rule, the statement was only implicit. One judge said merely, "The hearing allows you an opportunity to show you cannot return to your past work," and the other stated, "You have to show" that you are too disabled to work. Neither of these judges and no other judges in the study sample explained what the "burden of proof" means in a Social Security claim—that is, that claimants had the responsibility to provide evidence and testimony that makes a prima facie showing to the judge that their medical impairments prevent them from performing their previous work activity (*Gallant v. Heckler* 753 F.2d 1450 (9th Cir. 1984)).

Given that so few judges made opening statements and that even fewer explained the rules to which they were bound when making decisions, it was not surprising that 94 percent of the judges failed to offer claimants the opportunity to ask questions about the hearing process (61 out of 65 cases). This oversight may reflect the belief suggested by one ALJ at the Justice and Diversity training that asking claimants if they have questions about the process may encourage them to challenge the process too vigorously and, hence, undermine the judge's authority.

Left to devise their own opening statements, Social Security ALJs in the sample of cases studied did not satisfy even the basic *Hallex* mandates necessary to ensure the reviewability of hearings. Judges almost unilaterally avoided any statements that would engage claimants in a genuine community of minds. Rather than acknowledging the introduction's importance for raising expectations and setting standards for all that is to follow, these ALJs appeared to treat the introduction as an empty formality.

ALJs often justify procedural omissions on the grounds that claimants' attorneys have already informed their clients of the hearing procedure, and, indeed, ALJs did make opening statements of some sort in the hearings of eight of the nine claimants who appeared without representatives. Relying on attorneys to explain the process, however, is not wise. A small study found that when asked whether they felt prepared for their hearings, claimants expressed a need for judges to explain the process even when their attorney had previously done so (Mills 1988). Moreover, attorneys' and representatives' activities are far less regulated in this regard than are those of judges. But even if all representatives could convey to their clients the basic hearing procedure, judges would still have the responsibility in their introductions to engage in some way with the claimants to ensure anything like genuine justice.

Unrepresented Claimants

My findings reveal that ALJs' oversight of rules governing waivers of the right to representation undercut whatever effort they made to provide opening statements to unrepresented claimants. Social Security regulations and case law require judges to inform claimants of their right to be represented by an attorney before their testimony is taken (SSA 1992 I-2-652). In addition, ALJs must secure on the record unrepresented claimants' acknowledgment that they understand their right to representation and their unequivocal affirmation of their decision to proceed without a representative (SSA 1992 I-2-652). Finally, ALJs must inform claimants that attorneys can be retained on a contingency-fee basis or that attorneys may be available for free.[9]

Nine of the sixty-seven hearing transcripts and decisions I reviewed involved hearings of claimants unrepresented by counsel. In three of the nine hearings of unrepresented claimants, ALJs failed to mention that claimants had a right to an attorney. One of these cases involved an illiterate man who had no formal education, and a second case involved a woman whose IQ tested in the borderline mentally retarded range. People with borderline intelligence have been identified by federal courts as requiring special assistance in exercising their right to representation (*Vidal v. Harris* 637 F.2d 710 (9th Cir. 1981)).[10] In seven of the nine cases, judges failed to inform claimants that they could retain an attorney for free. In Mrs. Moore's case (89-6436, IL), for example, the ALJ told the claimant that there are lots of "attorneys in the phone book," and there is a "list of Legal Aid attorneys," but he never informed this claimant that attorneys could be retained on a contingency-fee basis or for free. When Mr. Prince (87-9662, IL), a claimant who had a fifth-grade education and was illiterate, asked whether the judge felt a lawyer was necessary, the judge responded, "I'm not here to give you advice." The ALJ then gave Mr. Prince a list of attorneys and informed him that he had 30 days to find a lawyer before his case would be rescheduled. Mr. Prince was offered no assistance in reading the list.

Of all the rules governing the right to representation, ALJs complied most frequently with the rule prohibiting them from attempting to dissuade claimants from obtaining attorneys or other representation, yet the judges still violated this rule in two cases. In Mrs. Moore's case (89-6436, IL), the judge promised to protect the claimant's rights, and in Mr. Prince's case (87-9662, IL), the judge said that it was the claimant's responsibility to make sure all the evidence was considered.

In six of the cases, judges failed to include in the transcript or decision the claimants' acknowledgment that they knew that they had a right to representation. In five of the cases, the judges did not obtain from the unrepresented claimants an unequivocal affirmation of their decision to proceed without a representative. In all the cases involving unrepresented applicants, ALJs neglected to ensure that claimants understood how counsel could assist with their cases. In no hearings, for example, did a judge inquire whether unrepresented claimants had fully read and evaluated the exhibit file containing their medical evidence and whether they had any objections to it. In the case of Mr. Costello, a man who was illiterate and had no formal education, the ALJ failed to inquire whether the claimant had even read the file (88-7350, IL). In other cases where judges did ask, they neglected to investigate with any vigor whether illiteracy or a lack of education may have hindered the claimants' review of the evidence in the file. Instead, as chapter 6 reveals in detail, the judges would rely on claimants' assertions that illiteracy or educational deficit posed no difficulty. It is the duty of lawyers who represent disability claimants to read, review, and critically evaluate the exhibit file. As my evidence reveals here, and in the next two chapters, it is difficult to imagine any of these unrepresented claimants not benefiting from the assistance of counsel.

One other relevant factor regarding the treatment of unrepresented claimants is worth noting: While no other study has ever analyzed the characteristics of unrepresented claimants, my randomly selected (albeit small) sample revealed that they are members of the most disadvantaged groups and hence need more, not less, assistance through the application process. Of the nine unrepresented claimants, seven were African-American and one was Cuban. Four of the nine unrepresented claimants were illiterate. Six of the nine unrepresented claimants were female. Six of the nine unrepresented claimants had not attended high school or did not complete their high school education; none had more than a high school education. The fact that claimants who entered the system unrepresented were also members of the most disaffected groups raises the possibility that disregard for the rules governing claimants' representation may be related to the judges' disinterest or may be deliberate attempts to further alienate these applicants from the hearing process in general and from representing their own best interests in particular.

Eliciting Testimony

Legally, judges are charged with developing the record to the fullest extent possible.[11] They are responsible, in other words, not only for collecting medical and other written evidence but also for eliciting oral testimony from claimants whose cases they hear. Indeed, eliciting oral testimony is the primary purpose of the ALJ hearing. Several rules establish the parameters of judges' efforts to elicit testimony, but to what extent do ALJs comply with these regulations? An analysis of this question provides additional insight into how the Social Security disability decision-making process works.

ALJ training materials (SSA 1993),[12] Social Security case law, and *Hallex* outline the rules that apply when ALJs elicit testimony. The training materials direct judges to address women and men by last names and appropriate titles. While *Hallex* in general permits ALJs to determine what testimony they elicit from claimants and witnesses at the hearing (SSA 1992, I-2-660 A), both *Hallex* and Social Security case law establish precise formal and substantial parameters that limit ALJs' inquiries.

To develop what reviewing courts have regarded as the full and necessary record (20 C.F.R. 404.944), an ALJ must elicit ample testimony on the key facts on which disability decisions fairly and impartially rest: the claimant's age, education, literacy, work experience, and impairment. *Hallex* further stipulates that the ALJ should make reasonable efforts to allow claimants to testify in their own ways if they have good reason (SSA 1992, I-2-660 A). While testifying, claimants may, for example, need to stand up, sit with their feet propped up on a pillow, or leave the hearing room for air or to get a drink of water.

Two additional requirements when eliciting testimony apply: claimants must be given the opportunity to explain their medical or disability problems without being hindered and to state their positions without being interrupted (*Ventura v. Shalala* 55 F.3d 900 (3rd Cir. 1995); *McGhee v. Harris* 683 F.2d 256 (8th Cir. 1982)). Being "hindered" at a hearing refers to ALJs either directly or indirectly interfering with claimants' efforts to explain their impairments. ALJs directly hinder testimony when they lead it in a specific direction or put words in claimants' mouths. In my experience, when judges hinder or interrupt claimants, it silences them; claimants then tend to underplay their complaints or characterize their impairments as less severe than they believe them to be. ALJs indirectly hinder testimony when they neglect to ask important or relevant questions, either to elicit information on key facts or to follow up on incomplete testimony. ALJs also hinder testimony more directly when they become argumentative, demanding, irritable, or accusatory. Interrupting testimony refers to instances where judges break into testimony with further questions, comments, or corrections.

Rules regarding hindering and interrupting are deeply embedded in the American sense of fairness and justice. Anthony Taibi describes this sense most astutely:

> The perception that natural justice includes the independent right to tell one's tale at a fair tribunal is as old as civilized society itself. In a democracy, the procedural process due to an individual can only be legitimately determined by the community's sense of fairness. To the extent that agency procedures are not consistent with what people think justice requires, those procedures are unfair. (1990, 932)

Certain rules are integral to the elicitation of evidence and proved key when evaluating judicial compliance, including:

1. ALJs should address women and men by last names and appropriate titles (Mr./Ms./Mrs./Miss/Claimant).
2. Claimants must receive an opportunity to describe their medical or disability-related problems without being (directly or indirectly) hindered.
3. Claimants must receive an opportunity to state their positions without being interrupted.
4. ALJs must make an effort to allow claimants to testify in their own ways if they have a good reason to do so.

5. ALJs must attempt to obtain all evidence pertinent to claimants' cases, including (a) age, (b) education, (c) literacy, (d) work experience, and (e) impairments.

Appropriate titles. When I evaluated whether ALJs complied with the gender-bias training materials that mandate that they address women and men by last names and appropriate titles, I found that the judges violated these rules in 24 of the 65 hearings (37 percent). While the violations ranged from the judge never referring to the claimant by name to a reference to one claimant as "grandmother," it was clear that ALJs often had little regard for this rule. The most serious violations involved two women of color (four hearing transcripts and decisions in total), one white woman, and one man of color. Each of these examples merits fuller explanation.

In the case involving the white woman, Ms. Thompson, the judge told the claimant and her witness, a friend, "Okay, I think I'll swear you ladies in together" (88-6104, IL). Ms. Thompson was a 56-year-old woman with an extensive work history. Being lumped together with her friend and reduced to the designation of "a lady" with all of its historical connotations of subservience, idleness, and fragility suggested the possibility that this judge viewed Ms. Thompson not as a deserving, previously hardworking disability applicant—that is, not as equivalent to the deserving stature of a man but rather as an undeserving "lady" who was typically dependent on others for her security and livelihood.

A similar violation occurred when another ALJ referred to Mrs. Moore, a 45-year-old African-American woman, as "ma'am" and "dear" (89-6436, IL). In so doing, it felt very much as though the judge was infantilizing her or treating her as subservient. *Dear,* a term used with children, and *ma'am,* used historically as a reference to black slaves or mammies, seem inappropriate terms for a judicial hearing in which all claimants should be treated with the same respect (Collins 1991). Clearly, judges should avoid even the appearance of racism or sexism.

In another example, also involving Mrs. Moore, the claimant testified that she was married, yet the judge consistently referred to her as "Miss." While some may argue that these distinctions seem trivial, Patricia Hill Collins (1991) has persuasively argued to the contrary.[13] The term *miss* has often been used to refer to African-American women in their roles as servants, nannies, and maids. By using *miss,* then, a judge renders an African-

American woman's true identity invisible—ignoring the fact that she is a married woman with a black family and verifying, instead, her unattached quality, which allows her to serve as nanny to her white employer. What is most distressing about this characterization of Mrs. Moore is that it is a clue that stereotyping is occurring, and the judges seem so completely oblivious to the prejudices they seem to be holding (von Hippel, Sekaquaptewa, and Vargas 1995).

In another instance, also involving Mrs. Moore and a different ALJ, a male judge took the "lady" reference one step further. Describing the lengths to which Mrs. Moore had gone to care for her family, the judge referred to the claimant as "a very nice lady that takes care of herself and her two handicapped family members." This comment stereotypes Mrs. Moore not only as a homemaker but also as someone who, if able to care for her family, is also able to work outside the home. In fact, two different judges reviewing Mrs. Moore's claim were so persuaded that her caretaking activities rendered her able to work that they overlooked medical evidence that proved Mrs. Moore's inability to work because of a listing-level impairment. In this case, the judges' stereotyping blinded them to the evidence they were mandated by law to evaluate. This case suggests the importance of making judges conscious of stereotyping clues and of forcing them to look beyond the stereotypes that lead to these unjust results.

In another case, an ALJ violated the rule of appropriate titles when he referred to the claimant, Miss Plain, a 51-year-old African-American woman (87-5258, IL), as "Grandmother," asking, "Grandmother, ever pick the baby up?" The ALJ's question apparently attempted to manipulate the claimant into assuming a grandmotherly posture to respond more honestly to an assessment of her physical capacity. This kind of question illustrates how simple violations of seemingly minor rules such as the use of appropriate titles open the door to stereotyping a claimant to a gender-essentialized role.

Two other violations occurred when ALJs referred to claimants, both of whom were African-Americans (one male and one female), by their first names (James, 88-1712, CA; Moore, 89-6436, IL). The fact that the worst of these appropriate-titles violations involved women and men of color (and four of the six worst cases involved women of color) suggests that ALJs may fail to show due respect to women of color and more particularly to African-American women.

Hindering and/or interrupting claimant testimony.   When I evaluated whether ALJs hindered or interrupted claimants in their testimony, non-compliance rates proved disturbingly high. ALJs hindered claimants in 40 of the 65 cases (62 percent) and interrupted them in 26 cases (40 percent).

Allowing claimants to testify in their own ways.   When I examined the transcripts for violations of the rules allowing claimants to testify in their own ways, I counted violations in 25 percent (16 of 65) of the cases. Two claimants were forced to testify in English despite their stated preference for testifying in their native language, and in one case the ALJ told the claimant to "Speak up!" after she testified that her throat hurt.

Eliciting testimony about claimants' age, education, literacy, work experience, and impairments.   Judges complied better with the duty to determine the claimants' age (13 percent noncompliance), education (25 percent noncompliance), and work history (16 percent noncompliance) than with the duty to inquire into claimants' ability to read (60 percent noncompliance) and impairments (43 percent noncompliance).

Analysis of ALJs' behavior when eliciting claimants' oral testimony again reveals systematic noncompliance with rules designed to ensure that all claimants are treated uniformly and with the necessary affectivity. As reported, judges commonly violated the rules prohibiting hindering and interrupting claimant testimony, mandating appropriate use of titles, and requiring ample development of the record, with the result that virtually no case was free of violations.

It is not surprising that claimants who are undereducated, linguistically challenged, and different from the judges hearing their claims would probably need more assistance in being drawn out. They are less likely than their counterparts to be schooled in professional etiquette and style. They are thus less likely to read judges' implicit instructions through body language, tone, and the like about when to offer testimony. These claimants are less likely to have confidence and competence to respond in ways considered appropriate in the legal arena—that is, with controlled and well-articulated testimony. As a result of these shortcomings stemming from intellectual, cultural, racial, and gender differences, this class of claimants is more likely to feel uncomfortable testifying before ALJs than others would and hence is likely to be more reticent and less forthcoming with relevant testimony.

While such claimants require more time, attention, and patience from ALJs, it appears that judges, who are most often white and male, may actually be less rather than more patient with these people. Thus, instead of drawing them out, ALJs often fall into patterns of hindering and interrupting these claimants. This is consistent with the social-psychology literature, which suggests that stereotyped people are asked fewer questions and that questions are asked in a way that tends to elicit confirmation of the stereotype rather than information that would disconfirm stereotyping or individuate people (Trope and Thompson 1997). As chapter 5 will illustrate, when thus directing unempowered claimants' testimony still fails to produce the desired information, ALJs can become abrupt, irritated, even aggressive.

That judges frequently hinder and interrupt claimants may indicate the undue pressure on them to process claims as quickly as possible. That they develop the record with respect to work history more fully than they consider literacy or impairment may speak to the pressure judges feel to deny as many cases as possible. With more information about claimants' work history, ALJs are more likely to find skills that can be transferred to other work, rendering the claimants employable and ineligible for benefits. Similarly, the less ALJs know about a claimants' literacy and impairments, the less information the judges will have to grant benefits. It is hard to see, however, how institutional pressures might explain ALJs' failures to comply with rules mandating the appropriate use of titles. Since the most serious violations of rules mandating appropriate use of titles affected women, particularly African-American women, it seems all too likely, at least in the cases I reviewed, that other factors that reflect larger cultural prejudices may, in some instances, affect the Social Security disability-hearing process.

Mandate to Obtain and Prefer Treating-Physician Evidence

On the condition that their opinions are supported by clinical and laboratory findings, the Code of Federal Regulations grants controlling weight to the opinions of treating physicians—that is, physicians who see a claimant over a period of time, prescribe treatment, and order and interpret tests (Social Security Rulings 1996, 96-2P). This preference is predicated on the assumption that treating physicians develop relationships with and knowledge of their patients and can therefore more accurately document the extent, nature, and degree of their impairments.

Judges are permitted to disregard opinions of treating physicians if the judges support their conclusions with persuasive medical evidence (Social Security Rulings 1996, 96-2P). To support such dismissals, judges typically rely on the opinions and reports of CEs (physicians contracted by Social Security specifically to help decide disability claims). CEs usually examine a claimant only once but perform several clinical tests (e.g., EKGs, blood tests), and they prepare detailed reports that take into account the entire medical record, the listings, and other Social Security rules. Claimants often cannot afford to obtain comparable medical/legal reports from their treating physicians and instead must rely on the treating physicians' office notes, which are often unspecific and illegible. This situation can make it more difficult for claimants to convince judges that the records of treating physicians are more persuasive than CEs' reports.

The Code of Federal Regulations and Social Security case law acknowledge this problem and, by holding ALJs responsible for developing claimants' medical records, seek to prevent ALJs from relying too conveniently on medical reports that make sweeping conclusions based on little or no previous history of the patient's condition. This responsibility translates into requirements to give claimants adequate time (up to 30 days) to obtain the evidence that they need from a treating physician or facility (SSA 1992, I-2-514A.1) and, in some cases, for judges themselves to write to treating sources and order reports needed to complete claimants' medical records (I-2-514.A.3).

Social Security case law has interpreted the circumstances under which ALJs should write to treating sources. In *Marsh v. Harris,* the court held that "where the ALJ fails in his duty to fully inquire into the issues necessary for adequate development of the record, and such failure is prejudicial to the claimant, the case should be remanded" (632 F.2d 296, 300 (4th Cir. 1980)). The *Marsh* court considered an unrepresented illiterate claimant to be "completely unschooled on the requirements for proving his case" (299). For that reason and because, if obtained, the report, "might well have contributed to a proper ALJ decision" (300), the court held further that it was not enough for the ALJ to attempt to contact the treating physician; the ALJ was himself held responsible for obtaining the report.

My research evaluated whether or not ALJs complied with the treating-physician rule by posing three basic questions. The first two questions examine the extent to which judges help claimants obtain information necessary to develop their medical records. The first question assesses how much time judges allow claimants to obtain needed records. A 30-day period, specifically designated in *Hallex,* is reasonable in light of the time it takes to obtain and submit copies of records and reports from treating facilities such as county hospitals, county clinics, and health maintenance organizations.[14] The second question examines the extent to which judges are willing to help claimants disadvantaged by education and/or intelligence secure the evidence they need by writing to treating sources on behalf of illiterate, poorly educated, or unrepresented claimants. The third question is designed to determine whether judges properly articulated reasons for rejecting a treating physician's opinion.

Allowing 30 days to obtain records.   Claimants in 26 transcripts reviewed for this research requested additional time to obtain and submit reports from treating physicians. In 11 of these 26 cases (42 percent), ALJs allowed fewer than 30 days to submit the new evidence. Most judges of the 11 hearings who violated the rule allowed claimants between 10 and 14 days to obtain and submit medical evidence. All but one of the eleven claimants denied a 30-day period were represented by attorneys; a judge requested that an unrepresented claimant with an IQ of 70 submit additional evidence within 14 days of the date of the hearing (Moore, 89-6436, IL).

Helping claimants obtain records.   Either because the claimant was not limited by literacy, education, or representation conditions or because the hearing transcript did not reveal the need for additional evidence from the treating source, the requirement on the judge to write to treating physicians for additional medical records applied in only three transcripts and decisions. In each case involving unrepresented claimants, one of whom had an IQ of 70 and an incomplete high school education, ALJs asked claimants to collect and deliver their own medical records (Moore, 89-6436, IL; Bell, 90-5548, IL; and Redd, 87-3348, IL).

Specifying reasons for disregarding the treating-physician rule.   In 22 of the 25 cases (88 percent) in which the treating-physician rule was applied, the ALJ did not comply with the third part of the rule, which requires judges to state in their decisions specific reasons for disregarding the opinions or reports of treating physicians.

As was evident in their treatment of unrepresented applicants, ALJs seemed to make little or no effort to insure more generally that needy claimants' cases were adequately developed and that the files contained treating-physician documentation. My findings that judges fail to assist claimants in developing their evidence seem particularly troubling in the disability cases of white women and people of color because, as previously discussed, research shows that they are less likely to get the medical workup and treatment necessary to provide persuasive documentation of disability eligibility (Ayanian and Epstein 1991; Blendon et al. 1995; Burns et al. 1996; Colameco, Becker, and Simpson 1983; Mirvis et al. 1994; Redman et al. 1991; Steingart et al. 1991; Unger and Crawford 1992; Whittle et al. 1993).

In some cases, claimants owed money to doctors and therefore could not obtain detailed medical reports because they could not pay for them. In many of these cases, judges did little or nothing to help claimants overcome this disadvantage, and in some cases ALJs discouraged claimants from obtaining evidence from their treating physicians.

The case of Mr. James (88-1712, CA) illustrates my point. Mr. James was an African-American applicant whose treating physician saw him "for years without payment." Because he was owed money, the doctor was unwilling to prepare a medical report for Mr. James's disability claim. Mr. James, like many disability applicants, was medically insured during his employment and briefly following an industrial accident. However, at some point his medical coverage expired, and he remained ill without the medical insurance he needed.

The effect on his disability case was devastating: the judge relied on the reports of several workers' compensation CEs to deny Mr. James's claim. What further disadvantaged Mr. James, however, was the judge's apparent preference for consultative evaluations: when Mr. James's attorney gave the judge the choice of obtaining a report from a treating physician or from the workers' compensation consultative evaluators, the judge insisted on the workers' compensation reports. While the judge said he would be willing to consider the treating physician's report, he did not insist on receiving it or offer to pay for it. This raises an important concern: Do judges circumvent reliance on treating-physician reports by discouraging claimants and their advocates from obtaining evidence prepared by treating physicians?[15]

In Mr. James's case, the ALJ ended up considering the treating physician's office notes but dismissed them as "relatively uninformative." The judge did not mention that Mr. James's attorney expressed the desire to obtain a more detailed and informative report but was apparently unable to afford one. Rather than obtaining a report from Mr. James's treating physician, the ALJ denied the claim on the findings and conclusions of a one-time visit to a few workers' compensation and Social Security CEs.

Mr. Tommie (89-4093), a poor, white Vietnam veteran, was also disadvantaged when he could not afford to obtain the medical evidence he needed: Mr. Tommie had been tentatively diagnosed with a number of ill-

nesses, including Graves' disease, AIDS, cancer, and Agent Orange exposure. No definitive medical findings could be made, despite visits to the
Veterans' Administration and University of California at San Francisco
Medical Center and various county clinics. Stanford Medical Center was
apparently his only hope. He was seen there once before his disability
hearing and could not return for lack of medical coverage. He planned to
marry an AFDC recipient to render him eligible for the Medicaid he
needed to visit the Stanford physicians. It can be assumed from the judge's
decision that Mr. Tommie did not visit the Stanford Medical Center in
time to provide the documentation the judge needed. The ALJ denied the
claim without ever mentioning that Stanford might have provided the necessary medical evidence.

In a similar case, involving an African-American claimant, Ms. Burr,
(87-10636, IL), the ALJ neglected to order the evidence that was needed to
evaluate her claim. Although the claimant in this case had a treating physician, the record was inadequate because the claimant lacked the money to
seek appropriate medical care from epilepsy specialists. Lack of funds
undoubtedly prevented her from developing a more accurate medical picture of her condition (as cited in the federal district court order).

In this case, a U.S. magistrate in federal district court ordered the ALJ
to arrange for Ms. Burr to be evaluated by a CE for the purpose of determining whether the claimant met the listing for epilepsy. Both Mr. Tommie's and Ms. Burr's cases highlight the importance of fully developing the
record so that even applicants with treating physicians can get the specialized information they need to have their claims fully evaluated.

In cases where a judge explicitly disregards a favorable treating-physician's report, another important issue is raised: how influential should CE
reports be when they conflict with the opinions of treating physicians? In
the case of Ms. Curran (88-2459, MA), a white woman, the judge disregarded the opinion of her treating neurologist despite the unusual fact that
he attended the disability hearing to testify on her behalf. The judge
rejected the doctor's testimony because the

> claimant may well have some chronic low back discomfort secondary
> to some obscure disorder, but her tendency to exaggeration was obvi-
> ous. She testified that she was unable to sit for more than 20 minutes,
> but she sat throughout the hearing, which lasted for more than one
> hour, in a normal position with no outward indications of discomfort.

As in Ms. Curran's case, the judge in the case of Ms. Smith (86-6054, IL) disregarded the favorable report of the treating physician and instead relied on a CE's report to deny her claim. Ms. Curran's and Ms. Smith's cases suggest that judges do indeed try to overcome treating-physician evidence by relying on one-time CE reports. However, in both cases, the federal district court found the judges' reasoning erroneous. The district judge in Ms. Curran's case, in which benefits were granted outright, held that the ALJ erred in substituting "his own opinion for that of uncontroverted medical evidence or opinion." In Ms. Smith's case, which was remanded, the district judge held that the ALJ improperly disregarded relevant evidence and should therefore reconsider it in light of the court's findings.

These cases seem to suggest that applicants who cannot afford to purchase detailed medical reports are both consciously and unconsciously neglected by ALJs who are indifferent to the rules governing the gathering of evidence for claimants. This issue is particularly important in cases involving claimants of color or white women, who are already at a disadvantage in obtaining the medical evidence they need to win a disability claim. Even white male claimants, as in Mr. Tommie's case, are disadvantaged solely on socioeconomic grounds.

Failure-to-Follow-Prescribed-Treatment Rule

The Code of Federal Regulations defines the parameters of the failure-to-follow-prescribed-treatment rule. They both acknowledge a claimant's failure to follow prescribed treatment as a justifiable reason to deny otherwise medically qualified claims and specify precise conditions or circumstances that justify or excuse a claimant's failure to follow prescribed treatment. Perhaps more than any other rule considered in this study, laws governing the failure to follow prescribed treatment are straightforward and, hence, establish clear criteria on which ALJs can systematically analyze an applicant's failure to comply with prescribed treatment.

The laws governing the failure to follow prescribed treatment stipulate that to deny claimants benefits on the grounds that they failed to follow prescribed treatment, the treatment in question must not only be prescribed but must also be "expected to restore [the] capacity to engage in any substantial gainful activity" (20 C.F.R. 404.1530; Social Security Rulings 1982, 82-59). Further, to deny applicants benefits on the grounds that they failed to follow prescribed treatment, judges must document certain relevant factors, including: (a) what treatment the claimant has not complied with; (b) who prescribed the treatment; (c) that the prescribed treatment is likely to restore the capacity for work; and (d) why the prescribed treatment is likely to restore the capacity to work (20 C.F.R. 404.1530; Social Security Rulings 1982, 82-59). I analyzed the hearing transcripts and decisions for ALJ compliance with these rules.

In addition to these documentation requirements, regulations and federal case law further require ALJs to give claimants an opportunity to explain their failure to follow prescribed treatment and to acknowledge in the decision any of several reasons the courts recognize as acceptable for not following treatment (20 C.F.R. 404.1530; Social Security Rulings 1982, 82-59). If an ALJ denies benefits because a claimant fails to follow prescribed treatment, the ALJ must acknowledge in the decision any of the following acceptable reasons given for failing to follow the treatment: (a) religious beliefs, (b) an inability to afford prescribed treatment, (c), a treating source's recommendations against such treatment, or the need to undergo (d) a high risk procedure, (e) certain cataract operations, (f) the amputation of an extremity, or (g) a previous and similar unsuccessful surgery.

Because the failure-to-follow-prescribed-treatment rule is so straightforward, I could unambiguously identify cases in which judges concluded that claimants failed to follow prescribed treatment and evaluate the judges' compliance in those cases with the relevant rules. A case was deemed relevant when judges used claimants' failure to follow prescribed treatment to deny claims. Judges in 8 of the 67 transcripts and hearings analyzed for this study (12 percent) concluded that claimants failed to follow prescribed treatment. Seven of the eight claimants who were found to have failed to follow prescribed treatment were racial or ethnic minorities.

Further analysis of findings revealed that judges violated the failure-to-follow-prescribed-treatment rule almost every time they invoked it. Hence, they failed to document who prescribed the treatment in seven of eight cases, to document why the prescribed treatment was likely to restore the capacity for work in all of the cases, and to give claimants an opportunity to explain why they did not follow the treatment in all of the cases. ALJs who failed to allow claimants to explain why they did not follow treatment obviously could not acknowledge in their decisions the claimants' justifiable reasons. In the course of their testimony, two claimants did give justifiable reasons for not complying with a particular treatment; in both cases, the judges failed to cite those reasons in their decisions.

My findings reveal that when ALJs invoke rules governing a claimant's failure to follow prescribed treatment, they almost always deny the claim and, moreover, that in each such case, the judges violate the parts of the rule that require them to fully evaluate the claimant's alleged noncompliance. Institutional pressures to deny cases and to decide cases quickly may at least partially explain why the ALJs in my research invoked this rule. That judges invoke the rule to deny cases seems consistent with the spirit of the rule, but the tendency not to fully evaluate these issues certainly does not. Whatever the reasons for doing so, systematic violation of rules in my small sample of judges raises questions at least of the possibility that other factors may be operating. When, as in the case of the failure-to-follow-prescribed-treatment rule, violations are made overwhelmingly in the cases of claimants of color, the assumption that no extrajudicial factors are operating is weak. A larger, more comprehensive study that looks more closely at these issues would be helpful in establishing with more certainty what is really operating.

Judgments of a Claimant's Credibility

The cases that come before Social Security ALJs are typically difficult and ambiguous. As experts in matters of disability, judges are expected to review each case in depth. To award or deny benefits, ALJs are legally required to rely heavily on the compilation of usually conflicting clinical evaluations and laboratory reports from treating physicians and workers' compensation and other medical professionals that make up the exhibit files. To deny benefits, not only must ALJs demonstrate in their decisions why unfavorable evidence supports their assertion that the claimants' conditions are not disabling, but judges must also justify why they have rejected evidence that supports the applicants' claims.[16]

This evaluation of evidence is no easy task. Guided by the sequential evaluation process, ALJs evaluate the testimony of claimants and, in some cases, of vocational and medical experts. This testimony, too, typically contains many variables and inconsistencies. To balance the conflicting accounts of medical records and testimony, the judge must determine whether the claimants are to be believed—whether, that is, their allegations of pain, fatigue, shortness of breath, or other symptoms are credible. A credibility determination is often the essential link between favorable and unfavorable testimony and evidence, between an award of benefits or a denial.[17]

But determining credibility is a complex matter. To do so, judges must rely on innumerable, indescribable, and immeasurable facts and feelings. Pain, fatigue, and other symptoms present a very difficult challenge to judges, because to determine whether such factors are, in any given case, truly disabling, a judge must "assess . . . as objective something that is really subjective, a complexly determined personal experience" (Stone 1984, 137). Indeed, when SSA (1995) evaluated the top five reasons for ALJ allowance rates, claimant credibility and the impact of pain figured prominently in their results. This finding suggests that subjectivity is particularly critical to ALJ decision making, and that credibility can both positively and negatively affect outcomes.

In the following section, I identify and explain the laws governing an ALJ's credibility inquiry that I incorporated into my study. I then present and interpret findings from my analysis of transcripts and decisions. Again, I find that judges' violations of basic rules impede the chances of all claimants to receive a fair hearing and decision. Strong quantitative evidence appears to confirm that in the hearing process, some of these violations may reflect the cultural assumptions of the judges deciding the cases. As findings are already beginning to suggest, such is true, in part, because these violations seem to affect certain historically disadvantaged groups more severely than others.

As indicated, credibility determinations are key because they underlie judges' other important decisions—for example, whether to agree with a treating physician or with a CE or whether to elicit testimony on a matter more likely to strengthen or on a matter more likely to weaken a claimant's case. But how do judges make credibility determinations? They watch claimants, ask and receive answers on a series of questions, and consider the comments of others who have viewed or examined the claimant. In so doing, judges are given discretion on the format, style, and questions they employ, but they are also bound by certain rules.

The most important rule governing credibility determinations requires judges explicitly to describe the medical and extramedical factors that influenced their thinking. One federal court described this requirement as follows:

> When the decision of an ALJ rests on a negative credibility evaluation, the ALJ must make findings on the record and must support those findings by pointing to substantial evidence on the record . . . . This rule is simply a specific application of a bedrock principle of

administrative law. A reviewing court can evaluate an agency's decision only on the grounds articulated by the agency. (*Ceguerra v. Secretary,* 933 F.2d 735, 738 (9th Cir. 1991))

Not only are judges required to state the factors that influenced their credibility determinations, but they are also required to base their determinations exclusively on relevant factors. Social Security rules, regulations, and case law have clearly identified some factors and behaviors as irrelevant and/or inappropriate for credibility determinations. For example, ALJs are prohibited from basing credibility determinations on race, gender, and socioeconomic status (42 U.S.C. § 405 (b) (1); 42 U.S.C. 1383 (c) (1); SSA 1992, I-2-601); thus, a claimant who receives welfare or workers' compensation benefits should not be categorically denied (*Coria v. Heckler* 750 F.2d 245 (3rd Cir. 1984); *Desrosiers v. Secretary,* 846 F.2d 573 (9th Cir. 1988); *Macri v. Chater* 93 F.3d 540 (9th Cir. 1996). Further, if ALJs examine a claimant's military service, prison history, or family background, they should expressly evaluate the relevance of this personal history to the credibility determination by explaining their reasons (*Ghant v. Bowen* 930 F.2d 633 (8th Cir. 1991); *Novotny v. Chater* 72 F.3d 669 (8th Cir. 1995)). ALJs are prohibited from automatically regarding housekeeping or caretaking abilities as ability to do paid work (*Ghant v. Bowen* 930 F.2d 633 (8th Cir. 1991); *Davis v. Callahan* 125 F.3d 670 (8th Cir. 1997)).[18] Moreover, an ALJ's observations, for instance, of a claimant who shows no physical manifestation of pain at the hearing called the "sit and squirm" test, are essentially irrelevant unless supported by medical evidence (*Perminter v. Heckler,* 765 F.2d 870 (9th Cir. 1985)).[19] Finally, ALJs are instructed to avoid using in their decisions emotionally charged words, pejorative terms, and personal judgments or opinions (SSA 1992, I-2-830).

In my study of these issues, I formulated seven rules that fall into two main groups. The first six comprise the "documentation rules," and the first two, which can be considered one subgroup, refer specifically to rules governing documentation of evidence that is clearly relevant to the credibility-determination process. The first rule is as follows:

1. When making a negative credibility determination, ALJs must state in the decision the factors about the claimants' character, testimony, or evidence that influenced the credibility determination.

For this first point, I analyzed whether ALJs stated the specific factors considered when making credibility determinations, including the trustworthiness of the claimants' character, the content and manner in which they gave testimony, and other nonmedical evidence. Testimony presented by the claimants' family and friends may also produce relevant extramedical factors influencing ALJs' decisions.

The second rule was formulated as follows:

> 2. When making a negative credibility determination, ALJs must document in decisions the medical evidence that supports the negative credibility determination.

Since reviewing courts hold ALJs responsible for documenting medical evidence in specific detail, I regarded incomplete analyses of medical records as noncompliance with this rule.

Rules 3, 4, 5, and, to a lesser extent, 6 comprise the second subgroup of documentation rules, the documentation of potentially or certainly irrelevant evidence. This subgroup measures the extent to which ALJs follow rules that limit their use of irrelevant evidence. The third rule was worded as follows:

> 3. When making a credibility determination, ALJs must document in the decision with testimony or medical evidence why housekeeping or caretaking activities constitute an ability to work.

The fourth and fifth rules relate to characteristics of race, gender, and family history and to status issues like socioeconomic status, military status, and prison history. Of all the areas examined, rules 4 and 5 most clearly revealed the influence in disability decisions of culturally based assumptions. Rules 4 and 5 were formulated as follows:

> 4. ALJs must never use race, gender, or socioeconomic status when making a negative credibility determination.
> 5. When relying on a claimants' military status, prison history, or family background, ALJs must obtain and explicitly evaluate details of those experiences to be sure they are relevant to the credibility determination.

Given the difficulty of detecting and the importance of determining the potential effect of subtle forms of institutional and/or cultural bias on the decision-making process, I applied what may seem at first a rather stringent principle for rules 4 and 5. I assumed that judges who asked questions about or commented on claimants' race, gender, socioeconomic status, military history, prison record, or family background presupposed ideas or obtained information related to these issues that was then consciously or unconsciously factored into their decision-making process.

This assumption is consistent with the social-psychological literature, which suggests that inadmissible evidence is difficult if not impossible to disregard. Johnson et al. (1995) studied the differential effects of exposure to inadmissible evidence. In their study, a group of subjects were directed to disregard the inadmissible evidence. The research revealed that in a simulated criminal trial, if subjects were instructed to disregard inadmissible evidence, they did not and in fact used that evidence to justify their perception that a harsher verdict was appropriate. It is noteworthy that the subjects denied that the inadmissible evidence had any effect. Johnson et al.'s study is consistent with the argument that judges may very well use the inadmissible evidence they collect and then deny that it has any effect.

For purposes of this part of the study I considered any judge who raised issues of race, gender, and social status in either the hearing or the decision to be in violation of rule 4. I reasoned that the use of such factors was unconscious (as the transcripts seemed to suggest) and negative in all instances. Issues of military, prison, and family history, the subject of rule 5, may in some cases be relevant to a credibility determination; thus, I counted as violations of rule 5 instances in which judges raised such issues but did not follow them up in sufficient detail to determine whether they were relevant to the claimant's credibility.

The sixth point reflects the prohibition against ALJs relying exclusively on their own observations and applying, as federal courts have termed it, the "sit and squirm" test, whereby claimants' credibility is judged solely on whether they sit and squirm throughout the hearing. Rule 6 was formulated as follows:

> 6. When making a negative credibility determination, ALJs must never rely exclusively on their observations of the claimant without citing support from the medical evidence in the decision.

Like rules 3 and 5, rule 6 concerns documentation of potentially irrelevant evidence. In a sense, however, rule 6 establishes a category of its own, personal-judgment rules (to which rule 7c also partially belongs).

The seventh and final rule concerning credibility determinations is taken directly from *Hallex* (SSA 1992, I-2-830); it refers to the language ALJs use to refer to or describe claimants in the hearings and in their written decisions. I refer to it as the harmful-language rule.

7. When making a negative credibility determination, ALJs should avoid using (a) emotionally charged words, (b) pejorative terms, and/or (c) personal judgments or opinions, even if the harmful language appears in evidence or testimony.

Hallex explicitly proscribes ALJs from using emotionally charged words or pejorative terms in hearings or decisions. ALJs are also prohibited from using personal judgments when evaluating claimants' credibility. I considered words to be emotionally charged if they were likely to insult or offend claimants unnecessarily. For example, in one case the ALJ referred to an illiterate and clearly unsophisticated African-American claimant as "somewhat evasive" and his testimony as "changeable" (Prince, 87-9662, IL). In another case, an ALJ, citing a medical report in the file, quoted the doctor as referring to the claimant as "greedy"; the emotional charge was inherent in the judge's suggestion that the claim was driven by greed rather than by the need for benefits to which the claimant was entitled (Neri, 84-20289, CA).

I considered comments that were clearly sarcastic and unnecessarily judgmental as those containing pejorative terms. In one case, for example, the ALJ told a claimant who testified that he was short of breath that smoking "could sure have something to do with chest pains" (Reed, 88-6170, IL). As noted earlier, rules 6 and 7c in a sense comprise a category of personal-judgment rules. Judges use their personal judgment when, for example, they substitute their own opinions or judgments for those of the medical evidence or the law. This situation often occurred when judges evaluated the allegations of drug addicts, alcoholics, or people with mental disabilities.

Findings

Overall credibility findings.   The overall findings for each of the seven rules are as follows:

Rule 1. In 29 of the 49 applicable decisions (59 percent),[20] judges failed to report the extramedical factors of character and testimony that substantiated and validated their negative credibility determinations.

Rule 2. In 26 of the 52 applicable hearings (50 percent), ALJs failed to report the medical evidence that supported their negative credibility determinations.

Rule 3. In all 16 decisions in which judges concluded that claimants could work because of their ability to keep house or take care of one or more other people, ALJs failed to explain how the housekeeping or caretaking activities demonstrated that these claimants could do paid work.

Rule 4. Judges violated the rule prohibiting them from using factors such as race, gender, and socioeconomic status in 39 of the 66 decisions reviewed (59 percent).

Rule 5. In all 33 decisions in which judges used military status, prison history, or family background to make credibility determinations, they failed to obtain and carefully evaluate details of those experiences to ensure that they actually were relevant to the credibility determination.

Rule 6. ALJs violated the rule prohibiting them from basing credibility determinations exclusively on their own observation of claimants in 19 of the 66 decisions (29 percent).

Rule 7. ALJs violated the rule prohibiting them from using harmful language in credibility decisions as follows: of the 66 relevant decisions, judges used charged words in 13 (20 percent), pejorative statements in 8 (12 percent), and personal judgments or opinions in 36 (55 percent).

Rules 1 and 2: Documenting relevant evidence.   As noted, credibility is the backbone of the judicial decision, for it is both the determination on which interpretations of ambiguous evidence rests and the most subjective of judicial decisions. The rules herein discussed provide the only mechanism for regulating credibility assessments. Rules 1 and 2 require ALJs specifically to document the extramedical factors that influence their decisions (e.g., trustworthiness of the claimants' character, content and manner of their testimony) and to present the medical evidence that substantiates and validates the judges' determination. Rules 1 and 2 are thus fundamental to making credibility determinations fair because they mandate that judges base these very influential but potentially highly subjective judgments on legally relevant and verifiable written (or recorded) evidence.

Against this backdrop, my findings reveal that in 59 percent of the cases in my sample, judges failed to explicate extramedical factors to substantiate and validate their negative credibility determinations, and in half of the cases judges failed to document the medical evidence that supported their negative credibility determinations. Hence, even though ALJs are mandated to support their negative credibility determinations with medical or extramedical evidence, a majority of the judges disregarded this requirement and instead relied on factors beyond the law. When judges disregard the only credibility rules that bind them to legally relevant criteria, it raises the question of the basis on which credibility decisions are made. ALJs' rates of noncompliance with rules 3, 4, 5, and 6, subsequently discussed more fully, confirm my unfolding thesis that many judges, at least those in my small sample of cases, relied significantly, at least in some kinds of judgments, on largely if not wholly irrelevant and illegal factors.

Rules 3, 4, and 5: Documenting potentially relevant and avoiding certainly irrelevant evidence. As indicated above, rules 4 and 5 and, to a lesser extent, 3 most clearly revealed the influence of normative assumptions in disability decisions. Given the importance of this outcome, I separately analyze my findings for each rule governing the documentation of relevant evidence and avoidance of clearly irrelevant evidence.

Rule 3: Housekeeping. Rule 3 grows out of a series of concerns raised by scholars and claimant advocates. Previously, I documented instances where judges denied benefits to both women and men who had testified that they had cared for a child or a spouse since becoming disabled (Mills 1993). According to Social Security case law, the ability of an applicant to keep house or to care for others does not necessarily indicate a capacity to do paid work. As one federal district judge concluded, "Ghant's ability to do housework is not necessarily substantial evidence that he can perform the requirements of light work. We have previously held that a person who is able to do light housework is not necessarily able to perform gainful employment" (*Ghant v. Bowen*, 930 F.2d 633, 638 (8th Cir. 1991)).[21]

In every denied case examined for this study in which ALJs questioned claimants about housekeeping and caretaking (regardless of the gender of the claimant), the judges failed to explain in their decisions why these activities constituted the capacity for gainful employment. Given that all of the judges who regarded housekeeping or caretaking activities as evidence of capacity to do paid work failed to adequately defend their conclusions and given that these rule violations disadvantaged every claimant in which the rule was invoked, it seems highly likely that normative or gendered assumptions about the people who perform housework and caretaking influenced judges' thinking and even their decisions. Judges simply cannot assume that performing tasks in the home, at one's own pace, and in an environment in which one can regulate one's activities is equivalent in any way to the demands of paid employment.

Rule 4: Race, gender, socioeconomic status. For further insight into the possible operation and influence of bias, I examined the transcripts and decisions for questions and comments that violate the clear prohibition against basing credibility decisions on the race, gender, or socioeconomic status of the claimant (rule 4). If a judge asked questions related to race, gender, or socioeconomic status that had no clear bearing on the disability determination, I counted that judge in violation of the rule.

I considered that judges factored race into their credibility determinations when they asked foreign-born claimants such questions as "Where were you born?" "When did you come to this country?" "Have you been naturalized?" and "When were you naturalized?" Though on the surface and out of context such questions seem harmless, it is nevertheless true that where disability claimants were born and when they came to this country are irrelevant at the ALJ-hearing level. While the issue may be relevant when a Social Security district officer first takes a claim (assessing such matters as eligibility for benefits), an ALJ can reasonably assume that a claimant who has appealed to the stage of a face-to-face hearing is legally entitled to benefits.

I also considered that ethnicity probably factored into the decision making of judges who assumed that a claimant who needed the assistance of an interpreter could and should at least attempt to speak English. As unlikely as it seems in this age and nation of diversity, the small number of ALJs reviewed in this study did in fact make such demands in 3 of the 17 hearings (18 percent) in which claimants required the use of an interpreter (Acevedo hearings 1 and 2, 87-2767, CA; Vatistas, 88-6532, IL).

Similarly, I considered judges in violation of the gender category of rule 4 when they gathered or commented on information specific to a claimant's gender role. For example, comments made about a woman's lifestyle choice as wife, girlfriend, mother, or homemaker, such as "claimant's lifestyle as mother and homemaker is essentially the same as in the past [i.e., before she became ill]" and "the claimant's not working at substantial gainful activity was one of choice, not one imposed upon her by debilitating illness" were considered gendered references and hence should have been considered irrelevant to the credibility determination. The second comment implied that the judge applied a different standard to women who previously worked only in the home than to men who previously performed paid work in the national economy. Against this standard, which suggests that women who have worked only in the home have never participated in "real" work, women's claims to disability are easily deemed less credible than men's. Social Security rules, however, do not penalize claimants who have not previously worked in the paid labor force. Rather, judges' inquiries into a claimant's work history, whether paid or unpaid, are relevant to the disability determination process only for the purpose of identifying skills that may be used or transferred to a paid work environment or, as described in detail in chapter 5, for purposes of accommodating or engaging the special needs of female claimants.

Other examples of comments that I counted as violations of the gender category of rule 4 include instances in which ALJs assumed that claimants were somehow limited to gender-specific work roles (e.g., when ALJs asked female claimants whether they could perform such traditionally female jobs as receptionist and male claimants if they could perform such traditionally male jobs as manual laborer) and when ALJs commented on physical appearance in gender-specific terms (e.g., when they noted that certain female claimants "looked good" but that male claimants "looked fit"). Also noteworthy as a violation of rule 4 was an ALJ's comment that if a claimant could walk in three-inch spike heels, as she was noted to have worn to the doctor, then clearly her back condition was not as debilitating as she had alleged (Davenport, 89-1268, MA). The assumption that a claimant's attire provides evidence of the severity of a claimant's impairment is more likely to disproportionately disadvantage women who are, regardless of a physical or mental impairment, under more social pressure to dress or otherwise present well.

Violations of the part of rule 4 that prohibits ALJs from using socioeconomic status as a factor when making credibility determinations were relatively easy to detect. The source of claimants' income is relevant to judges' disability determination only if they are working. The Social Security district office may decide that claimants are not entitled to SSI or DI because they receive other income or benefits, but an ALJ is not in a position to do so. The source and amount of a claimant's income should not be a factor in judging a claimant's credibility. Consequently, I counted all such questions as "How much welfare do you receive?" and "How long have you received it?" as violations of the rule.

A more subtle violation of this rule occurred when an African-American claimant with a fifth- or sixth-grade education could not respond with certainty to the question about which grade he had completed (Prince, 87-9662, IL). In his decision, the judge interpreted the claimant's inability to remember as evasive and manipulative rather than as a broad reflection of an impoverished education or intelligence.

While several of these examples seem minor when viewed out of context, as I illustrate in chapters 5 and 6, the ALJs in my sample of cases often made several—not just isolated—comments that suggest a penchant for prejudice.

Rule 5: Military, prison, family history.   While the issues regulated by rule 4—race, gender, and socioeconomic status—are certainly irrelevant to the Social Security decision-making process, the issues regulated in rule 5 have not always been thought so. However, judges who gather testimony or make comments on a claimant's military, prison, or family history are obligated to explore the issue in enough detail to reasonably assess whether such evidence is relevant to the determination process.

With rule 5, like rule 4, I assumed that judges who asked, directly or indirectly, about claimants' military status, prison history, or family background factored something of that information into their decision-making processes, whether or not they explicitly mentioned these factors in their decisions. Thus, I marked in violation of rule 5 any ALJ who asked about or commented on these issues but failed to obtain sufficient details about them to assess the relevance of the issues to the disability decision-making process. For example, if a judge asked if a claimant had served in the military but did not establish the relevance of the claimant's military record (or lack thereof) to the disability determination,[22] I assumed that the judge believed that military status in and of itself was relevant to the decision-making process when in fact it is not.[23] Similarly, if ALJs asked claimants if they had prison histories but did not establish whether that prison history had any bearing on the claimant's credibility, I concluded that the judge believed that a prison history in and of itself was relevant to the decision-making process, which it is not. A prison record can and should influence a judge's credibility determination but a prison term should not in and of itself taint a claimant's credibility (*Ghant v. Bowen* 930 F.2d 633 (8th Cir. 1991)). For example, approximately 20 years before his hearing, one claimant in my sample had served time in San Quentin for assault with a deadly weapon and robbery. He had since worked and not returned to prison (James, 88-1712, CA). I question whether the judge in that case could fairly assume that the claimant's prison history, which the judge mentioned in passing in the decision, necessarily discredited his testimony, especially since the judge did not ask follow-up questions to establish the relevance of the crime to the claimant's behavior after he was released.

Rule 5 also regulates a judge's questions regarding a claimant's family background, another aspect of credibility that is not in and of itself relevant to a disability determination. A question like "Is there a family history of bipolar disease?" is clearly related, whereas "Does your child/wife/husband/mother/father work or receive welfare?" is not. Again, I marked in violation any judges who asked unrelated family history questions but failed in their decisions to link the information gained specifically to the issue of the claimants' alleged disabilities.

Judges invoked rule 5 in half of all cases reviewed for this study (33 out of 66 cases) and, like rule 3, they violated it each time they invoked it. In light of this finding, my study suggests that judges be strictly monitored when relying on factors such as military status, prison history, and family background and that they be mandated, as in the case of race, gender, and socioeconomic status, to explicitly consider how such factors influenced their decision-making process. Chapter 7 describes how judges might explore the relevance of such factors in greater detail.

Rule 6: Documenting personal observations.   As noted, ALJs violated the rule prohibiting them from basing their credibility determinations exclusively on their personal observations of claimants in 19 out of 66 decisions. This finding, which reveals the extent to which ALJs rely on their personal observations of claimants, confirms the pattern established by this credibility analysis: when ALJs are left unregulated, a number of them are likely to rely not on documented and legal medical or nonmedical factors but rather on their eyeball assessment of the claimant. This finding, together with the fact that ALJs used race, gender, or socioeconomic status in more than half of the cases, leads to the development of a pattern in which my small sample of ALJs seem to use prejudicial assumptions when making credibility determinations. These issues are developed more fully in the next two chapters.

Rules 7a, 7b, 7c: Avoiding harmful language.   The pattern of noncompliance with the harmful language rules (charged words in 20 percent of the cases, pejorative statements in 12 percent of the cases, and personal judgments or opinions in 55 percent of the cases) is consistent with results reported earlier in this chapter—that ALJs hindered claimants' testimony in 62 percent of the cases and interrupted claimants in 40 percent of cases examined. Like hindering and interrupting claimant testimony, the ALJ's use of harmful language reaffirms the power imbalance between judge and claimant, further undermining the capacity of claimants to present their cases as effectively as possible. I believe that claimants are entitled to judges who come to the decision-making table with an awareness of their penchants for prejudice and regulate them according to what the circumstances may demand.

The use of personal judgments found in 55 percent of the cases poses similar problems. ALJs' personal judgments are supposedly irrelevant to the decision-making process. However, violations of these rules underscore the difficulty judges have in keeping those personal judgments out of the hearing process. Again, I suggest that if judges were given the tools to become conscious of how their personal judgments affected the hearing process, they could draw on their personal resources when the hearing called for it and temper those judgments when it did not.

My findings reveal how judges consistently neglect uniformity in a number of areas: when making introductions; when providing assistance to unrepresented claimants; through both deliberate and unconscious efforts to circumvent rules regarding the gathering of evidence; in applying the compliance-with-prescribed-treatment rule; and in credibility determinations. My results also suggest that negative affectivity, especially ALJs' prejudicial emotions, creeps into the hearing process as it is currently formulated through such unconscious dynamics as hindering testimony and inflicting personal judgments.

The next chapter explores in much more textual depth the experiences of unrepresented claimants and those claimants needing special assistance in the elicitation of their testimony. This closer reading reveals the kinds of difficulties judges have in expressing positive affectivity toward those claimants whose backgrounds differ from those of the judges. Chapter 6 complements the findings in chapters 4 and 5 by revealing exactly how stereotyping operates in the hearing transcripts and decisions and how the judges' penchant for prejudice, even in my small sample of cases, overshadows the entire system of Social Security justice.

CHAPTER 5

Disengaging Discourses

No previous research has documented in any detail how well judges' fulfill their affirmative duty to engage or accommodate claimants when hearing and deciding their cases.[1] How effective or ineffective are Social Security judges in providing affective or positive justice to the claimants whose cases they deny? To present my findings, I draw on the texts of hearing transcripts and decisions as well as the relevant federal court decisions that support my evolving thesis that judges are emotionally incapable of affirmatively accommodating the special needs of claimants and of taking their differences into account when the law or other compelling circumstances demand. I focus my discussion on two areas visited in the previous chapter: judges' difficulties in accommodating unrepresented claimants and judges' problems in attending to claimants' needs while eliciting their testimony.

Judges' Failure to Engage or Accommodate
Unrepresented Applicants

As previously noted, Social Security regulatory and case law clearly establishes that ALJs are required to accommodate unrepresented claimants. *Hallex* establishes the methods ALJs must follow to ensure that they protect claimants' right to an attorney; these methods include the requirement that judges "secure on the record an unrepresented claimant's acknowledgment of the right to representation and affirmation of the claimant's decision to proceed without a representative" (SSA 1992, I-2-652). Federal courts have further described this responsibility. In the *Cruz* case, a federal district judge in California remanded the decision of an ALJ, ordering him to reconsider the evidence in this non-English-speaking claimant's case, on the grounds that he had "little if any understanding of the deficiencies in the evidence presented and of how counsel could have assisted him" (*Cruz v. Schweiker* 645 F.2d 812, 813 (9th Cir. 1981)). Similarly, the *Vidal* court remanded a case involving a claimant who could not read well, had an IQ that measured between 73 and 78, was not familiar with hearing procedures, and was unable to challenge the conclusions of the VE (*Vidal v. Harris* 637 F.2d 710, 714–15 (9th Cir. 1981)). Other courts have required judges to inform claimants of their right to free or contingency-fee counsel and to assist them in obtaining lawyers.[2]

The text analysis in this section supplements my findings in chapter 4, which suggest that the ALJs in my sample of cases seem consistently incapable of complying with rules mandating them to assist unrepresented claimants. Here I consider excerpts from six hearing transcripts and decisions to illustrate the ways in which ALJs fail to uphold their positive duty to engage and accommodate unrepresented claimants.

Ms. Acevedo (87-2767, CA), a 54-year-old Spanish-speaking applicant, was assisted only by her sister-in-law, who spoke limited English, when appearing before an ALJ. Through an interpreter, the judge presented the issue of exercising or waiving the right to representation as follows:

> *ALJ:* The hearing is going to be informal. The testimony's going to be given under oath and it is now being recorded by a tape recorder. Now when we received your application we sent you a notice on June 11th, 1986, and we indicated in the notice that if you wished to you could be represented by a lawyer or other qualified person. We also indicated in the notice and included a list of organizations that would help you in securing a lawyer if you wished to. Now, it's left entirely to you whether you wish to have a lawyer. But I do wish to be sure that this is what you wish. Now do—do you wish me to hear the case without a lawyer?
>
> *CLMT:* Well, I feel that I have enough evidence right now without needing assistance—any legal assistance.

On the face of it, this dialogue seems to satisfy the legal requirements that the claimant acknowledge and waive her right to an attorney. However, testimony that came later in the transcript raises an important question about whether the claimant could adequately acknowledge that she indeed was waiving her right to counsel. The following testimony immediately followed her comment about not needing legal assistance:

ALJ: We also indicated in a notice of hearing that you could come to the office any day between 3:30 and—excuse me, 8:30 and 3:30 to review the file. Now, do you have any objection to any of the documents you saw in the file?

CLMT: Since I don't read English, she is the one who read it [referring to her sister-in-law].

ALJ: I beg your pardon?

CLMT: I do not read English, she is the one who read it.

ALJ: Well, all I'm asking is do you have any objection to the documents that we have regardless of—regardless of who read it. I'm indicating that we asked you to come or we suggested to come to the office if you wish to read the file. Now again I'm asking do you have an objection to the documents you saw in the file?

CLMT: Well, I didn't see them. [The translator says:] She gave them to her [referring to her sister-in-law] so she can read them.

ALJ: Do you have an objection to any of the documents in this file?

CLMT: No.

The situation of the Acevedo case is very similar to that of the *Cruz* case, in which the federal court mandated that the ALJ assist a claimant who did not have the benefit of representation and who, because of a language barrier, could not fully appreciate the process. In the Acevedo decision, the ALJ ignored this mandate, reporting in the decision:

Although fully advised of her rights to an attorney, the claimant *voluntarily* waived such rights and chose to proceed without representation. (emphasis added)

But can a Spanish-speaking claimant "voluntarily" waive her right to counsel when she fails to realize that the exhibit file, which she is unable to read, is the basis on which the judge will decide the case? Throughout the hearing, Ms. Acevedo often became confused and obviously could have benefited from the assistance either of the judge or of counsel. Her confusion became especially apparent in this passage:

ALJ [asking questions through the translator]: Where does she work? Your answer, where does she work? She isn't testifying. Do you know where she works?

CLMT: Where she works?

ALJ: Works? Your sister.

> *CLMT:* My sister.
> *ALJ:* No, I'm not asking her. I'm asking her. Look—look at this—
> *CLMT:* I don't remember.
> *ALJ:* Okay. Wait a minute. Do you remember that I said if you don't
>   know you're supposed to say I don't know.
> *CLMT:* Well, I don't know.

Furthermore, whenever Ms. Acevedo relied for assistance on her sister-in-law, her only representative at the hearing, the judge seemed to chastise her. At one point, the ALJ even suggested the possible removal of the sister-in-law:

> *ALJ:* Now you said that you have problems sleeping because of the
>   pain. What pain—what—what hurts you? You were in an automobile accident, I believe, weren't you? Okay, what hurts you?
> *CLMT:* Everything.
> *ALJ:* No. You know, if you don't stop looking at your sister I'm going
>   to have your sister to go out. I want you to answer the questions.
>   You answer the questions to the best of your ability, and if you
>   can't answer you just say I don't know. Don't look at your sister to
>   give you the answers. Okay. We were talking about where you have
>   the pain or what hurts you. Okay, now what hurts you, your back?
>   Your feet? What?

This passage raises serious questions regarding the judge's compliance with such cases as *Cruz,* which require the ALJ to be particularly attentive especially to the needs of an unrepresented claimant with an inability to speak English well. In fact, assuming that Ms. Acevedo's sister-in-law was the only "counsel" or "representative" she had, the ALJ's threat to remove her could be construed as depriving the claimant of her right to counsel. On appeal, Ms. Acevedo's attorney argued that the case should be remanded on the ground that the ALJ failed to discharge the duty of upholding claimants' rights. A federal district court granted that remand.

A second case of an unrepresented claimant involved Mr. Costello (88-7350, IL), an illiterate white man who had no formal education. The ALJ's decision in the Costello case contained several statements that contradicted testimony in the transcript, suggesting that the judge failed to accommodate Mr. Costello in much the same way Ms. Acevedo was neglected in the process. First, in the hearing, the ALJ neglected to inform the claimant of his right to an attorney; however, in the decision, the ALJ reported that the claimant was informed of his right to counsel and voluntarily waived it. Second, during the short time the hearing lasted (approximately 15 minutes), the ALJ never asked the claimant about his most severe impairments—his knees, heart, depression, alcoholism, and inability to complete tasks. Then in the decision, the judge wrote:

> The claimant is alert and oriented. The claimant also has a history of alcohol abuse, now in remission. . . . The ALJ finds that the claimant seldom experiences deficiencies of concentration, persistence or pace resulting in failure to complete tasks in a timely manner (in work settings or elsewhere). . . . The ALJ finds that the claimant has never experienced any episodes of deterioration or decompensation in work or work-like settings which have caused him to withdraw from that situation or to experience exacerbation of signs and symptoms.

The contradiction here between the lack of testimony and the conviction of the judge's decision seems particularly troubling because the claimant, without the assistance of counsel, relied entirely on the ALJ's inadequate evidentiary development of the case. A third, explicit contradiction in the record can be found in the ALJ's conclusion that the claimant "takes no medications." One of the few things the ALJ and the claimant discussed was his list of medications.

Given the number of inconsistencies in this record and the number of times the judge construed facts against the claimant without eliciting testimony to support them, the judge seems obviously in this case to have failed to satisfy the standard set forth in *Cruz,* which requires the judge to "scrupulously and conscientiously probe into, inquire of, and explore for all relevant facts" and to "be especially diligent in ensuring that favorable as well as unfavorable facts and circumstances are elicited" (*Cruz v. Schweiker* 645 F.2d 812, 814 (9th Cir. 1981), citing *Vidal v. Harris* 637 F.2d 710, 713 (9th Cir. 1981)). In this regard, the ALJ clearly failed to accommodate the claimant, who as uneducated, illiterate, and unrepresented had several special needs that required particular attention.

Not all cases reviewed for this study indicated the same disregard for the rights of unrepresented claimants and unwillingness to accommodate. Yet even when ALJs took special care to ensure that unrepresented claimants voluntarily waived their right to counsel, the judge could discover in later testimony that the claimants were unable to represent themselves. The following interchange between a more sensitive judge and Ms. Price (89-4298, IL), an illiterate African-American woman, on the issue of obtaining the claimant's acknowledgment and waiver of her right to counsel seemed to start this hearing off well:

> *ALJ:* There are several preliminary things that we need to mention before we begin though. One is that you appear this morning, representing yourself.
>
> *CLMT:* Yes.
>
> *ALJ:* Now, you have received information from us—from us about the possibility of getting represented by an attorney or another representative if you want to be. Most people are represented by attorneys or other representatives in these hearings but—
>
> *CLMT:* All right.
>
> *ALJ:*—one need not be and it's my responsibility to make sure that all of the evidence is considered and that you receive a fair determination of your claim whether or not you have a representative—
>
> *CLMT:* All right.
>
> *ALJ:*—but one thing that we do need to do is to make sure that you have completely understood your right to be represented if you want to be represented by an attorney or another representative. Now, did you know that you could be represented by a lawyer or somebody else in this hearing if you wished?
>
> *CLMT:* Well, I knew it but I didn't have no money or anything and I didn't try to get one.
>
> *ALJ:* All right. Well, money is generally not a barrier in these cases to be represented because there are—there are any number of organizations and attorneys that will take a case like yours without being paid anything at the beginning.
>
> *CLMT:* I understand.
>
> *ALJ:* Now, if you want to investigate that possibility further, I will be glad to continue the hearing so that you can get a representative but as I say, you don't—
>
> *CLMT:* Well—
>
> *ALJ:*—you don't need—
>
> *CLMT:*—if it's all right with you, I can just go on through with it—
>
> *ALJ:* Sure.
>
> *CLMT:*—for today.
>
> *ALJ:* Okay. That's—

CLMT: That will be fine.

ALJ:—fine. Yeah, I'm not trying to talk you into that.

CLMT: I understand.

ALJ: I'm just—

CLMT: I know what you—

ALJ:—I'm just making sure that you understand that you could be represented if you wanted to.

CLMT: That will be just fine.

ALJ: All right. We'll find that you have understood the right to counsel and that you've waived that right and that you are prepared to proceed this morning.

However, almost immediately after this very supportive discussion about the right to an attorney, the claimant and the judge were confronted with Ms. Price's inability to represent herself. Here is the claimant's response to the judge's question regarding whether she objected to any of the exhibits contained in the file:

ALJ: Now, Miss Price, you had an opportunity to look over the exhibits that are associated with your claim, did you not?

CLMT: Yes, sir.

ALJ: Are you aware of any other evidence, particularly any medical evidence, that might be included in the file but isn't here now?

CLMT: Well, I got—I think they got them all pretty near but—all of them in there that I have because I mostly suffer with my—my back, my numb—my back gets numb. I have a hernia because of it. I can't lift. My doctor told me not to lift nothing and my—really—really what bothers me is this side. It just gets numb. At times, I can't pick up nothing with this—

ALJ: Okay. Now, we'll—we'll talk more about those things in a few minutes but for the moment, you're not—you haven't been in the hospital or been examined by any doctors that would have resulted in reports that we don't have, have you?

CLMT: No, sir. I haven't been—

ALJ: Okay. So you think that we have everything we need to?

CLMT: That's right.

ALJ: All right. We'll find that the record is complete and we'll admit into the record Exhibits 1 through 17.

Ms. Price, who had only a fourth-grade education and could not read, here appeared incapable of discussing the exhibit file. Instead of speaking about the file as containing the evidence on which the decision depends, she responded to the judge's question about the contents of the file with testimony regarding her impairments. In this instance alone, Ms. Price was clearly disadvantaged by her lack of counsel. Furthermore, her hearing lasted only 20 minutes. Beyond the initial supportive introduction, in which the judge attempted to accommodate Ms. Price's inexperience in these matters and her apparent lack of education, he did little or nothing, once he discharged his duty of obtaining the acknowledgment and waiver, to accommodate Ms. Price's needs during the hearing. Her case was ultimately remanded by the federal district court for further proceedings.

In a fourth case involving an unrepresented claimant, Ms. Moore (89-6436, IL), the ALJ appears on the surface to attempt to meet the requirements set forth by the *Cruz* and *Vidal* courts, but he probably in fact did not even comply with the *Hallex* requirements to obtain an acknowledgment and waiver:

> *ALJ:* You're willing to proceed without an attorney, is that correct?
>
> *CLMT:* Yeah.
>
> *ALJ:* That you signed a document here today, saying that you do not wish to be represented.
>
> *CLMT:* No. I didn't know how to go about getting one. I don't have no money for an attorney.
>
> *ALJ:* Well, there's over—what 7,000 or 8,000 attorneys in the phone book, and we sent you a letter, originally, giving you the list of Legal Aid Attorneys. You had ample opportunity. You had another trial before another Judge so you know about whether or not you're entitled to an attorney.
>
> *CLMT:* Yeah, but I—at the time I didn't feel like it was—one would know enough about the case to take it.
>
> *ALJ:* All right. Well, I want you to know that whether or not you have an attorney, I will do everything in my power to protect your rights. I want you to understand that. That's my job. I won't let—I won't let the government, I won't let anybody take advantage of you. So with that understanding, you're willing to proceed without an attorney. Is that correct?
>
> *CLMT:* Right.

Here, the judge professed that he would "protect" the claimant, as the *Cruz* and *Vidal* decisions require. However, the judge did so by infantilizing the claimant. Instead of responding to the claimant's ill-informed reasoning (she did not think an attorney could represent her because no attorney was familiar with her case) and instead of explaining that his role as claimant's protector may and often does conflict with his duty to act as judge, prosecutor, and defense counsel, the ALJ rushed to provide an unqualified promise to take care of her.

The quick pace and shallow presentation of the judge's response to Ms. Moore's explanation for not seeking counsel suggests that the ALJ may have made his promise to protect the claimant to avoid postponing the case to give the claimant an opportunity to get an attorney. Since cases are tracked by the local OHA for the length of time a judge has them, and since judges are pressured to move cases along, a midhearing postponement would not only cause the judge to "lose" the hour or so set aside for a given hearing but would also prolong the time it takes the judge to handle the case.[3] Such factors might have weighed into the judge's decision to subtly pressure the claimant to proceed without counsel.[4] If this statement influenced the claimant's decision to proceed, the judge clearly failed to fully accommodate her special need for patience in helping her to obtain counsel.

Although this judge never prepared a decision because he was taken off the case (probably due to illness or some other benign reason), the ALJ who ultimately decided the case recommended that Ms. Moore be denied benefits. However, the claimant's case was effectively argued in federal district court, and the case was remanded to an ALJ for additional workup on the grounds that "in reaching his decision the ALJ had a heightened duty to develop a full record because plaintiff was not represented by counsel and was unfamiliar with hearing procedures" (referring to *Lashley v. Secretary of Health and Human Services* 708 F.2d 1048 (6th Cir. 1983)).

In a fifth case involving an unrepresented claimant, Mr. Bell (90-5548, IL), a literate African-American SSI applicant, the ALJ seems, as in the Acevedo case, to satisfy the *Hallex* requirement to obtain an acknowledgment and a waiver of the claimant's right to counsel. Again, however, as in Ms. Price's case, it later became clear that the claimant was unable to represent himself and that the judge failed to discharge his duty of accommodating and, hence, engaging an unrepresented claimant:

ALJ: Mr. Bell, we sent you a letter back in—where is that—back when we sent you the notice of hearing, that you had the right to be represented by an attorney or other representative, although that's not required. And you've appeared here today without a representative. Do you wish to proceed anyway?

CLMT: Yes, I wish to proceed.

ALJ: Thank you.

This dialogue seems typical of the interchange between ALJs and unrepresented claimants in the cases I reviewed and outwardly satisfied the *Hallex* requirements. However, consider the following interchange between the judge and a vocational expert (VE) about Mr. Bell's ability to do his previous work:

ALJ: Now, I'd like to describe for you an individual who is not Mr. Bell. But he has these characteristics. He's 47 years of age, he has a GED and he has a past work record as you just explained it. The listed person has the limitations described by Dr. Shana upon examination on his residual functional capacity form attached to the examination, I will pass to you . . .

VE: Thank you.

ALJ: Do you have such an individual in mind?

VE: Yes, I do.

ALJ: Could such an individual do any of Mr. Bell's past work?

VE: I just have a question [referring to the report the judge has passed to him, which we can assume was not passed to the claimant since there would be only one copy of that report in the hearing room]. Nothing is checked off on page 2. Am I to assume that—

ALJ: Right.

VE: All of those would be "no."

ALJ: Yes.

VE: Okay, yes, he would be able to perform all of his past work given that.

ALJ: Any further explication?

VE: No.

ALJ: All right, sir [referring to Mr. Bell], now it's your turn to ask her about her opinion, if you wish. Do you have any questions?

CLMT: No, I don't think anything is relevant to—

ALJ: I'm sorry?

CLMT: I don't have anything that is relevant to—you're speaking about another person than myself?

ALJ: Well, we're talking about a hypothetical person, an imaginary person, but who has your characteristics.
CLMT: Oh, I see.
ALJ: Because she advises me.
CLMT: Um-hum.

In short, Mr. Bell was not familiar enough with hearing practices and procedures to follow the discussion of his own case. When he waived his right to an attorney, in other words, he did not fully comprehend his need for representation, and the judge did little or nothing to help him understand it more fully. Surely, at the point that he expressed his misunderstanding of the method the ALJ used to interrogate the VE, Mr. Bell could easily have been informed by the judge that such practices were a means of inquiring whether a VE believed that medical problems similar to Mr. Bell's precluded work activity and, if so, more specifically what work activity it precluded.

Indeed, a VE's presence at a hearing can make or break the case for a claimant; consequently, careful cross-examination of a VE can be extremely important to a claimant's ultimate success. Since disability claimants rarely consult with experts on vocational matters unless judges invite VEs to hearings, claimants almost never have evidence in their exhibit files to contradict the VEs' testimony. Unless, then, the unfavorable testimony of a VE present at the hearing is persuasively cross-examined, the opinion of one VE will likely figure prominently in the judge's decision and ultimately in the mind of an appellate court.

Even if the judge denies the applicant's claim, careful cross-examination of a VE at a hearing can still have critical importance to claimants who decide to appeal their cases to federal district courts. On appeal, a court's standard of review is whether there was substantial evidence at the hearing level to deny the case. Cross-examination of a VE at the hearing is therefore also important to establish a record for appeal. Conversely, if the testimony of a VE at the hearing goes without cross-examination, it is likely to stand unopposed as the substantial evidence on which a federal district court would rely in making its decision.

Mr. Bell never pointed to other medical records or reports (other than one doctor's report on which the VE's testimony was based and which may not have considered all of Mr. Bell's impairments) to cross-examine the testimony of the VE at his hearing. In the end, Mr. Bell's claim was denied, and his case was never heard in federal district court. Mr. Bell attempted to represent himself on further appeal; however, his federal district court file indicates that he failed to properly complete the paperwork.

The Bell hearing highlights several of the ALJs' problems in their efforts to accommodate unrepresented applicants. The first problem can be traced to the ALJ's opening statement. The ALJ in Mr. Bell's case neglected to fully explain to the claimant what role the VE played in the process and the fact that both the judge and Mr. Bell would have an opportunity to ask the VE questions about whether she believed, based on the medical records and reports, that he could do his previous work.

A second problem pertains to the ALJs' convention of phrasing questions to VEs in a way that is likely to mystify the claimant—that is, by referring to the claimant as a hypothetical person. Many judges follow this procedure to avoid appearing to have decided the case in advance. By questioning VEs in hypothetical terms, judges can characterize applicants with whatever impairments the ALJs believe are severe, excluding from consideration those impairments believed not to be severe. The ALJ hearing Mr. Bell's case might, at a minimum, have explained this convention and its purpose to the claimant.

Third, ALJs may help or hinder claimants with instructions relevant to materials they must procure to complete their files. For example, the ALJ hearing Mr. Bell's case failed to properly assist the claimant when asking him to get his doctor to fill out an additional medical form. The judge gave Mr. Bell the form without explaining its relevance to his case (in fact, it was key) and then said only, "All right. . . . And if nothing comes back, I'll make my decision anyway." The judge did not explain that some doctors may be unwilling to fill out medical forms without being compensated; that both OHA and DDS have funds for compensating doctors who fill out medical forms; or that DDS and OHA, as standard practice, will send the form for claimants (SSA 1992, I-2-520).

In the final case of an unrepresented claimant to be reviewed here, that involving Mrs. Redd (87-3348, IL), a literate African-American claimant, the ALJ initially neglected to ask Mrs. Redd whether she was aware of her right to be represented and whether she waived that right. Roughly five minutes into the hearing, the ALJ said:

> *ALJ:* And you were advised of your right to appear with an attorney. And you've elective [*sic*] to be here on your own [inaudible], is that correct?
> *CLMT:* Yes sir.

ALJ: Alright.
CLMT: I didn't think I needed one.
ALJ: Alright.

The judge did nothing to follow up Ms. Redd's comment that she didn't think she needed an attorney. Again a judge seemed to meet the minimum *Hallex* requirements but did not take the time to accommodate Ms. Redd as the *Cruz* and *Vidal* cases demand. In response to the question, "Did you review the exhibit file?" Ms. Redd answered, "Briefly." This response should have alerted the judge that Ms. Redd did not fully understand the importance of the medical evidence in her case. Ms. Redd's case was remanded by federal district court because

> the ALJ failed to develop a full record and failed to give [claimant] a fair hearing. [T]he hearing record suggests that the ALJ spent minimal time and effort developing the record and implied before the testimony was complete that he would rule against [claimant]. The remand . . . should be adequate to correct the deficiencies of the hearing.

From these cases, it is clear that some judges do not adequately accommodate or engage claimants by meeting even the minimum requirements set forth in the *Hallex* rules that require ALJs to obtain an acknowledgment and a waiver of a claimant's right to representation. Other judges meet the minimum requirements set forth in *Hallex* to obtain waivers from claimants. However, judges use different tactics to obtain waivers. One judge reassured the claimant that he would "protect" her, without explaining that he must play contradictory roles, including that of defense lawyer, prosecutor, and judge. That judge also did not truly give the claimant the option to freely "choose" not to be represented. Instead, he reassured her with a promise to protect her and then said, in effect, "Knowing what I've just told you, you want to proceed, right?" He afforded her little or no choice in the matter.

Other judges obtained the acknowledgment and waiver and hence satisfied *Hallex* requirements but did not probe further into an understanding of whether claimants truly appreciated their need for counsel. When judges hear that claimants have reviewed the exhibit folder "briefly" or did not or could not review it at all, the judges should at a minimum honor rules mandating them to accommodate the claimants and become and remain alert to signs of whether or not such claimants really understand the process and appreciate their need for counsel. Insincere or incomplete efforts to accommodate unrepresented claimants reveal, on the one hand, the heavy burden ALJs bear when having to assist such claimants through the process and, on the other, the inadequate job they do to satisfy their duty.

Judges' Failure to Engage or Accommodate Claimants while Eliciting Testimony

The requirement on ALJs to inquire fully into each issue and, hence, to accommodate claimants with special needs extends to the practices judges follow to elicit testimony.[5] Specific ways in which judges failed to accommodate claimants with special needs included leading the claimant, infantilizing the claimant, acting unnecessarily judgmental and rude, failing to follow up on relevant questions, and implying that the claimant's perspective was wrong.

Leading the Claimant

Leading a claimant is a technique used by ALJs to ask questions that "lead" a claimant to say or not say certain things. Generally, the answers elicited to leading questions are used against claimants to deny their application for benefits. This technique is particularly devastating when it is used with claimants who have special needs.

A clear example of a judge leading a claimant is the hearing of Miss Plain (87-5258, IL), a case also mentioned in chapter 1. Miss Plain was an unrepresented, illiterate African-American nurse's aide with a third-grade education. At the hearing, the claimant testified that she had not worked since 1966 because "would be nobody hire me no more." The judge, wanting clarification of why the claimant had not worked, asked the following question: "And during that time, did you, did you not work because nobody would hire you or did you not work because you were raising a family?" suggesting that her lack of work history was related to factors other than illness.

Here is how the judge pursued his questioning regarding her ability to work at the time of the hearing:

ALJ: Now, have you got a job now, if there was a job now available in a nursing home—would you work now?
CLMT: No because I can't be able to lift patients like I used to be.
ALJ: Could you do any other things, besides lifting a patient? What

else does a nurse's aid do in the hospital, so you wouldn't have to lift anybody. Any other jobs there?

CLMT: That's the only thing I would know to do, just change a patient and lift them because I can't read.

ALJ: Can you answer the telephone?

CLMT: Yes, I can answer the telephone.

ALJ: Could you—

CLMT: But I can't—

ALJ: Could you be a receptionist?

CLMT: I can't sit long enough for that because my legs and thighs get real numb. I have to stand and move around.

Here it seems likely that the judge's leading questions are designed to persuade the claimant that she can work, despite her myriad of limitations. Could Miss Plain realistically be a receptionist without being able to read and write? If the judge truly was interested in learning what jobs Miss Plain could do, wouldn't he have considered her illiteracy and related educational factors when questioning her about her ability to do alternative jobs?

Infantilizing

Judges also commonly infantilized claimants—that is, treated them like infants to minimize their testimony, to delegitimize their stories. Judges most frequently infantilized claimants with such special needs as lack of counsel and an inability to speak English well. This problem surfaced in chapter 4, when I described some of the inappropriate titles that ALJs used to refer to claimants. This section describes other, more complicated interactions in which ALJs infantilized claimants.

Ms. Acevedo (87-2767, CA) was unrepresented. She required the assistance of an interpreter at the hearing. As previously noted, her sister-in-law was also present. The judge treated the claimant like a small child when she said, "Okay. Wait a minute. Do you remember that I said if you don't know you're supposed to say I don't know."

The judge hearing the case of Ms. Alva (84-0617, CA), a claimant who also required an interpreter, also infantilized the claimant:

ALJ: When is the last time you saw Doctor Robinson?

CLMT: I think it was in April, in April I think.

ALJ: Of this year?

CLMT: Yes.
ALJ: Ms. Alva, please pay attention to what I'm asking you. When is the last time you saw Doctor Robinson?

It seems in this passage that instead of accepting the claimant's memory lapse, the judge scolds her as though she were a small child who is deliberately withholding information.

In another case, involving Mrs. Moore (89-6436, IL), an African-American woman with a tenth-grade education, the judge infantilized the claimant relying on a slightly different approach: "I don't want you to walk out of here and say, oh my goodness, I forgot to tell him something. Now, you take your time." While this comment in and of itself may be benign, the judge's comments following the claimant's testimony that she smoked are illuminating: "Do you really? Can I get you to quit? Can you quit smoking, for your own good health?" She responded, "I don't know. I have a lots of pains over my—" Then the judge tried a different tactic, saying, "Well, everybody does that, but cigarettes—that cuts into your income. Do you realize that you must spend—what? Ten, fifteen, twenty dollars for cigarettes, a month?" When the judge asked whether the claimant's physician told her to quit, the following dialogue ensued:

CLMT: Well, he didn't tell me that to quit, but he says slow down.
ALJ: Is that all? That's an unusual doctor nowadays.
CLMT: Well, he always said, you know, cut it down. That's what—that's all I ever remember him telling me.
ALJ: He didn't tell you to quit?
CLMT: Well, he probably did.
ALJ: All right.
CLMT: I would say he did.
ALJ: And you haven't?
CLMT: No I haven't.
ALJ: All right.

The judge did not ask why Mrs. Moore continued smoking despite her doctor's advice to quit; it is as though the judge, as with a child, was not interested in her explanation (which is certainly relevant to a disability determination that will deny benefits to an applicant who does not follow the prescribed treatment of a treating physician) but rather felt the need to lecture her. At the end of this interaction, one cannot be sure whether the doctor ever really told Mrs. Moore to quit or whether she conceded so because the ALJ convinced her that it was true.

These transcripts revealed that some judges, in their efforts to accommodate claimants with special needs, actually instead infantilize and probably alienate them. Even more problematic is the recognition that these practices ultimately affect the outcome of a claimant's case; in Mrs. Moore's hearing, the judge essentially forced her to concede that smoking constituted a failure to follow prescribed treatment.

Acting Unnecessarily Judgmental

In transcripts in which judges seemed unnecessarily judgmental, I inferred, particularly in cases involving claimants with special needs, that the judge believed he knew better and wanted to give advice. The special needs of these claimants usually involved mental impairments, including drug and alcohol addictions. The advice given in these instances could at least as easily be read as an uninvited intrusion into personal matters as an effort to accommodate claimants, especially considering that the advice given typically seemed to reveal the judges tendency to stereotype. In the case of Mr. James (88-1712, CA), for example, after the claimant's wife testified that her husband used cocaine "too often," the judge responded as follows: "Well, can you give us some idea how often is too often? I mean, is that—frankly once every 10 years is too often as far as I'm concerned." In the same transcript, the judge gave Mrs. James the following lecture:

> *ALJ:* Now, before we close, let me point out to you Mrs. James, just as it—you can certainly ignore what I'm going to say, and you may well. But, I want you to understand that it comes as [*sic*] a disinterested observer. Not—not a lawyer for any side here. And I have no stake in it other than to judge what's going on. But, you're an enabler [phonetic]. You're causing a lot of this. And you ought to— I would suggest that you go to Alanon [phonetic]. If you don't believe me, because I think they will tell you the same thing that I'm going to tell you. That people don't drink regularly without someone helping them on the way. And you're a large part of that. And sure you can decide that all of the doctors in the world are wrong, and there must be a diagnosis. But, that's not the way most people approach a medical problem, I can tell you that. Most people go to a doctor, and the [*sic*] accept the doctor's word for what's wrong with them. And they feel better if the doctor [says] there's nothing

wrong. And it's a lot better to have it in your mind than in your body. Because, you can cure minds. You can cure attitudes and you can cure emotions. But, if there is something really wrong with your body it's a lot hard[er] then if you're—people are telling you, I'm not the doctor, but there sure is a slew of doctors that said there's nothing wrong physically with your husband. Or at least nothing that major wrong.

CLMT'S WIFE: That they can find.

ALJ: No, not that they can find. Nothing major wrong period. As I say you can shop forever and somebody will agree with you. There's enough doctors, lawyers, and people in the world, so you can always find someone for enough funds to agree with you.

CLMT'S WIFE: Well, I am a professional.

ALJ: I'm not—wait a minute, I'm not telling you to argue.

CLMT'S WIFE: No.

ALJ: I'm just telling you, because I want to tell you because it will be on my conscience if I didn't say something. I'm telling you talk to Alanon, because—or any of the groups that deal with alcoholics. But, you don't get to be one—you don't abuse alcohol or drugs without someone in the family enabling you. That's where you fit in. You ought to understand your role in the process, because he's not going to get better unless dynamics in the family change. And I mean both of you working at it.

CLMT'S WIFE: Well, I don't drink.

ALJ: No, you're causing him to drink.

CLMT'S WIFE: No, I don't drink. The pain is causing Arthur to drink.

ALJ: Oh, people always find a reason to drink.

CLMT'S WIFE: The pain is causing Arthur to drink. And I also go back to say that I am a professional. And I see my husband in pain. And I want to know why he's in pain. He's been in pain too long.

ALJ: Well, okay. I think I have . . . much more insight [in]to what's going on.

CLMT'S WIFE: He's been in pain too long.

ALJ: And I appreciate it.

CLMT'S WIFE: You know, it doesn't make sense. And it's like his body is not getting any better.

ALJ: It's not going to. I can tell you that. . . . Until the family dynamics change, he's not going to get any better.

CLMT'S WIFE: Well, he has no family problems. My going to get his liquor, that's—

ALJ: That's not a problem?

CLMT'S WIFE: That's not a problem. I can stop doing that right now. But, he still has a physical disability.

ALJ: Well—

The judge then proceeded to lecture the claimant:

> *ALJ:* Mr. James, let me say one thing. . . . You know whether or not your going to get Social Security benefits is obviously within my control. But whether or not you recover [is] within your control. You got to start taking some active interest in your recovery, or it's not going to occur and you are running out of employable time, you're 47 years old. Regardless of what I do or don't do, you're going to become less and less attractive to [future] employers as time goes along. An awful lot of doctors seem to feel you can make it. . . . that's a vote of faith in your ability to recover. . . . I think Mr. Waxman [the claimant's attorney] has done an excellent job in try-ing to get you in an appropriate program. . . . You ought to look into your own vocational recovery. . . . And while you have to wait a long time at County Hospital, it's there for you. You're going to have to make some efforts, cause it isn't going to happen without your effort.

In this passage, a man alleging an alcohol addiction in a Social Secu-rity disability claim and his wife were subjected to a lecture by an ALJ. This seems a clear violation of both the affirmative duty of judges to posi-tively accommodate and engage claimants and the rules mandating judges to avoid personal judgments. To accommodate in this case would have been to inquire into the nature of the claimant's mental impairment and addiction patiently and with understanding and to apply the law. Ideally, in a more affectively oriented legal system, described in more detail in chapter 7, the judge would also be encouraged to describe why he was con-cerned about the claimant's persistent and disabling addiction in a manner that revealed the judge's sensitivity to and personal experience with situa-tions similar to that of the claimant. Given prevailing rules and interpreta-tions, however, the judge's disapproval of the claimant's behavior and expression of that disapproval seemed both alienating and prejudicial.

In another case, one involving a white woman who also was an alcoholic, Ms. Degryse (88-2082, MA), the ALJ dismissed the applicant's claim because she gave alcoholism as her primary excuse for not filing a timely request for hearing. The Appeals Council reversed this decision, concluding that the claimant's alcoholism was good cause for filing a late request for hearing. However, once the case was returned to the judge, the judge subjected the claimant to a series of abuses. Before the claimant's testimony was taken, the ALJ required the paralegal representing the claimant to go through her analysis of the five-step sequential evaluation process on the grounds that he "hate[s] to walk into these things blind [referring to the testimony to be taken]. What is it we're going to be looking for?"

In another case heard by the same judge, which involved a female applicant alleging diabetes and high blood pressure (Galasso, 88-0280, MA), the judge proceeded, as do most judges, by taking the claimant's testimony. No questions were asked of this claimant's representative about the five-step sequential evaluation process, and the judge made no comment about hating to walk into hearings "blind." It is possible that the judge was punishing either Ms. Degryse or the paralegal for having challenged his dismissal before the Appeals Council or that he resented having to hear the claim of an alcoholic and wanted to make it as difficult for her as possible.

Another example of how this ALJ was harshly judgmental in the Degryse case is illustrated in the following testimony, in which the judge asked the claimant about her pulmonary problems and her smoking:

> *ALJ:* And he does pulmonary function tests on you, you say, fairly regularly?
> *CLMT:* Yeah, he does.
> *ALJ:* What does Dr. Sabba say about smoking 2 packs per day?
> *CLMT:* I shouldn't be doing it.
> *ALJ:* Well, I think that's probably an understatement, isn't it?
> *CLMT:* It certainly is. I have tried to quit, it never worked. That's why we have the catapras [phonetic] patch.

Again, the judge's language in this case implies his disdain for the claimant's lifestyle ("Well, I think that's probably an understatement, isn't it?").

Another case, this one involving an uneducated, illiterate African-American man, Mr. Prince (87-9662, IL), raises similar problems. The judge opened the hearing as follows:

ALJ: Is that the loudest you can speak?

CLMT: Yes.

ALJ: Now, Mr. Prince, let me tell you so we don't have, cause it is very disconcerting. You're going to have to hold your voice up. If you can't do it we'll have to postpone the hearing because you have to speak up, do you understand.

The judge goes on to ask Mr. Prince how far he went in school:

ALJ: How far did you get in school?

CLMT: About six grade; seven, almost to seven something like that.

ALJ: Did you finish the sixth grade?

CLMT: I don't know. I really don't know. I really don't know cause I start to work then.

ALJ: You don't know how far you went in school?

CLMT: About the sixth grade.

ALJ: Did you finish the sixth grade?

CLMT: I was still in it when I quit.

In this passage the ALJ seems judgmental about the fact that this man, to whom school was obviously never very relevant, could not remember how many grades he completed.

These cases suggest that ALJs may be judgmental about claimants with special needs such as mental impairments, including addictions, illiteracy, and lack of education, when in fact the law requires not personal judgment or disrespect but accommodation; the judges in my sample did not go far enough to meet the requirement to positively accommodate claimants with special needs.

Being Rude

Examples of rude judges abound in the transcripts. This manifestation of failing to accommodate claimants is, again, particularly troubling when it involves claimants with special needs.

Judges' rudeness takes many forms in the transcripts. In the case of Mr. Hilton (89-2370, MA), the judge used language in his decision that only a college- or law-school-educated person would understand. Yet the judge used this elevated language in a decision written for an illiterate claimant:

Evaluating his pain within the guidelines of *Avery, supra* [a standard for cases involving allegation of pain in that district], the Administrative Law Judge finds that the nature, duration, and frequency of the claimant's pain are *de minimis,* and that there is little evidence of more than minimal true functional limitation secondary to his allegations of pain, based on his own description of his daily activities.

Judges also very often make sarcastic comments and innuendos when eliciting the testimony of claimants with special needs. The following claimant, a native speaker of Portuguese, Ms. Marques (89-01257, MA), was doing her best to answer the judge's questions:

> *CLMT:* When my daughter comes home around two-thirty she gives me lunch.
> *ALJ:* What is that?
> *CLMT:* The pains, I don't know the pains, what she makes.
> *ALJ:* What you do eat for lunch, madam? Tell me a typical week of eating!
> *CLMT:* More or less Portuguese food.
> *ALJ:* We are going to get this sooner or later, aren't we?
> *CLMT:* Fish—

The judge's comments ("We are going to get to this sooner or later, aren't we?") were unnecessary and rude. They may well have alienated the claimant, which would likely hinder her testimony further.

Likewise, in trying to find out how much Miss Plain (87-5258, IL) did to care for her grandchildren, several of whom lived with her, the judge in that case adopted a sarcastic tone that showed disdain for the claimant's lifestyle, asking, "Do you do anything to your grandchildren? Do you feed them, do you dress them, do you bathe them?" She responded, "No, their mothers do that." Then the judge said: "Their mothers do that. Their mothers are in the home all day too? They're not working?" She responded: "One of my daughters, be home at all times."

The judge hearing the case of Mr. Reed (88-6170, IL), an uneducated African-American man, likewise turned sarcastic. Mr. Reed described his previous job, and then the following exchange took place:

> *ALJ:* I take it these boxes were put into another box for shipping?
> *CLMT:* What's you say?

ALJ: Weren't the boxes that you made put into another box to be shipped out to these customers?
CLMT: No.
ALJ: What did you do with the boxes after they were formed?
CLMT: That's what I'm explaining now.
ALJ: Well, get to it.

Subsequently, the conversation continued:

ALJ: You're putting them on a pallet.
CLMT: Yeah.
ALJ: Okay. At least we got that far.

In context, all of these claimants seem to be struggling as well as they can to negotiate the complex hearing procedure. The ALJs' rudeness through sarcasm can hardly be expected to facilitate the process and probably has the opposite effect.

ALJs also show rudeness toward claimants with special needs by growing visibly impatient with them. The ALJ taking testimony of the following claimant, Ms. Burr, an African-American woman suffering from both physical and mental impairments (87-10636, IL), seemingly could not hurry her story along fast enough:

ALJ: How long were you hospitalized there or were you, did you continue to go to Cook County Hospital after that?
CLMT: No, I was in there for about a week. And Cook County, they didn't give me no seizure medicine, they sent a psychiatrist in—
ALJ: Uh huh.
CLMT:—and I didn't see why I needed a psychiatrist.
ALJ: Alright and then what happened, just tell me that?
CLMT: Because I told them that I—
ALJ: I know what you told them but, I mean, what did you do next, you stayed there for about a week and then you left?"

Likewise, the ALJ grew impatient when taking the testimony of Mr. Prince (87-9662, IL):

ALJ: When did you start falling?
CLMT: I've been falling for a good while.

ALJ: What's a good while?

CLMT: Bout—

ALJ: Now, how long Mr. Prince?

CLMT: I don't know the exact year and—

ALJ: Mr. Prince, you have to try and tell me as best as you can recall, how long it's been since you've been falling.

CLMT: Only been, I been falling four or five years and so on.

ALJ: Okay. And how often do you fall?

CLMT: Well, like I be, I just get out of breath and stuff and it locks my leg and I just get weak and it all depends. Sometimes I be walking and grab something.

ALJ: Okay. How often does it happen that you fall?

CLMT: When this feeling hits me.

ALJ: How often does it happen?

CLMT: Well, lately is just come like every two or three weeks or something like that.

ALJ: no, —

And later in Mr. Prince's testimony:

ALJ: How long have you had the cramps [in your legs]?

CLMT: Four or five years, I guess.

ALJ: Okay. Every day you've had them four or five years?

CLMT: I have cramps every day.

ALJ: Has that been true for four or five years?

CLMT: Yeah, but I didn't know what it was.

ALJ: No, please, Mr. you have to answer my questions, do you understand.

CLMT: I am trying to answer them the best I can.

While questioning Mr. Rodriguez (87-878, IL), a Puerto Rican claimant with an eighth-grade education, another judge grew similarly impatient:

ALJ: What problems, if any, do you have climbing stairs?

CLMT: Very much, I get to uncomfortable, you know I get—

ALJ: Do you have chest pains from climbing stairs?

CLMT: Yes.

ALJ: Just answer yes.
CLMT: Yes.

It is hard to imagine that the impatience conveyed by these judges could help these claimants come forth with their testimony and realize as fully as they might the burden of proof on them to demonstrate their claims.

In each of the following three passages, ALJs demonstrate a different form of rudeness, a propensity to put claimants to the test unnecessarily and place considerable pressure on them. The judge hearing Mr. Reed's case (88-6170, IL) pressed as follows:

ALJ: All right. What's the heaviest thing you had to lift?
CLMT: I would say mostly maybe one box would weigh 2–3 pounds.
ALJ: An empty cardboard box or a pressboard box would weigh 2 or 3 pounds, 14 inches?
CLMT: Some of them would have like wax on them or something like that. Maybe, double wall, some of them would be. It wouldn't be that often—
ALJ: Let me ask you this. What's a gallon of milk in a paper carton weigh?
CLMT: A gallon of milk?
ALJ: In a paper carton. Give me your answer as quickly as you can. You don't get any prize. It just tells me what kind of judge at weight you are.
CLMT: I'd say maybe five pounds.
ALJ: Three pounds as a matter of fact.

Later in the transcript, the judge pressed still harder:

ALJ: Where do you have arthritis in your legs?
CLMT: It's in my hip and low back and down my spine.
ALJ: What's the difference between your lower back and spine?
CLMT: Well the spine is in the center of your back . . .
ALJ: . . . I don't know the difference between the spine and the low back. What distinction are you making?
CLMT: I said right above the hip.
CLMT: Above the hips.
CLMT: Right.

> *ALJ:* What's that, the spine or the lower back?
> *CLMT:* The lower back.
> *ALJ:* Okay. Now where's the spine then?
> *CLMT:* Right in the center.
> *ALJ:* Same spot?
> *CLMT:* No, down, I said the spine is in the center of your back.
> *ALJ:* Yes, the spine is in the center all the way from your neck to your tailbone. And so that includes your lower back I would think.

In this passage, as in the following one, it appears that the judge may be more concerned with revealing the claimant's ignorance than with eliciting testimony about his condition.

> *CLMT:* I have emphysema.
> *ALJ:* Emphysema. What's that?
> *CLMT:* It's like a respiratory problem, breathing, something with the lungs.
> *ALJ:* Okay. What else?
> *CLMT:* And asthma.
> *ALJ:* You have emphysema and asthma?
> *CLMT:* Yeah, that's what the doctor tells me.
> *CLMT:* What's the difference between those two things? If you know.
> *CLMT:* I don't know.
> *ALJ:* Okay. I don't know either.

Finally, judges show rudeness by becoming accusatory. In the following passage also from Mr. Reed's hearing, the judge, during testimony elicited by claimant's attorney, makes an accusation against the claimant, only to recognize his error. The really troubling point is that the information the judge seeks to extract from the claimant is easily verifiable by a doctor and does not require the judge's rude tone:

> *ATTY:* Now do your medications help at all with the pain?
> *CLMT:* Sometimes they slow it down but it don't never stop.
> *ATTY:* And you said that you're taking Tylenol, is that Tylenol number 3?
> *CLMT:* Yeah.
> *ATTY:* With Codeine?

ALJ: Wait, wait, wait, hold it, stop. If you're going to testify, Counsel, we'll swear you in. Where do you get Tylenol number 3 without a prescription?

CLMT: From the same doctor—I said I had it, I told you I take Tylenol.

ALJ: You told me you take Tylenol but you didn't put a number on it. That makes a big difference.

ATTY: So you meant to say Tylenol number 3?

CLMT: Yeah, I meant to say that.

ALJ: You meant to say that.

CLMT: Yeah.

ALJ: Where's the bottle?

CLMT: I told you, I said I didn't bring it.

ALJ: Why? You brought all your other medicine?

CLMT: I thought I had it in there. Sorry, I thought I had it in there.

This interchange concluded as follows:

ATTY: How many of those [Tylenol with codeine] do you take a day?

CLMT: About one every four hours.

ALJ: Will this testimony ever stay consistent? You told me in your testimony, Tylenol, yeah, I'm sorry, my apologies, one every four hours was the same thing you testified.

These findings of judges being rude to claimants, particularly to claimants requiring accommodation given their special needs, suggest that ALJs may be hindering the testimony of claimants with special needs, and in the process, putting these vulnerable claimants at a distinct disadvantage in the hearing and decision-making process.

Failing to Follow Up

In several cases, ALJs failed to follow up testimony of claimants or were indifferent to testimony that claimants with special needs perceived as important. In the case of the unrepresented claimant Ms. Acevedo (87-2767, CA), for example, the claimant testified that she had visited a psychiatrist, but the ALJ never followed this testimony up. Instead of asking the claimant why she visited a psychiatrist or what came of the visit, the judge concluded, "We have reports from him." This finding seems contrary to law, given the judge's duty to adequately develop the cases of an unrepresented applicant (*Vidal v. Harris,* 637 F.2d 710 (9th Cir. 1981); *Cruz v. Schweiker,* 645 F.2d 812 (9th Cir. 1981)).[6]

In the case involving Ms. Degryse (88-2082, MA), an alcoholic, the ALJ failed to follow up on a number of pertinent comments. In one passage the ALJ seemed concerned only with the quantity of alcohol consumed and not with whether Ms. Degryse became drunk or passed out (i.e., the physical manifestations of impairments stemming from her consumption) or with why she drank. The decision explained his interest in the quantity of alcohol she consumed: the judge concluded that the claimant's credibility was tarnished because her income prevented her from ingesting the level of alcohol she testified to drinking.

Another judge disregarded the testimony of Ms. Alexander (90-1220, CA), who reported that she went to a psychiatrist because she wanted to run her husband over with a car. The judge followed this disturbing comment with "How do you sleep at night?" Later in this case, the claimant testified that she lived downstairs in one apartment and her son lived upstairs with her mother, his grandmother. The ALJ never followed up with her about how or why this claimant could not care for her son and what the situation might suggest about her ability to function in general. Finally, Ms. Alexander testified that if she had a little extra money, she liked to "you know, free-base." The judge responded by asking, "You like to what?" And the claimant repeated, "Free-base." While it is obvious that the judge did not know what "free-basing" was, he never asked the claimant to explain.

In the case involving Mr. DeAlmeida (87-3402, CA), a Portuguese claimant, the judge failed to follow up on two important comments. First, the claimant testified that he had a strange feeling in his head, "as if there's a ball emptying and filling up, emptying and filling up." The judge then turned the questioning over to the attorney without asking for further clarification. Second, neither the judge nor the attorney followed up when the claimant said, "I have other problems that I should not be discussing here. My sexual life is not what it used to be" when asked whether he had other problems as a result of his diabetes. Questions on the subject could certainly have been asked sensitively and could have provided relevant testimony regarding the effect of Mr. DeAlmeida's diabetes on his functioning. In fact, the judge was so oblivious to this testimony that he erroneously concluded in his decision, "there has been no change in [Mr. DeAlmeida's] family life."

In the case involving Mrs. Karkar (89-3486, CA), a Jordanian woman with a sixth-grade education, a judge failed to follow up the following testimony:

> *CLMT:* I got sick when I was working, and since then, I just can't concentrate on anything.
>
> *ALJ:* So you—the main reason you couldn't do it would be because you wouldn't be able to concentrate on the job. Is that correct?
>
> *CLMT:* No, it's because I am sick and nervous.
>
> *ALJ:* When you say you are sick, what are you referring to?
>
> *CLMT:* I feel pressure coming to my chest and my—my arms—they get very nervous and tense, and I cry and I scream.
>
> *ALJ:* You take this medication for your nervousness and your anxiety. Does it help you?

In this passage, the ALJ failed to ask the claimant how often she cried and screamed or what made her do so. Instead, he superficially probed the issue by asking her if the medications helped.

In a similar case involving Mr. Slevin (84-3092, CA), a man suffering from manic-depressive disorder, the claimant revealed a number of detailed stories about his depression, outlining how on one occasion he could not leave his hotel room for two days because of his debilitating sadness. The judge asked no follow-up questions to these relevant and important stories.

In another case, Ms. Galasso (88-0280, MA), an Italian-speaking claimant, asked the judge to look at her hands in general and to look at the bones of her fingers in particular. The judge responded, "I'm not a physician and I would have to say that I don't see anything at this distance which is obvious to me, if you care to describe some." The attorney also asked the judge to look at Ms. Galasso's hands. What is noteworthy about this passage is not whether the judge should or should not have examined her hands but rather his expressed indifference. He concluded the interaction by saying, "Wouldn't mean anything to me."

In Mr. Costello's case (88-7350, IL), the judge asked this unrepresented, illiterate claimant with no formal education to describe any other problems he has. The claimant testified, "I have, I have a ulcer in my stomach. I had it for a long, long time. Sometimes, you know, I forget things, you know." Instead of following up on Mr. Costello's memory problems, the judge responded, "Go ahead. Anything else?"

In the case of Ms. Moore (89-6436, IL), the claimant alleging a mental impairment answered the question "what's bothering you that you can't go to work?" with "Well, I have the—they say it's not [inaudible] in the fact, but I do have constant back pain. Maybe it could be my nerves; I don't know what it is." The judge asked: "Constant rot—where's the pain? Right?" without ever following up on her testimony that her nerves might be bothering her. The judge concluded, "the claimant showed no obvious sign of significant pain or distress either at the hearing or at the prior interviews conducted by Social Security representatives." Can a judge make an eyeball assessment of a claimant's pain or distress if he fails to ask her to elaborate on her nervousness?

These cases are particularly troubling because they involve claimants who do not have the emotional or linguistic capacity to give testimony to fully document their cases; judges further hinder these claimants' testimony by failing to follow up on relevant comments that should have elicited interest.

Implying That the Claimant's Perspective Is Wrong

Judges also often responded negatively to claimants by implying that their perspective was wrong, even though it was frequently later revealed that the judge's negative response was incorrect. One way ALJs imply that claimants' perspectives are wrong is by disregarding them in the decisions. For example, Ms. Acevedo (87-2767, CA) testified that the physician she sees is a specialist. In the decision, however, the judge said that the physician was not shown to have a medical specialty. The federal court decision shows the claimant to be correct, referring to her doctor as an orthopedic surgeon.

The methods judges use to elicit testimony affects, in most instances, both the process and the outcome of the cases. Particularly in cases involving claimants with special needs, judges who lead claimants, infantilize, are unnecessarily judgmental, fail to follow up relevant questions, and imply that claimants' perspectives are wrong can inappropriately prevent an already vulnerable claimant from providing the testimony needed to fully develop the record. These practices reveal the difficulties judges seem to have when required to accommodate or engage claimants and raises serious questions about ALJs' ability to carry out their mandate to provide a hearing process that is fair to all applicants.

These examples provide qualitative evidence that at least some judges fall far short of their affirmative duty to positively engage or affirmatively assist disability claimants who have special needs. Taking this analysis one step further, these findings provide additional evidence that this sample of Social Security ALJs has tremendous difficulty accommodating claimants and consequently systematically disadvantages certain groups in the hearing and decision-making process.

Unrepresented claimants who are uneducated, are linguistically limited, and/or have alleged mental impairments seem to be severely disadvantaged as they try to negotiate the complicated hearing and decision-making process. My findings show that while judges generally satisfy, at least on the surface, their duty to obtain claimants' acknowledgments and waivers of right to representation, the ALJs do little to help such claimants sincerely participate in the hearing process once the acknowledgment and waiver are obtained.

In addition, the methods ALJs use to elicit testimony indicate that judges put claimants with these special problems at a particular disadvantage. It is not uncommon in cases involving these claimants for ALJs to lead testimony to the point of manipulating it, to infantilize claimants, to be unnecessarily judgmental about behaviors or lifestyles, to be rude, to fail to follow up on relevant questions, and to imply that the claimant's perspective is wrong or to ignore it, particularly when doing so serves the purpose of denying them benefits.

My qualitative data suggest that ALJs' failure to accommodate claimants stems, at least in part, from judges' prejudicial images regarding certain applicants, the evidence they present or do not present, or the impairments they allege. These findings suggest that certain claimants, including the uneducated, the linguistically limited, people alleging mental disabilities, people of color, and women may enter the Social Security disability hearing and decision-making process at a disadvantage. These findings imply that the most vulnerable members of our society, who may present their cases to ALJs without the benefit of the resources available to other claimants, may be confronted with judges who neglect their affirmative duty to accommodate.

The next chapter explores in more depth the stereotypes detected in the hearing transcripts and decisions that may at least begin to explain the results of the numerous quantitative studies that suggest that certain disability claimants are disadvantaged, and even discriminated against, in the process. This evidence too, may help explain why Social Security judges seem to have difficulty engaging claimants demanding special attention.

CHAPTER 6

Signifiers of Stereotyping

In the real-life application of Social Security's uniform and affective procedures, safeguards such as the right to an opening statement, the right to representation, and the right to assistance in developing relevant evidence and testimony can be rendered empty formalities by adjudicators who neglect the mandates both for uniformity and for affectivity. The evidence presented in chapters 4 and 5 offers a glimpse of exactly how uniformity can operate prejudicially and how the veil of impartiality reveals bias. In addition, an institutionalized disdain for the emotive dimensions of judging can contribute definitively to judges' inability to appropriately engage claimants in the ways the rules require.

In this chapter, I expose more directly how Social Security ALJs, at least in the sample of cases I analyzed, seem predisposed to negative stereotyping of certain types of impairments; members of certain racial and ethnic groups; people who are illiterate or uneducated; members of both genders, but especially women; and people receiving benefits like workers' compensation and welfare. In this chapter, I draw on the qualitative evidence of bias found in the hearing transcripts and decisions I reviewed.

Qualitative Evidence of Stereotyping in ALJ Decision Making

To illuminate exactly how and in what form bias specifically takes in ALJ decision making, my research concentrated on how judges stereotyped claimants during the hearing and decision-making process, particularly when denying these claims. Since all previous studies documented quantitatively the existence of bias in denied claims, as described in detail in chapter 3, I thought it useful to do a qualitative text analysis of how that bias manifested in the day-to-day functioning of the judicial bureaucracy. I focused on five areas in which judicial prejudice was qualitatively indicated in transcripts and decisions: type of impairment, race and ethnicity, education/literacy, gender, and receipt of benefits like workers' compensation and welfare.

Before proceeding with a presentation of my findings, however, it is important to note three things. First, the stereotypes I identify do not actually fall into such neat categories as the five headings suggest. For example, because the cases in which assumptions about obesity surface happen to involve female claimants, it is difficult to determine whether the stereotypes identified actually apply to the impairments alleged by the applicants or to the claimants' gender. Although I categorize my findings in one way or another, stereotypes are actually fluid and, as such, call for a much larger-scale study to verify the tentative findings reported here.

Second, few of my findings of stereotypical ideas amount to signs of outward or direct bias; rather, they usually indicate that the prejudices, if operational, are subtle and in many if not most cases hidden from the judges themselves.

Also because stereotyping is difficult to detect, I rely not only on evidence of their potential operation from the ALJ hearing transcripts and decisions but also on the findings and conclusions of the federal courts reviewing these decisions. This additional evidence often bolsters my interpretation of the presence and negative effect of stereotyping on the outcome of the cases.

Finally, while many of the assumptions ALJs hold mirror assumptions held elsewhere in society, it is important to remember that under the current construction of impartiality, judges are mandated to put aside all such notions and to consider only the relevant facts and law of each case (42 U.S.C. § 405 (b) (1); 42 U.S.C. § 1383 (c) (1); SSA 1992, I-2-601). For the purpose of promoting a better understanding of the conditions that might give rise to bias in the Social Security hearing and decision-making process, these qualitative analyses clarify how deeply embedded prejudicial assumptions may be and the pressing need to address their unconscious effect on the hearing and decision-making process.

Type of Impairment

More than with any other impairments alleged, ALJs seemed to hold the most preconceived assumptions about applicants who had alcohol or drug addictions, who were mentally ill, or who were obese. Qualitative analysis of the transcripts and hearing decisions suggest, and the federal court decisions available in most of these cases confirm, that ALJs' stereotypical assumptions about these impairments may well have influenced the judges' decision-making process and the outcomes of some cases.

Drug and Alcohol Addictions

Until 1996, when Social Security regulations eliminated benefits for people addicted to alcohol and drugs, alcoholism and drug addiction were considered disabling impairments within the meaning of the Social Security rules.[1] Eliminating benefits to people with drug and alcohol addictions may itself support my contention that some ALJs rejected the claims of these applicants simply because of their discriminatory attitudes regarding the nature of addiction as a disabling impairment. Indeed, it was the ALJ's complaints to Congress that addicts were misusing their benefits that motivated Senator William Cohen to investigate this issue which ultimately resulted in the passage of legislation eliminating benefits to people with drug and alcohol addictions (Mills and Arjo 1996).

Prior to the passage of the Amendments that eliminated these benefits, two requirements were necessary to obtain benefits: first, the alcohol or drug use was severe because it had caused a disabling impairment (rendering the claimant unable to do full-time work); second, the drug or alcohol use was beyond the claimant's control (Social Security Rulings 1982, 82-60). In practice, some judges required people addicted to alcohol or drugs to have become physically debilitated with evidence of a disease like pancreatitis. In other cases, judges required an underlying mental impairment. My research examined the cases for instances in which judges failed to comply with the old laws governing addictions, as these were the relevant rules at the time the study was undertaken.

The connection between drug or alcohol use and mental illness is well established in the medical literature. The need to drink or abuse drugs to alleviate the symptoms of trauma is quite common (Harrison, Hoffman, and Edwall 1989). Similarly, depression is often prevalent among drug addicts (Malow et al. 1990). Moreover, before the change in the law, it was well established in the Social Security cases (*Cooper v. Bowen,* 815 F.2d 557 (9th Cir. 1987))[2] and in the medical literature (American Psychiatric Association 1994), that drug and alcohol abuse is often involuntary and that it can affect both adults and children (Elliott and Coker 1991).

Thus, claimants who proved that they were alcoholics or drug addicts, that the addiction caused a disabling impairment, and that the addiction was beyond their voluntary control should have been legally qualified for benefits. However, these rules presented sufficient difficulty for some judges who did not consider alcoholics and drug addicts to be "deserving" of benefits to disregard the rules and rely instead on prejudicial assumptions.

The ALJ who heard the case of Ms. Degryse (88-2082, MA), a 40-year-old white woman, revealed the stereotypical assumptions he held that alcoholism can only affect older people and was only deserving of benefits if it manifested in a physical illness. For example, the judge asked Ms. Degryse's representative, "Why would I find your client disabled?" The representative responded, "She is a severe alcoholic." The judge then asked, "She's a younger worker?" and "Is there any impairment, physical impairment, which would prevent your client from working?" Then the paralegal stated, "Well the alcoholism." And the ALJ asked, "Physical?"

During this exchange, the judge limited his inquiry to the age of the claimant and the presence of physical symptoms. Since stereotyping occurs in both what is and what is not said, in what is asked and what is not asked, I inferred that by not making a similar effort to inquire into the claimant's mental illness as he made into her physical problems, the judge was prejudicially assuming that only physical illness was important when considering the severity of an alcohol addiction. Further, by asking whether the claimant was "younger," I inferred that the claimant's youth was relevant to his assessment that she was less deserving of benefits.

As noted, the medical-legal literature reports that claimants suffering from drug or alcohol abuse can be affected both physically and mentally (Social Security Rulings 1982, 82-60; Harrison, Hoffman, and Edwall 1989; Malow et al. 1990) and that people can be affected by a drug addiction as young as infancy (Dorris 1989; Elliott and Coker 1991). In Ms. Degryse's case, the attorneys representing Social Security in federal district court believed something was amiss in the ALJ's decision; they recommended that the federal district judge remand Ms. Degryse's case and order the ALJ to issue her a fully favorable decision, and the judge complied.

In a similar case, a judge found the alcoholism of Mr. O'Connor (89-4412, IL), a 47-year-old African-American man, not disabling. The ALJ reasoned that because the claimant's alcoholism had not impaired his brain function (Mr. O'Connor's neurological tests were normal) and he could perform some daily activities, the claimant was not disabled. This decision erroneously disregarded Social Security Ruling 82-60, which provided that alcoholism or drug addiction is disabling when "anatomical, physiological, or *psychological* abnormalities can be shown . . ." (emphasis added). As in Ms. Degryse's case, Mr. O'Connor's case was remanded following an appeal to the Circuit Court of Appeals; the three-judge court held that the ALJ had considered Mr. O'Connor's alcoholism "mechanically." The inquiry, the court of appeals decision instructed, was not whether Mr. O'Connor had been brain damaged but whether he could work.

Two other cases illustrate the point that biased assumptions regarding claimants' ability to control their alcoholism seemed to affect ALJs' decision making. One case involved Mr. Harper (89-4374, IL), a 53-year-old African-American man who alleged that he was suffering from alcoholism. The ALJ concluded that despite a "level of depression [that] was notably elevated, he did not appear to be significantly depressed in manner and behavior." In violation of rules prohibiting ALJs from making personal judgments and invoking the prejudicial assumption that all alcoholics can control their drinking, this ALJ found that the claimant's alcoholism was "of his own choice" and that any mental limitations imposed by his alcoholism would be resolved should he stop drinking. The judge made these conclusions despite evidence in the record that Mr. Harper curtailed his alcohol use only when the "pain made him feel like something might bust" and that he continued drinking while taking Antabuse, a drug that induces nausea and vomiting when mixed with alcohol. The ALJ summarized his assessment and admitted to his biased attitude when he proclaimed, "it is not the purpose of the Social Security Act to support an alcoholic habit."

The federal district court disagreed with the ALJ. The court considered the ALJ's observations regarding Mr. Harper's depression to be based on "selected portions of Harper's psychological and psychiatric reports, ignoring those parts of these reports which contradict it." Citing several instances in which Mr. Harper continued to consume alcohol despite severe physical problems, the court concluded that the claimant was unable to control his drinking, and it was not, as the ALJ interpreted, a matter of choice. The federal district court judge further found that the ALJ's comment that "it is not the purpose of the Social Security Act to support an alcoholic habit" constituted a clear violation of the rules: "the ALJ must apply the law established by the Social Security Act and its underlying regulations . . . and it is beyond question that claimants who are alcoholics and who cannot control this problem may be disabled and entitled to benefits."

Another case exemplifies how far afield the assumption that all addiction is controllable may lead a judge. Mr. James (88-1712, CA), whose case was described more fully in chapter 5, was a 48-year-old African-American applicant with chronic back pain who alleged that his drug and alcohol use was a means of managing pain. As discussed earlier, the judge lectured the claimant's wife, calling her an "enabler" and informing her of the importance of attending a program like Alanon. While it may be impossible to intuit with any certainty what role race, education, or class played in the latitude the judge took in lecturing Mrs. James (the judge was white, the claimant and his wife were black; the judge was a law school graduate, the claimant was a high school dropout, and his wife was a nurse; the judge earned $120,000 a year, the claimant and his wife were fighting for an annual disability pension of $12,000), the judge probably would not have felt such freedom in a case involving a claimant with heart disease or a brain tumor. It is as if an allegation of an alcohol, drug, or other addiction gives judges an opportunity to admonish claimants and their spouses for their lifestyles. Indeed, this judge even ventured the interpretation that Mr. and Mrs. James were "codependent," suggesting the stereotypical assumption that people addicted to alcohol or drugs and their partners are blameworthy and deserve to be lectured.[3] This judge ended his lecture to the claimant's wife with the comment, "I think I have much more insight into what's going on [than you do]."[4] The ALJ denied benefits in Mr. James's case, arguing that the claimant's drug use was controllable and a conscious choice. The federal district judge hearing Mr. James's appeal disagreed and remanded the case for further workup, holding that the claimant's "grossly exaggerated" pain justifying his related drug use signaled an uncontrollable addiction rather than a controllable one, as the ALJ had suggested.

Mental Illness

Similarly, prejudicial assumptions also seemed to influence judges in several cases involving claimants who alleged mental impairments. Informed by the *Diagnostic and Statistical Manual of Mental Disorders* (American Psychiatric Association 1994), Social Security rules and regulations reflect current medical literature and clearly recognize mental illness as a disabling impairment (20 C.F.R. 404, subpt. P, app. 1, 12.00). However, some judges seemed to override or disregard the rules governing mental impairments in favor of prejudicial assumptions about mental illness reflective of cultural stereotypes.

In the case of Mr. Slevin (84-3092, CA), a 29-year-old white male suffering from manic depression, the ALJ concluded that the claimant's mental condition was not severe despite a well-documented history of the disorder, an extended history of drug and alcohol abuse, violent outbursts, extended periods with no social contact whatsoever (as previously noted, at one point Mr. Slevin locked himself in a hotel room for several days and refused to leave), and incarceration for possession of a weapon. Despite an assessment by his treating physician, Dr. Pappas, that the claimant's functioning "was moderately severe, interfering with his ability to perform basic work activities," the judge concluded that there was "no evidence of a 'severe' psychiatric problem in [the medical reports] aside from an underlying attitude problem."

The federal district judge who reviewed Mr. Slevin's case on appeal disagreed with the ALJ, concluding as follows:

> [T]here is not substantial evidence to support the ALJ's finding that claimant's mental disorder was not severe. Dr. Pappas' assessments of Mr. Slevin's impairments, corroborated by senior therapist Kenneth Jones and Dr. Burke, show a significant limitation to his mental abilities. None of the evidence relied upon by the ALJ can overcome this diagnosis.

The ALJ's effort to override the views of the claimant's treating physician and the opinions of two other treating therapists with his own personal judgment clearly reflected the judge's penchant for prejudice, which disregarded both the law in question and the facts of the case. That this judge should interpret the claimant's severe mental problem as an "attitude" further reflected an uninformed, stereotypical perception of mental illness, one more to be expected of a layperson than of a judge who is trained to evaluate the severity of mental as well as physical impairments.[5]

While Mr. Slevin's case demonstrates one way that judges used stereotypes when evaluating mental illness, several cases demonstrated the use of a different assumption—namely, that if the mental illness stems from a social problem, it is less deserving of benefits. Notably, one claimant, Ms. Burr (87-10636, IL), wanted to discuss how a previous rape had caused her to fear leaving the house at night, but the judge asked no follow-up questions to this relevant testimony. Mr. James (88-1712, CA) attempted to explain how several deaths in his family and bankruptcy had deeply shaken his psychological stability, but the judge in this case, too, asked no follow-up questions. The conclusion that mental illness cannot stem from such social problems as rape, death, and financial problems clearly runs contrary to the medical literature and to Social Security law (see American Psychiatric Association 1994; 20 C.F.R. 404, subpt. P, app. 1, 12.00).

Obesity

Obesity is an impairment that ALJs tend more often to recognize in the cases of women than of men, but, like drug and alcohol addiction and mental illness, ALJs' response to obesity often seems fraught with biased assumptions. As previously noted, drug and alcohol addictions no longer render a claimant eligible for disability benefits under current rules. Similarly, the Social Security Administration is proposing to rescind the Obesity listing (20 C.F.R. 404, subpt. P, app. 1, 9.09) on the grounds that "there is no generally accepted current medical and vocational knowledge which establishes that even mass obesity, per se, has a defined adverse effect on an individual's ability to work . . ." (63 Fed. Reg. 11854 (1998, March 11)). As with drug and alcohol addictions, this proposed change in the law bolsters my finding that ALJs have difficulty applying the obesity rules. Moreover, this proposed change may reflect the biases of the culture at large, and the ways in which those attitudes creep into the hearing and decision-making process (Snow and Harris 1985; Unger and Crawford 1992). Nevertheless, under current rules, ALJs are mandated to evaluate claimant's obesity as a disabling impairment, recognized by the Listings of Impairments.

Without consulting claimants about their ability to lose weight, ALJs in the cases of several women—for example, Miss Plain (87-5258, IL), Ms. Petrie (87-9100, IL), and Mrs. Moore (89-6436, IL)—concluded that their obesity was remediable or should have been better controlled. This assumption regarding obesity is widely held in our culture (Wadden and Stunkard 1987; Rothblum et al. 1990).

In the case of Mrs. Moore, the ALJ concluded that the claimant's obesity was not only remediable but a significant cause of another physical limitation, the claimant's shortness of breath. His preconceived assumption that obesity caused shortness of breath (which it does in some but by no means all cases) made him overlook the possibility that she really did suffer from pulmonary disease. By assuming that her obesity was the sole cause of all her other impairments and adopting this stereotypical view, the ALJ overlooked a very important piece of evidence and denied her claim on that basis.

The federal district court remanded Mrs. Moore's case, stating, "The ALJ clearly overlooked the [pulmonary function] test [which revealed a listing-level pulmonary impairment]. . . . Instead, the ALJ expressed his opinion that plaintiff's shortness of breath was due to her being over-weight." The court then cautioned, "An ALJ may weigh the medical evi-dence in the record in arriving at a conclusion on the ultimate issue of dis-ability, but he may not make his own medical findings."

Race and Ethnicity

Evaluating whether ALJs were biased with regard to race and ethnicity posed difficult problems because judges made few explicitly racist com-ments. Thus, when reading the transcripts and decisions for indicators and clues of such assumptions, relying on what is said and not said, asked and not asked, I used as my guide the mandate on judges to avoid even the sug-gestion or perception that bias entered the hearing and decision-making process. Comments made by Gwendolyn S. King, former commissioner of the SSA, who responded to the attacks on ALJs following the 1992 GAO race-bias study, convinced me that judges are currently mandated to avoid even "the mere suggestion of bias," which King believed "must be dealt with vigorously and decisively" (King 1992, 75).

Despite quantitative studies suggesting racial bias against African-American claimants, in my review of the records ALJs made few or no explicitly stereotypical comments about African-American applicants. However, ALJs' manner of addressing certain claimants, whether by "Miss," "Ms.," "Mrs.," "Mr.," or "Claimant," as noted in chapter 4, did seem based on negative connotations, particularly of African-American women, and suggested the possibility that nonblack claimants received more respect than African-American claimants in the hearing process. Cases conjured up essentialized images of African-American women as domestics, grandmothers, and mammies.

My finding that immigrants were often the target of biased assump-tions, no matter how subtle or minor, is particularly troubling in light of social-science literature, which reflects the difficulty immigrants often have adapting to the American culture and lifestyle and to its expectations (Hulewat 1996; Padilla et al. 1988; Saldena 1995; Smart and Smart 1995; Thomas 1995). Judges' stereotypical ideas about Latinos clearly surfaced in at least three hearings involving interpreters, in which ALJs assumed that claimants could or should speak English and, as a result, did not fully translate the proceedings for them (Acevedo 87-2767, CA 1 and 2; and Vatistas 88-6532, IL).

In Ms. Acevedo's case, for example, the ALJ asked the claimant's husband how long he had been working in the country, "about two years, three years, four years?" The husband responded, "22, 23 years." In asking this question it seems the ALJ erroneously assumed that Ms. Acevedo's husband's lack of English-language skills meant that he was a recent immigrant. Hidden in this judge's question was the assumption that someone who has lived in the United States longer than four years should be able to speak English.

In a case involving Ms. Mendoza (87-2376, CA), a 55-year-old Spanish-speaking applicant with a second-grade education, the ALJ concluded that the claimant's "activities and interests are essentially normal for her cultural and educational background," implying some unstated, preconceived idea of what is "normal" for a woman of a given educational and cultural background. This statement suggests that the ALJ, a well-educated white male who did not bother to familiarize himself in this hearing with the activities and interests of this particular claimant, probably imposed his own stereotypical assumptions about what constitutes the norm for a claimant of some unspecified, general type to formulate his conclusion. When evaluating whether such comments are biased, it must be remembered that judges are mandated to inquire "fully into the issues" (20 C.F.R. 404.944) and that the hearing process should be "consistently applied with the utmost integrity" (King 1992, 76). Given the lack of inquiry into this claimant's activities, this ALJ appears not to have honored that mandate. It is likely that his assumptions influenced the outcome of the case. The federal district court, persuaded that something went seriously awry in this case, ordered Social Security to pay the claimant benefits without a second hearing or further explanation of its action.

One other racial comment merits mention. In a case involving a Latina claimant, Ms. Alva (84-0167, CA), the ALJ noted that there are large numbers of Spanish-speaking people living "in this community." In no case did a judge state that there were large numbers of white people living in a particular geographical area, suggesting that this judge might hold some preconceived albeit incompletely articulated assumptions about the "Spanish-speaking people" who live in that community.

Education and Literacy

To fully and adequately evaluate claimants' cases, the law requires ALJs, when and if appropriate, to inquire not only into claimants' level of education but also into their literacy (20 C.F.R. 404, subpt. P, app. 2, 201.00 (h)).[6] In several cases reviewed for this study, judges did not adequately investigate either of these issues and, as a result, some judges may have improperly assumed claimants' ability to read.

Individuals who cannot read or who have weak educational backgrounds are more likely to exaggerate than understate their ability to read and write, either for fear that their illiteracy will be used against them or because they will feel humiliated by such an admission (Kozol 1985). According to Social Security rules, however, illiterate and severely undereducated claimants are more entitled to benefits than literate and educated claimants because there are fewer jobs in the national economy for people who lack those skills. In any given case, then, where literacy and education are at issue, there is no telling without careful inquiry how claimants' testimony on their literacy may be slanted.

In some cases, ALJs did not inquire into claimants' ability to read. In other cases, judges made inadequate inquiries. For example, the ALJ made an incomplete inquiry in a case involving a Puerto Rican claimant, Mr. Rodriguez (87-878, IL), who spoke some English but who had failed the eighth grade while attending school in Germany. This ALJ asked, "How well do you read in English?" The claimant responded, "not to[o] good, but fairly I guess." The judge asked, "Well, if you had to give yourself a grade, concerning your ability to read in English. Would you give yourself A or a B or a C, or D or F?" The claimant answered, "To me I would say a B." The ALJ then asked about writing in English, and the claimant responded, "Like a C." This type of self-evaluative measure tells a judge or a reviewing court little or nothing about a claimant's ability to read in a work setting. Objective questions, like whether claimants took oral or written driver's license tests or whether they can fill out employment applications without assistance, would more fully inform adjudicators of claimants' abilities. In this case, the judge violates the Social Security mandate to investigate whether claimants are literate, suggesting the possibility that the judge dismissed Mr. Rodriguez (and his claim) by showing no particular interest in his true ability to read (20 C.F.R. 404.1564).

One theory is that using the claimant to judge his own capacity to read may be predicated on the biased assumption that claimants who are uneducated or have difficulty reading will feel comfortable enough informing judges of their own ability. Research shows that just the opposite is true (Alfieri 1994; Kozol 1985; National Center for Education Statistics 1993).[7] Moreover, anecdotal evidence from literacy advocates reveals countless incidences where people who are illiterate go to great lengths to hide their limitations. In one case, an illiterate woman signed her children away to an adoption agency, in part because she was too afraid to admit to the agency that she did not know what she was signing (Adams 1994).

This was evidenced in Ms. Price's case (89-4298, IL, described in chapter 5) when the claimant seemed to cover up the fact that she could not read when she responded to the judge's question about whether she had any objections to the exhibit file by describing her impairments. In another case, the ALJ took this assumption one step further and imposed the expected answer on the claimant. Thus, the judge asked Ms. Smith (86-6054, IL), an African-American claimant with a ninth-grade education, "you can read and write, can you not?" She responded, "A certain amount, yes." When the judge asked whether she read the newspaper, she answered, "yes, I—I—yes, I can read." Then he asked, "If you were unable to come to the hearing because you were ill today, could you write me a note that I would understand about your absence?" The claimant said, "I think I could do that." With that response, the judge was satisfied that the claimant could read and write. What was prejudicial about this judge's statements was his assumption that the claimant would be forthcoming with the fact that she had trouble reading or writing—his lack of a full investigation into this issue seems to have been influenced by the biased assumption that all people should be able, without feeling stigmatized, to evaluate their ability to read and write.

Gender

Several gender stereotypes emerged in the transcripts and decisions, including that gender or traditional gender roles are relevant to inquiries about daily activities or ability to do a particular job; caretaking or housekeeping activities constitute, without corroborating evidence, an ability to do paid work, and women who "look good" or men who "look fit" are likely not to be disabled.

In several cases, ALJs asked certain questions and not others depending on claimants' gender. For example, female applicants were asked about their ability to knit and crochet while male applicants were asked about their hunting or fishing activities. Asking female applicants knitting questions and male applicants questions about hunting or fishing is not as benign as it may seem. Take for example, male and female claimants alleging musculoskeletal impairments. Chances are that a back condition would preclude any applicant, male or female, from hunting or fishing, but that condition would not necessarily preclude the more sedentary activities of knitting or crocheting. Judges who inquire only into male applicants' ability to perform strenuous activities such as hunting and fishing (which all such applicants, male and female, are unlikely to be able to do) may erroneously conclude based on incomplete information that male applicants' inability to fish or hunt constitutes an inability to work. Likewise, judges inquiring only into female applicants' ability to perform less strenuous activities like knitting and crocheting (which all such applicants, female and male, are probably able to do) may erroneously conclude that the female applicants' ability to knit or crochet constitutes an ability to work. In this regard, gender-specific questions are more likely to disadvantage female applicants.

In other cases, judges suggested jobs that claimants might be able to do based on traditional gender roles. Hence, a female claimant might be asked whether she could be a receptionist or a hearing assistant, while male claimants might be asked if they could do physical labor. When judges asked such questions of VEs or even of claimants based on gender stereotypes, female applicants were almost certain to be disadvantaged. An individual with a disability is much more likely to be able to do light jobs traditionally held by women, including clerical and sales positions, than heavier occupations traditionally performed by men. It seems, in other words, much more credible for claimants with back conditions to allege that they are unable to perform the work of a physical laborer than that of a receptionist or hearing assistant.

Judges also often imposed assumptions about gender roles when they inquired into claimants' ability to do housework or to take care of other people. For example, in denying benefits to Mrs. Karkar (89-3486, CA), a 56-year-old Jordanian woman, the ALJ considered the claimant's caring for her sick husband as evidence of capacity to work as a home health-care attendant; however, both the claimant and a witness testified in the hearing that Mrs. Karkar could move only very slowly while working in the house. The federal district court concurred with the claimant and remanded the case, holding that the ALJ had never established that the claimant could work. Assumptions about caretaking and housekeeping abilities are more likely to exclude women than men from disability eligibility, for, regardless of their physical or mental impairment, most women continue to do light housework and family care.[8]

Several other cases had gender implications. For example, in general, I found that women who tended to do more day-to-day activities, despite their allegations of physical and mental impairments, were more likely not to be found disabled on this evidence than men; judges tended to interpret a female claimant's housework as evidence of her choice to be a home-maker—that is, in effect to regard her as employed and therefore ineligible for benefits, whereas judges tended not to use these assumptions in the cases of male claimants. On another gender-related case, a claimant's credibility with regard to her back impairment was questioned because she was noted to have attended the doctor in high heels (Davenport, 89-1268, MA). The judge erroneously but stereotypically assumed that she wore such attire by choice without questioning whether dressing up to go to the doctor may have been related to a deeply ingrained pressure on women to look good regardless of their physical or mental incapacity.[9] The stereotype inherent in this assumption is that attractive women must not be disabled and are not deserving of benefits. Such an assumption is fraught with biases; indeed, judges are mandated not to rely exclusively on their personal observations but are required to inquire beyond how claimants' look.[10]

Receipt of Workers' Compensation or Welfare Benefits

Although the rules and case law limit the relevance of such factors (*Desrosiers v. Secretary,* 846 F.2d 573 (9th Cir. 1988)), claimants in my sample who received workers' compensation or welfare seemed fairly clearly disadvantaged in the Social Security hearing and decision-making process.

The ALJs hearing the cases of Ms. Curran (88-2459, MA) and Mr. LaPensee (89-2492, MA) articulate the disadvantage some workers' compensation recipients faced. In the case of Ms. Curran, a 50-year-old registered nurse alleging a back impairment, the ALJ wrote in his decision, "failure to improve [medically] may be based on reasons other than medical, such as receipt of workers' compensation benefits." Ms. Curran's treating physician believed so strongly in her case that he attended the hearing and testified on her behalf. The judge ignored the physician's testimony and the treating-physician rule, concluding that a treating physician is required to accept a patient's symptoms at face value and therefore is less credible. The federal court reviewing this case rejected this interpretation of the treating-physician rule and the conclusion that the claimant's receipt of workers' compensation benefits hindered her desire to return to work, finding, "the observation . . . about a class of people [i.e., workers' compensation recipients] generally . . . is remarkably weak evidence."

The ALJ hearing the case of another workers' compensation recipient, Mr. LaPensee (89-2492, MA), a 32-year-old white male, appeared to hold the same view. He assessed the credibility of the claimant as follows: "[This claimant] is quite content to collect workers' compensation and . . . has no motivation for return[ing] to work." Mr. LaPensee's case, too, was remanded by federal district court for further workup.

The ALJ hearing the case of Mr. Davidson (88-0280, MA), a 59-year-old white male, did not articulate the presumption that workers' compensation beneficiaries are lazy and unmotivated to work. However, this judge's cross-examination of the claimant seemed relentless on one point; the ALJ became extremely aggressive and seemed to leave no stone unturned in his effort to discover whether Mr. Davidson had a workers' compensation appeal pending. The ALJ asked at least four times whether Mr. Davidson had hired a lawyer or filed a lawsuit.

Finally, the ALJ hearing the case of Ms. Galasso (88-0280, MA), a 55-year-old Italian woman, commented that the claimant had received a "nice Christmas present" when she received her workers' compensation settlement check on December 24. Such a sarcastic and irrelevant comment from a judge certainly suggests that he was prejudiced—assuming that workers' compensation is more like a present than a settlement owed as a result of an injury at work.

Receipt of welfare benefits also seemed to disadvantage certain applicants. Judges seemed eager to learn whether claimants depended on government benefits, and although never stated explicitly, the information gathered from such inquiries must have been useful or these very busy judges would not have bothered to ask. Speculating one step further, those who answered the welfare question in the affirmative may have been treated or judged prejudicially; this seems even more evident in the cases where the ALJs questioned claimants about whether other members of their families depended on welfare. It seems plausible that the people who are most likely to rely on such benefits, such as poor white women and people of color, are at a distinct disadvantage when such factors are considered.

My findings seem to mesh with previous studies that suggest that judges' stereotypes emerge in the cases of claimants who are the target of prejudice in the culture at large. The fact that judges have difficulty managing their bias and that it reveals itself as often as it does provides support for my thesis that the ethos of impartiality as it is currently embraced must be reformulated to take account of the unrecognized and repressed bias that permeates hearing and decision texts and subtexts. The next chapter explores, theoretically and practically, how to resolve the problems these tensions suggest. Through calculated policies and trainings, these suggestions begin to imagine a more balanced and individualized process—one that resembles the uniform but engaged, rule-bound but passionate, justice that is the American ideal.

CHAPTER 7

Planning for Prejudice

While the 67 transcripts I reviewed are not in any way representative of all denied cases in the Social Security system, my sample reveals a systematic pattern of prejudice that merits attention, particularly when my qualitative findings are considered together with the disturbing results of previous studies and the evidence of bias detected in Social Security doctrine. From the point of view of judges, the veil of impartiality protects them from allegations of personal bias, especially in the Social Security context, where the claimants are so obviously dissimilar from the judges, and hence very unlikely to evoke blatant sympathies or prejudices.

My account deconstructs prevailing interpretations and practices of impartiality and bias and suggests the myriad of ways that judges who interact with claimants, however briefly, fail to appreciate the subtle ways in which biased attitudes creep into the hearing and decision-making process. Bias not only essentializes and stereotypes claimants but also prevents ALJs from engaging these vulnerable groups in a way that the legal process positively demands.

Summary of Findings: Patterns of Noncompliance, Disengagement, and Stereotyping

Derived from a small sample, the findings of this study are tentative but nevertheless revealing. Overall, they suggest that judges frequently ignore mandated rules and do so regardless of claimants' race, gender, education, and socioeconomic background. In short, overall rates of noncompliance suggest that the rules promulgated to ensure impartiality and fairness are systematically disregarded.

For example, ALJs gave either no opening statement or an incomplete

148

opening statement in 47 out of 65 hearings (72 percent). Further, my findings revealed that ALJs did little in the way of compliance with the rules designed to put claimants at ease; in seven out of the seventeen relevant hearings (41 percent), for example, ALJs did not introduce claimants to interpreters, and in 48 out of 65 of the cases (74 percent) claimants were never informed that hearing assistants were present to run the recording equipment and to take notes. Judges did even less to encourage claimants' active involvement in the hearings: in only four out of sixty-five hearings did judges ask claimants if they had questions about the process (94 percent noncompliance), and in only two cases did ALJs inform claimants that they had the burden of proving their claims (97 percent noncompliance).

My findings also revealed that although most judges in my sample made opening statements in hearings involving unrepresented claimants, the ALJs undercut any positive effect such explanations could have had when they failed to comply with the very important rules governing the waiver of claimants' right to representation. In three of the nine cases (33 percent) involving unrepresented claimants, ALJs failed even to mention that the claimants had a right to be represented by counsel. In addition, in seven out of eight cases (88 percent), ALJs did not mention the availability of counsel and particularly of free counsel. In no case did the ALJ take the time to explain the benefit of having an attorney, particularly that unrepresented claimants are less likely to obtain new evidence which, in turn, can affect the outcome of their claim (GAO 1997). It is noteworthy that, for the most part, unrepresented claimants in my sample were uneducated and African American, so that the judges were particularly insensitive to the demands of people who were educationally challenged and racially subordinated.

When eliciting testimony from claimants, the ALJs in my sample similarly systematically violated important rules designed to ensure the fairness and impartiality of the process. Women, especially African-American women, were subject to judges' preconceived assumptions, as evidenced particularly by ALJs inappropriate use of titles. In addition, ALJs hindered claimants in 40 out of 65 cases (62 percent) and interrupted them in 26 out of 65 cases (40 percent) I examined. The judges also took the time to develop only certain aspects of claimants' cases, like work history (only 16 percent noncompliance), that provide evidence needed to reject claimants while neglecting other aspects of the case, such as impairments and literacy (43 and 60 percent noncompliance, respectively), that would more likely produce evidence to support disability claims.

Likewise, when I studied compliance with two procedural rules, my investigation also revealed that ALJs in my sample developed only those aspects of disability cases likely to support a denial of benefits. Overall, the rule requiring ALJs to allow claimants sufficient time to obtain records was violated in 11 out of 26 cases. In addition, in all three relevant cases, ALJs did not help claimants obtain the records needed to adequately develop the evidence for their claims. Similarly, in 22 out of 25 relevant cases, ALJs did not give specific reasons for disregarding the evidence of the claimant's treating physician. My sample revealed that women and people of color may be most disadvantaged by these results because they were disproportionately represented in the relevant samples; however, a larger study is necessary to confirm these tentative findings.

High levels of noncompliance were also detected when I examined ALJ compliance with the failure-to-follow-prescribed-treatment rule. Judges violated the rule in almost every one of the eight cases in which they invoked it, failing to document who prescribed the treatment in seven cases, to document why the prescribed treatment was likely to restore the capacity for work in all eight cases, and to give claimants an opportunity to explain why they did not follow the treatment in all eight cases. In the course of testifying, two claimants did give justifiable reasons for not complying with particular treatments; in both cases, the judges failed to cite those reasons in their decisions.

I found that at least half of the judges did not comply with the rules regarding documenting of relevant evidence, which require ALJs to present in their decisions the medical or extramedical factors that influenced their credibility determinations. In 26 of 52 applicable decisions ALJs failed to report the medical evidence that supported their negative credibility determinations, and in 29 of 49 applicable decisions judges failed to report the extramedical factors that substantiated their negative credibility determinations. Without such documentation, reviewing courts were deprived of the information they needed to evaluate whether the judges' credibility determinations were based on substantial evidence. I found instead that some judges relied, at least in some measure, on such illegal and irrelevant evidence as race, gender, or socioeconomic status in 39 out of 66 decisions (59 percent). Other judges inappropriately considered housekeeping (16 out of 16 cases) or military status, prison history, and/or family background (33 out of 33 cases) without adequately investigating its relevance to the case. The use of personal observations in 19 out of 66 cases (29 percent), charged words in 13 out of 66 cases (20 percent), pejorative statements in 8 out of 66 cases (12 percent), and personal judgments or opinions in 36 out of 66 cases (55 percent) was also a problem. Each of these violations raised questions about what stereotypical and other negative assumptions may have influenced the disability decision-making process.

My qualitative analysis explored this question in greater detail. Indeed, the judges in my sample failed to accommodate certain historically oppressed groups that the law mandates be engaged. ALJs skirted their responsibility to unrepresented claimants and when they elicited testimony from members of groups who have a difficult time expressing themselves in general because of their marginal position in the society at large. Especially in the elicitation of evidence, I found judges leading claimants' testimony to the point of influencing it, being unnecessarily judgmental and rude, not following up on important issues, and implying that the claimants' perspective was wrong and/or should be ignored. In these cases, I discovered that ALJ hearing practices particularly affected the cases of people with little education, people who were illiterate, and people alleging mental impairments. As previously noted, ALJs also failed to engage all claimants but particularly African-American and female claimants when they neglected to be carefully attentive to developing medical evidence. Instead of doing more to accommodate women and racial minorities, my findings reveal that some ALJs do less.

Moreover, I found that judges most often explicitly used stereotypical assumptions when addressing claimants alleging mental impairments (including addictions) and obesity and when addressing members of racial and ethnic minorities, including African-Americans. The judges also frequently imported such assumptions in hearings and decisions involving claimants with educational or linguistic limitations. Both genders were subject to stereotypical assumptions about the kinds of work they could do and about their daily activities. Recipients of such benefits as welfare and workers' compensation were also subjected to ALJs' stereotypical ideas. In many of these cases the judges' prejudicial assumptions not only affected their hearing of cases but their decisions as well.

This study answers the question of whether a close examination of hearing transcripts and decisions helps explain why women and African-Americans (and possibly other marginalized groups not previously studied) have been disadvantaged by Social Security ALJs' hearing and decision-making practices. In sum, this study detected in the hearing transcripts and decisions reviewed very few signs of clear-cut discrimination.

When closely analyzed, however, the hearing transcripts and decisions reveal patterns of noncompliance with key procedural and substantive rules designed to ensure fairness and impartiality. In addition, the case records reveal that judges' stereotypical ideas about most if not all marginalized groups probably lie behind many of these rule violations. Judicial intolerance and stereotyping was also revealed in the judges' difficulty in accommodating and engaging claimants with special needs.

My quantitative and qualitative findings combined suggest that some claimants are afforded worse treatment than others in the ALJ hearing and decision-making process. Given that judges stereotype and complicate rather than ease the efforts of disadvantaged groups (women, African Americans, other racial and ethnic minorities, welfare and workers' compensation recipients, illiterate claimants, and people with mental disabilities, including addictions) to tell their stories, there is no doubt that bias underlies at least some of these violations.

Given the ever-present institutional influences on ALJs discussed in passing throughout this study, my work would be incomplete without a further exploration of their implications for my conclusions. Judges are under tremendous pressure to process hundreds of claims each year. But they are also under pressure to deny them (Bernoski 1997; Pear 1997; Tolchin 1989). Under such circumstances, it is not surprising that corners are cut and rules are violated. When trying to deny cases, it is easier not to explain the process, not to help a claimant obtain a lawyer, not to elicit testimony, to rely on CEs and reject the treating physician's evidence without full explanation, and so forth. These institutional factors, however, in no way undercut my finding that judicial bias, informed by larger cultural assumptions and prejudices, probably enters into and influences the ALJ hearing and decision-making process. These pressures in effect encourage judges to inject their personal feelings into the process.[1] As a result, my preliminary findings suggest that claimants who are disadvantaged in society at large because of their race, ethnicity, intelligence, education, and gender are further disadvantaged in the Social Security system.

In addition to the pressure to decide and to deny many claims, the requirement that ALJs assume multiple roles likewise seems to encourage the importation into the process of assumptions and beliefs. When playing defense counsel, prosecutor, and judge, ALJs' ability to adjudicate in a truly fair and impartial manner is necessarily compromised. An extension of this problem is that it is more difficult for ALJs to maintain their authority as judges when playing three roles. It is possible that in an effort to maintain their authority and control, ALJs are inclined to establish their own rules: abbreviated opening statements, no explanation of the right to counsel, and so on. These unstated but observed practices deny claimants the opportunity to participate fully in the hearing process, especially when they are accompanied by the failure to accommodate and the propensity to stereotype.

One other institutional influence surfaced in the course of this study—that is, a rather pervasive assumption or belief among judges that at least some of the rules and mechanisms established to promote fairness are empty formalities. As previously noted, this concept was first introduced by Mashaw et al. (1978) when they found that ALJs failed to give opening statements and failed to properly assist claimants who required counsel (66). My findings reveal that nearly 20 years later, judges may still adhere to this belief, which certainly contributes to the high levels of noncompliance with at least some rules. Even SSA's (1995, 1997) DHQRP studies involving as many as 9,000 cases suggest that ALJs fail claimants, both procedurally and substantively. Most startlingly, this SSA self-assessment revealed that in 1995, 20 percent of unrepresented claimants were not adequately informed of their right to counsel. Given the suggestion in my study that these unrepresented claimants are from the most vulnerable groups, these assumptions about the rules might be a partial explanation for the findings of bias detected in previous studies.

The practice that seems to have developed as a result of these assumptions—judges in effect establish their own individual sets of rules to follow to differing degrees—is hardly conducive to fair and uniform decision making. Further, the association this study discovered between ALJ disregard of key rules and stereotyping and failure to accommodate claimants with special needs suggests that a cavalier or even relaxed attitude toward the rules can indeed result in exactly what the rules are supposed to prevent—the introduction of prejudicial assumptions that may influence the process.

Can Lawyers Plan for Prejudice?

As a method for recognizing and grappling with the bias I detected, conscious self-reflection (subsequently described in more detail) would provide judges with the tools they need to realize the nonessentialized justice they claim to uphold. The social-psychological literature presented in chapter 1 suggests that conscious self-reflection, at least in the case of low-prejudiced people, will help ensure that negative stereotyping is not imported into the decision-making process (Devine 1989). Indeed, one study suggests that suppression can actually have the effect of heightening stereotyping (Macare et al. 1994). It is arguable that the impartiality doctrine is a form of suppression and therefore only exacerbates the problem it seeks to correct. Indeed, SSA's (1995, 1997) denial of the problem and systematic refusal to address bias in its self-assessment and related quality review activities further contributes to this suppression and to the belief that judges can be impartial.

Of course the problem is that such a critical analysis requires that judges be willing to imagine a different or more engaged and hence enlightened judging process. This raises the question of whether judges, hired from pools of attorneys who are trained to value reason over emotion and rules over experiences, can fairly adjudicate the claims of some of our country's most subordinated people. As chapter 1 showed, attorneys are taught to isolate idiosyncracies and are trained in law schools by professors unsympathetic and often hostile to the plight of the poor and to the experiences of people of color. Judges are even more antagonistic toward the idea that they should reflect on their stereotypes.

People with disabilities who apply for benefits and appeal to ALJs are disproportionately poor and nonwhite and suffer from complex medical problems and intergenerational psychological conditions, such as depression, because of poverty. It seems fairly obvious that a cadre of mostly white male judges lacks the tools necessary to understand and process layers of disadvantage and disease and that ALJs' reliance on naive and professionally reinforced stereotypes is not only an unthinking expedient but also based on a mixture of fear of difference and denial of one's experience.

Thus, if judges are to retain the privilege of hearing disability claims, they must be educated about the limitations of their legal training. The distance from emotion and from experience inculcated at law school is of little or no value in preparing a lawyer to become a judge and to exercise the affective and interactive dimensions of judgment. I believe that judges must begin to use the stereotypes of their unidimensional legal education more consciously—they must become aware of how they were taught to disregard clients' cries or their own whimpers. They must recognize that they were admonished in their first-year law school courses and often throughout their legal educations when they took account of the feelings of the faceless claimants, plaintiffs, or defendants in a case method of legal pedagogy that is all too quick to erase the poverty, race, and gender of those whose lives are affected by legal judgment.

Disability adjudication is systematically flawed as long as judges in general and ALJs in particular are encouraged to disregard or repress the emotion—the passion, if you will—necessary to provide hearing conditions that accommodate claimants' limitations. I argue that these judges must learn to grapple with complexity and difference and that they need the tools to be self-critical. They must render judgments that think beyond the medical diagnosis as it narrowly applies to the rules. And they must consciously consider how their personal stereotypes may unconsciously influence their assessment of racial difference in relation to disease, of gender's influence on the course of certain maladies, and of subordination's effect on depression. They must be forced to understand exactly how these racist, sexist, classist, and other influences positively or negatively affect the evaluation of a claim by reflecting on them both during the hearing and in the decision. To expose this process to scrutiny, to make explicit what is now repressed and rendered unspeakable, will free judges, attorneys, and claimants to hear and present cases in an environment where suggestions of bias and instances when judges fail to accommodate claimants are safely and publicly exposed. Adjudicators must comprehend and hence tolerate the complexities of experience and of cultural context to which they are routinely subjected, and they must learn techniques for self-assessment.[2] Doing so will ensure a system where difference is anticipated and acknowledged and where all participants struggle to understand the text of their own intolerance.

In sum, policymakers should no longer take for granted the assumption that lawyers, trained in a formalistic, rule-bound tradition, can or should judge disability or other claims, particularly when the judges are expected to adjudicate large numbers of claims involving groups likely to be stereotyped or people who are illiterate and requiring special accommodation. If any professional group could supply adjudicators for disability hearings, it would more likely be that of therapists or social workers rather than lawyers, and I will now turn to aspects of these professionals' training.

Reflections on Affectivity

Feminist and critical race theories have provided the frameworks for mapping new methods of critical consciousness in jurisprudence. Psychoanalytic and postmodern traditions have also substantially contributed to the possibility of judicial reform. The conscious self-reflection that I advocate draws on these traditions, moving one step closer to realizing the affective justice that Cardozo, Brennan, and the legal realists imagined, an affectivity in judging that feels and responds, touches and imagines. Such conscious self-reflection also draws on the social-psychological literature that so persuasively reveals the importance of self-reflection in overcoming stereotypes.

Given the evidence and pervasiveness of the bias detected in the cases I reviewed, Social Security judges, at a minimum, should be taught to develop a critical consciousness in relation to their hearing and decision-making practices. Judging, according to this model, requires a radical restructuring—that is, adjudicators must evaluate the facts and apply the law while considering the unconscious dimensions that the litigants and their stories evoke. This more critical approach is relevant not only to the judges hearing and deciding cases but also to the legislators writing and passing laws. To advocate that lawmakers also undertake such a self-reflective attitude is to avoid the problem described in chapter 3, in which unexamined bias is so often detectable in the core of the rules, such as the listings and the Grid.

Here I want to make explicit the methods I use to unravel and reveal judicial prejudice and therefore to avoid the negative consequences it can have on the people who are inadvertently touched by it. Although implicit in feminist, critical race, and psychoanalytic traditions, these methods are often unarticulated, particularly in the theoretical literature, as having practical application. They include three interlocking and confluent considerations.

First, this more affective justice requires judges or legislators to do critical self-analysis, thereby situating their privilege, assessing their points of view. Such analysis reveals what is usually taken for granted or viewed as normative. That the canvas of one's core identity is multilayered and complex should go without saying. Privilege involves what are often conflicting dimensions rendered opaque by their long and undissected history, including such identity issues as one's relationship to one's nationality, race, geography, gender, age, socioeconomic status, education, religion, language, parental status, occupation, and sexual orientation. Hence, to reveal and reflect on these issues is to understand how, for example, one's Ivy League education affects one's relationship to an African-American heritage or to the experience of being a woman. But to reflect on one's biography is to reflect both on one's personal or core identity and on one's institutional or occupational affiliation and culture, especially for lawyers and judges, whose professions are riddled with cultural influences and values that, as I have demonstrated, are likely to affect how they judge claimants who appear before them.

Second, and inextricably intertwined with the first requirement, is the necessity for legislators and adjudicators to stand in the shoes of their constituents, their litigants. This requirement is more than empathy. This work requires that one examine one's history for instances of oppression and so experience and reexperience the shame, fear, and humiliation that affect most human beings. The reexperiencing of shame, no matter how repressed or ancient, will allow adjudicators and legislators to feel the brittle feelings of the vulnerable (and often angry) people they will encounter either directly or indirectly in their constituencies.

One aspect of feeling the feelings of others requires assuming that the most vulnerable citizens feel their oppression, in one form or another, consciously or unconsciously. It is therefore safe for legislators or adjudicators to assume that women, people of color, and members of other disaffected groups (including, as my study revealed, people who are illiterate or who suffer from mental illness, including addictions to drugs and food) will experience forms and layers of oppression. While it is safe to assume this experience of oppression, such an inquiry demands that when judging or legislating, it is useful to attempt to understand everyone's unique experience or relationship to the negative prejudice they encounter. Such understanding is easily accomplished after doing one's own work of recollecting personal experiences of shame and oppression. Armed with this recovered history, judges or legislators can at least begin to understand claimants, litigants, or citizens by hearing their stories, regardless of how temporary or brief the interaction and regardless of how different their biographies seem from those of the judges or legislators.

A third dimension of this work that provides the link between the first two forms of self-reflection insists that legislators and decision makers understand the interrelationship between their privileged status and position and their recovered history and more specifically, how that personal drama intersects with the stories of their subjects. This concept might best be understood in light of the psychoanalytic principle of countertransference (Jung 1966). Countertransference occurs in relationships between patients and psychoanalysts when the latter bring to the therapeutic relationship their own biographies or histories.

For example, if the patient is discovering a history of child abuse during the treatment and the therapist has lived a similar trauma or has perpetrated child abuse, there is, unless otherwise rendered conscious, an anticipated and expected effect of the therapist's trauma on the unveiling of the client's history. Needless to say, therapists are always "on duty" to recognize issues of countertransference—they are trained to render these issues conscious to themselves when doing therapeutic work with clients. The best therapists not only become aware of the effect of such personal issues on treatment but actually take the time to work out the countertransference in their own professional treatment.

I am arguing here and have previously argued (Mills 1996) that judges, lawyers, and lawmakers could benefit from a more conscious justice that reflects the intersecting and dissimilar histories of those who meet in the juridical theater. Toward this end, a form of legal countertransference can help the system move closer to realizing the importance of unveiling intersecting oppressions for all to see and underscores the need to acknowledge experiential similarities, both positive and negative.

For example, I recently attended a legislative forum at UCLA (Mills 1997). Representatives from the Los Angeles City Attorney's and District Attorney's offices also attended, as did Sheila Kuehl, a member of the California Assembly. The subject of the forum was mandatory prosecution of domestic-violence cases. Previously I had taken the position that victims of domestic violence should be given an opportunity to decline to prosecute batterers after counseling sessions with the prosecutor's office in which they explored the violence in their lives and their propensity to tolerate it. I argued that any coercive action on the part of the state that did not consider the battered women's feelings mimicked the actions of the abusers or even surpassed them, unwittingly forcing battered women to choose between batterers, a familiar form of violence in their lives, or the state, an unfamiliar but similar violently inflicted relationship (Mills 1998). I feared that all too often the state's coercive action through such policies as mandatory prosecution led battered women to rescue batterers, sending future incidents of violence between these intimates away from the law's monitoring eye.

The prosecutors who defended mandatory prosecution policies found my position untenable because they felt incompetent to function as counselors or therapists to battered women who felt sympathetic to or emotionally, culturally, or financially intertwined with their batterers. The prosecutors preferred the "big stick" approach, or law-and-order method, and rejected my suggestion that the system learn to be more flexible (Jackson 1996; Wills 1997).

While the prosecutors' denial of my argument for flexibility was in and of itself disturbing, the form of their argument was particularly revealing. These prosecutors, part of a nationwide movement to establish specialized domestic-violence units in district attorneys' offices, essentially argued that they were incapable, because of their lack of training, of providing a "feeling" environment that encouraged battered women to explore their complex and multilayered emotions, an exploration that would likely help them achieve a sense of empowerment and even of action. The prosecutors vehemently defended their belief that their duties did not include discussing with battered women, the victims of these crimes, what action they could or should take (Jackson 1996). Rather, it was the prosecutors' job to represent the state, to defend its laws, to protect these women—whether or not they wanted protection—by exacting an appropriate punishment (Wills 1997). A clinical colleague who attended the forum astutely observed that lawyers in general—and these prosecutors in particular—did seem incompetent to enter a feeling relationship with these victims. She intuitively observed that law training seems to deprive people of their natural capacity to hear and empathize, to feel and respond.

Prosecutors, judges, other court personnel, and policymakers must be taught to address what they perceive as differences and similarities between themselves and the parties who appear before them. They must address their emotions, repressed and otherwise, and how they affect the understanding of clients, how legal professionals' feelings influence their judgments of claimants. In this next section, I present a brief sketch of a training program that might help judges and other juridical personnel resolve the tensions between personal experience and prejudice and the experience of lawyering and judging.

Affective Training Program

While training for judges is an integral part of their job, there is virtually no literature on its effectiveness—especially with regard to bias training. These training suggestions are offered to those who believe that judges should accept that they, like all other human beings, hold certain stereotypical assumptions that are likely to surface when discharging their duties. Those judges who deny this reality or who are unwilling to explore these issues should be considered unqualified for carrying out the duties of judging, which require a sensitivity and engagement that all adjudicators should strive to achieve.

An affective training program for judges, lawyers, and/or legislators would necessarily include the dual goals of providing trainees with frameworks for exploring systematically how organizational and professional culture and identity (such as race and gender) influence hearing dynamics, decision making, and the legislative process. To do so, judges, legislators, or lawyers would begin with themselves—gaining insight into their personal core beliefs, values, and behaviors and simultaneously being educated on the core beliefs, values, and behaviors of different cultures. The analytic concepts and self-reflection exercises are then blended through opportunities for participants to develop practical strategies for coping with the countertransference issues that are bound to arise in their work.[3] This targeted effort can help them learn to comprehend, anticipate, and address issues raised by their subjects' or constituents' similarities and differences.

The training would demand the participants' active participation, requiring disclosure of what may be perceived as very personal material. Given the overall sensitivity of such a request, judges, lawyers, and legislators should be assigned to training situations in which they feel safe and secure to explore their old wounds as well as their more privileged or enlightened experiences. The training should last two to three days to ensure the kind of honesty, intimacy, and full disclosure necessary to achieve real and deeply felt personal growth. The faculty selected for such a training must be knowledgeable in the experiences of many cultures as well as sensitive to the norms and assumptions likely to surface in a group composed primarily of Caucasian men.

The training session should begin with opening exercises that promote safety among group members. The session might begin with a brief introduction in which participants self-identified (explained how they situated themselves in the culture at large). This process would involve the telling of a story or experience in which the participant recalled being shamed or humiliated. In addition, some introductory remarks by the trainers in which they too disclosed stories or experiences would help facilitate safety and honesty.

The session following the initial introductions should involve a discussion of cultural categories and overlapping boundaries. Such categories should be broadly defined in this era of identity politics, including nationality, race, geography, gender, age, socioeconomic status, religion, language, parental responsibility, and so forth. Specific questions that the faculty should encourage participants to address include family history as it relates to cultural/ethnic and gender identity as well as how one's family of origin tended to relate to communities perceived to be different from itself. For example, if prosecutors for battered women were involved in the training, it would be helpful for them to explore their own personal repressed histories of violence, which would likely contribute to their stereotypes about and fears of battered women. An exercise that challenged how people categorized others would be particularly helpful, including a gamelike exercise that requires participants to seek the acknowledgment or initials of people participating in the training who might fall within certain categories ("an African-American woman," "a person who is battered," "a white man"). Subsequent discussion should address how participants perceive each other and themselves. This exercise can begin the process of making prejudice conscious.

In the third session, it is helpful for trainers and participants to explore the organizational or professional culture of the group being trained. *Organizational culture* would refer to the larger culture to which judges and legislators belong. For example, Social Security judges are part of the Social Security system and therefore are influenced by its basic premises. *Professional culture,* in the case of ALJs, would refer to identification with other judges or with lawyers. Once the culture to which participants belong is identified, it is easier to unravel its norms and assumptions and to determine how they might influence and interfere with how judgments are made. Judges, lawyers, and legislators participating in the training can help identify cultural dynamics—its basic assumptions, operating principles, methods for resolving conflicts.

The final sessions of the training should involve a description of how countertransference works and how to help participants identify and intervene to understand it. This is very deep emotional work and requires participants to become aware of unspoken dynamics and subtexts. In the words of George Eliot, the process would be like "hearing the grass grow and the squirrel's heart beat": "we should die of that roar which lies on the other side of silence" (1871/1992, 177–78). To assist judges, lawyers, and legislators untrained in self-analysis in hearing the roar, it may be helpful to label large sheets of paper with the names of groups such as "ALJs," "policymakers," "battered women," and so on and ask participants to record the stereotypes they have heard about each of the groups represented. This exercise can be used as a jumping-off point for persuading participants that these assumptions float in the culture at large, that people are subjected to them unconsciously, and that attitudes are affected through the unconscious.

Deliberate self-reflection becomes the only method by which to purge stereotypes entirely from experience (Devine 1989). This process marks the beginning of the training's deeper experience, providing the opportunity to design special sessions that relate to the specific work of the groups being trained, such as mock Social Security or legislative hearings or mock client interviews. These situations become the opportunity for teaching participants exactly how to identify the unconscious dimensions of the hearing, decision-making, or lawmaking process to become more sensitive to the complexities of these dynamics.

The training program should end with suggested methods for participants to become more conscious of these latent aspects of decision or lawmaking. For example, some judges may want to use checklists to remind them that when adjudicating claims of parties who evoke prejudices within them (both positive and negative), they should "check" themselves to ensure that they have not been unwittingly influenced (Mills 1993). Similarly, judges could use such a checklist to encourage themselves to be more engaging in hearings in which they are mandated to accommodate claimants. For example, if they have claimants who cannot read, the checklist would help them ensure that they exhibit and express a level of accommodation that the claimants require. These tools or methods can make conscious what is now unconscious, can force judges, legislators, or lawyers to ask themselves what particular situations evoke or demand. They can then more consciously respond accordingly.

My own experience working with judges in training sessions and endeavoring to understand their resistance, their tendency to deny bias, and to sabotage self-reflexive exercises has led me to question the appropriateness of law school or legal training for judges. The exercises outlined here are based on therapeutic techniques and draw on my experience as a therapist. Again, judges unwilling to explore these issues may not be appropriate candidates for judging.

When completed, the training should have accomplished three goals. First, it should help judges, legislators, or lawmakers be self-critical, both of their repressed histories, which signal their hidden personal differences, and of their legal training, which prevents them from embracing their own stories, let alone narratives of the Other. Second, the training should provide an opportunity for participants to understand how dynamics work: experiences of oppression are similar, only inverted, twisted, turned inside out; hearing others' experiences evokes personal histories. To make this process conscious is to reveal the legal countertransference that underpins current juridical psychodynamics. Third, such training should inspire each individual judge, lawmaker, or lawyer to develop a method for hearing the silence that this study reveals. Through mental checklists and/or computer forms, this training should teach participants to deliberately reveal what everyone would prefer to repress and to address it through exposure. Together, these training goals and deliberate methods should expose a penchant for prejudice and will enable adjudicators, lawmakers, and lawyers to use universal biases in a just and deliberate manner.

The current construction of impartiality and its overriding importance in the judicial hearing and decision-making process helps to explain not only why judges stereotype (there is no obvious mechanism for them to reflect on what they do) but also why they fail to accommodate claimants with special needs (the unconscious stereotyping prevents judges from engaging the claimants they reject due to stereotyping). Accommodation presupposes close attention and sensitivity to individual difference, and sensitivity implies involvement on an emotional level. Hence, the mandate for accommodation contradicts the current notion of impartiality, and as the mandate to accommodate expands, so does the tension between these two components of justice. This tension, as I have argued, may well explain why judges in my study had difficulty accommodating claimants with special needs and why stereotyping reveals itself in the way it does.

Together, the forces of postmodernism and psychoanalysis, critical and feminist studies, and multiculturalism render the current rationalistic legal system dysfunctional. This dysfunction provides the impetus for rethinking modernist approaches to impartiality and for building a system of adjudication that values not only reason and intellect but also passion and emotion, a passion and emotion that celebrate self-reflection and yearn to uncover the insidious ways bias hides in crevices and collects in corners. Given deeply embedded judicial or legalistic resistance to that emotion, only through externally imposed self-reflection, with mandated methods that reinforce it, can a legal system that respects all differences be constructed.

In sum, I argue that current notions of impartiality must be enlarged to embrace the inevitable presence of judicial emotion in the form of stereotyping in legal proceedings. Accommodation, as a concept and as a working principle, takes us closer to a form of justice that ensures that those who live at the margin are protected from stereotyping and that judges have the mind-set necessary to ensure a fair and open process.

New methods for judging vulnerable groups are urgently needed, given the disturbing history of these Social Security judges, who seemed largely incapable of judging the claims of vulnerable people. The synthesis of law and emotion, the marriage of distance and accommodation, and the recognition of bias in all forms is the only path in which the medieval maxim *corde creditur ad iustitiam* will be realized. In this vein, believing in the heart is the path to justice.

Notes

Introduction

1. For a recent discussion of a related issue, see 20 C.F.R. 410.670 (c) and Pear 1997. In this latest development, SSA is suggesting that ALJs follow agency policy even when it conflicts with circuit precedent, unless an Acquiescence Ruling has been issued authorizing ALJs to follow the circuit court decision. Remedial training and disciplinary action has been threatened for noncompliance with agency policy (Pear 1997). Acting President ALJ Ronald Bernoski (1997) of the Association of Administrative Law Judges, expressed concern over this matter at a congressional hearing on issues related to OHA backlogs and decisional inconsistencies.

2. There is some evidence that the presence of an SSA attorney would relieve ALJs of this complex burden. See, for example, GAO 1997.

3. It has been suggested that because these cases have been appealed, they are not representative of typical hearings or decisions. I am not contending that my case sample is representative, only that it reveals some of the dynamics that occur between ALJs and claimants.

4. More recent statistics reveal similar trends. Approximately 88 percent of the ALJs are men and approximately 90 percent are white (Balkus 1998).

Chapter 1

1. *Hallex* is not binding on judges; it communicates guiding principles and serves as a reference source. However, its significance should not be underestimated. When SSA developed its data collection form to test ALJ compliance with the rules, *Hallex* figured prominently in its hearings review process (SSA 1995, 1997).

Chapter 2

1. As part of its Disability Redesign Plan (see note 2), SSA is testing the use of a "predecision interview" with a claimant by a DDS examiner in an effort to increase consistency in decision making between DDS examiners and ALJs (GAO

1997). Apparently there is some evidence to suggest that a face-to-face interview positively affects ALJ award rates (GAO 1997).

2. For an overview of some of the incremental steps Social Security is or is proposing to take through its Redesign Plan, see Apfel (1998). For a critique of the Plan, see Mashaw 1996. For recent proposed or final rules relating to the hearings and appeals process, see 62 Fed. Reg. 48963 (18 September 1997); 62 Fed. Reg. 49598 (23 September 1997); and 62 Fed. Reg. 50266 (25 September 1997).

3. See *Cruz v. Califano,* Civ. No. 77-2234 (E.D. Pa. 1979), a class-action lawsuit, which required SSA to provide certain Social Security and SSI notices in Spanish to Spanish-speaking claimants to remedy the fact that they had received notices in English, which they were unable to read, and hence were unaware of their appeal rights and procedures. Notices are not available in languages other than English and Spanish, however, SSA personnel have suggested the need to develop strategies that address the particular needs of diverse communities with large numbers of non-English speaking applicants (NOSSCR 1995). Recent congressional action suggests that these special services, including Spanish-language notices may be eliminated in the near future (NOSSCR 1996).

4. ALJs have rendered increasingly higher percentages of favorable decisions over the years. In 1958, they granted 4.1 percent of the cases they heard. In 1967, they granted 13.9 percent. By 1965, they granted nearly 30 percent of the cases they heard. By 1970, they granted 44 percent (Dixon 1973, 40). In the 1980s, ALJs' favorable decisions rose to 50 percent (U.S. Senate 1982, 146–47). By 1993, ALJs on average granted 74 percent of the cases they heard (GAO 1997). More recently, ALJ allowance rates have decreased (NOSSCR 1998). For a discussion of this issue, see chapter 2.

5. The cases I rely on for support for this argument vary according to circuit. I have attempted to cite cases from as many jurisdictions as possible to ensure that my argument is derived from broad principles of law. Recently, Social Security has attempted to limit the application and relevance of federal court decisions by limiting ALJ reliance on circuit precedent. See 20 C.F.R. 410.670 (c); Pear 1997; see also Introduction, note 1.

6. The two cases cited are the most famous illustrations of this point. See also *Miranda v. Secretary of Health, Education and Welfare* 514 F.2d 996 (1st Cir. 1975); *Heggarty v. Sullivan* 947 F.2d 990 (1st Cir. 1991); *Cutler v. Weinberger* 516 F.2d 1282 (2d Cir. 1975); *DeChirico v. Callahan* 134 F.3d 1177 (2d Cir. 1998); *Jozefick v. Shalala* 854 F. Supp 342 (M.D. Pa. 1994); *Sims v. Harris* 631 F.2d 26 (4th Cir. 1980); *Craig v. Chater* 76 F.3d 585 (4th Cir. 1996); *Clark v. Schweiker* 652 F.2d 399 (5th Cir. 1981); *Lashley v. Secretary of Health and Human Services* 708 F.2d 1048 (6th Cir. 1983); *Born v. Secretary of Health and Human Services* 923 F.2d 1168 (6th Cir. 1990); *Smith v. Secretary of Health, Education and Welfare* 587 F. 2d 857 (7th Cir. 1978); *Nelson v. Apfel* 131 F.3d 1228 (7th Cir. 1997); *Sellars v. Secretary of Health, Education and Welfare* 458 F.2d 984 (8th Cir. 1972); *Shannon v. Chater* 54 F.3d 484 (8th Cir. 1995); *Cox v. Califano* 587 F.2d 988 (9th Cir. 1978); *Crane v. Shalala* 76 F.3d 251 (9th Cir. 1995); *Dixon v. Heckler* 811 F.2d 506 (10th Cir. 1987); *Hawkins v. Chater* 113 F.3d 1162 (10th Cir. 1997); *Cowart v. Schweiker* 662 F.2d 731 (11th Cir. 1981); *Graham v. Apfel* 129 F.3d 1420 (11th Cir. 1997).

See also *Hess v. Secretary of Health, Education and Welfare* 497 F.2d 837 (3d Cir. 1974); *Brock v. Chater* 84 F.3d 726 (5th Cir. 1996); and *Binion v. Shalala* 13 F.3d 243 (7th Cir. 1994) for relevant legal elaborations and distinctions.

7. For other relevant cases on this point, see *Cruz v. Schweiker,* 645 F.2d 812 (9th Cir. 1981); *DeLorme v. Sullivan* 924 F.2d 841 (9th Cir. 1991); *Thompson v. Sullivan,* 987 F.2d 1482 (10th Cir. 1993).

8. A legal mandate is not the only reason why judges should make a concerted effort to accommodate claimants with special needs; as officers of the court, it is judges' ethical and social obligation to enable claimants to tell their stories in an environment that does not stifle what often requires great effort for people with special needs to report (Durston and Mills 1996).

9. See note 6 for relevant citations.

Chapter 3

1. See, for example, *Shore v. Callahan* 977 F. Supp. 1075 (D. Or. 1997) for the kinds of problems applicants encounter with Chronic Fatigue Syndrome. See also NOSSCR 1998 for a general discussion of the issues applicants face when they allege these impairments.

2. The GAO gender-bias study (1994) confirmed that 20 years later, the same problems could be detected in the disability decision-making process—namely, that "women had occupations that, among older applicants, had lower allowance rates regardless of gender" (4).

3. For other descriptions and interpretations of gender bias in the Social Security system, see *Williams v. Shalala* 997 F.2d 1494 (D.C. Cir. 1993); see also Becker 1989; Coughenour, et al. 1994; Dubin, 1993; Golin 1995; Jackson and Deller-Ross 1996; Lee, Porath, and Schaffner 1994; Masson 1995; Zelenske and Udell 1994.

4. Mashaw's (1995–96) more recent work on administrative adjudication seems more compassionate to claimants. He acknowledges that certain "immutable adversities" persist in mass justice systems that make it difficult to pursue the often conflicting values of accuracy, timeliness, and fairness (22). He makes several suggestions, including the implementation of quality assurance programs that identify problems and seek solutions and the adherence to program values and principles rather than technical rules. These ideas support my thesis that judges should be held accountable for their hearing and decision-making practices. In addition, these notions acknowledge that we need much more than rules to ensure that an engaged adjudicatory process is pursued.

5. SSA's decision to peer review these cases suggests that they may be reluctant to address the issue of bias directly.

Chapter 4

1. In two of the fifty federal court cases, (Allen, 89-2788, IL and O'Connor, 89-4412, IL), claimants appealed their federal court decisions affirming the ALJ's denial of benefits to the Court of Appeals. The Court of Appeals' decisions were contained in the file folders with the federal court records.

2. It is interesting to note that the racial and ethnic backgrounds of the claimants were readily available in the record, either through identifiers in the medical records or through Social Security records documenting the need for a translator. There is therefore little doubt that adjudicators know the racial or ethnic make-up of the claimants' cases they are adjudicating.

3. The GAO (1989) compiled a statistical analysis of the national pool of disability applicants who had been denied benefits. I used these statistics to compare the national pool of denied applicants to my sample. These were the only statistics and characteristics available for comparison. The only other statistics SSA compiles and publishes are of the recipients and beneficiaries of Social Security benefits. Since my study is specifically designed to look at denied applicants, the most relevant comparison is with other denied applicants.

4. The term *other* is used by Social Security to designate all people of color except African Americans. I use this term only for the purposes of comparison.

5. I could find no current data on the variations of ALJ award rates. I base this conclusion on my own practice and on the experience of my colleagues who still represent disability applicants.

6. The GAO (1997) opines that one reason ALJs grant more cases than DDS examiners is that claimants are represented at hearings by attorneys who aggressively pursue new evidence that the judge considers. This finding suggests that claimants who are represented by counsel at the ALJ hearing level may have a higher likelihood of success on their claims. This would comport with my experience as an advocate.

7. ALJs seem particularly influenced by treating physician evidence. A study by the Social Security Administration (1995) reveals that a treating physician's report was one of five primary influences on the ALJ to award or deny benefits.

8. For a discussion of this and related issues, see chapter 2, note 3.

9. Federal court cases that have addressed the issue of retaining an attorney directly, include *Yother v. Secretary of Health and Human Services* 705 F.2d 460 (6th Cir. 1982); and *Binion v. Shalala* 13 F.3d 243 (7th Cir. 1994). For cases on the right to representation more generally, see *Heggarty v. Sullivan* 947 F.2d 990 (1st Cir. 1991) (per curiam); *Robinson v. Secretary of Health and Human Services* 733 F.2d 255 (2d Cir. 1984); *Dobrowolsky v. Califano* 909 F.2d 403 (3d Cir. 1979); *Brock v. Chater* 84 F.3d 726 (5th Cir. 1996) (per curiam); *Yother v. Secretary of Health and Human Services* 705 F.2d 460 (6th Cir. 1982); *Binion v. Shalala* 13 F.3d 243 (7th Cir. 1994); *Carter v. Chater* 73 F.3d 1019 (10th Cir. 1996); *Graham v. Apfel* 129 F.3d 1420 (11th Cir. 1997) (per curiam).

10. For similar cases on this point see *Thompson v. Sullivan* 933 F.2d 581 (7th Cir. 1991); *DeLorme v. Sullivan* 924 F.2d 841 (9th Cir. 1991).

11. See chapter 2, note 6 for support for this contention.

12. These materials are now disseminated to all ALJs through the Justice and Diversity Training Series, which gives ALJs sensitivity training on race and gender issues (Skoler 1994).

13. For a definitive work on the topic of the social and cultural significance of such terms, see Collins 1991, chap. 4, "Mammies, Matriarchs, and Other Control-

ling Images." My references to claimants as "Miss" and "Mrs." are consistent with their responses to questions regarding their marital status. When I am in doubt, I use "Ms."

14. This interpretation is based on my 10 years' experience as an attorney for Social Security disability claimants, during which time I supervised the processing of more than 500 cases.

15. For case law related to this point, see *Bosch v. Secretary of Health and Human Services* No. 85 CV 3536 (E.D.N.Y. 1988); *Holloway v. Heckler* 607 F. Supp. 71 (D. Kan. 1985).

16. For a sample of relevant cases supporting this contention, see *Ferraris v. Heckler* 728 F.2d 582 (2d Cir. 1984); *Murray v. Heckler* 722 F.2d 499 (9th Cir. 1983); *Brandon v. Bowen* 666 F. Supp 604 (S.D.N.Y. 1987); *Byron v. Heckler* 742 F.2d 1232 (10th Cir. 1984); *Reed v. Secretary of Health and Human Services* 804 F. Supp. 914 (E.D. Mich. 1992). See also *Allen v. Heckler* 749 F.2d 577 (9th Cir. 1984) for an argument limiting the application of *Murray v. Heckler.*

17. Deciding any case involves a dialectic between evidence and credibility: a claimant's credibility is inextricably intertwined in the evidence, and the evidence is influenced in the judge's mind by the claimant's credibility. This process is complex; however, for purposes of my analysis, it is important only to recognize that a give-and-take occurs between the two.

18. Several federal court cases address the issue of household chores. I am not arguing that daily activities are not relevant to the consideration of a claimant's ability to do paid work, but rather that the ability to do these chores does not necessarily translate to the ability to work. See for example, *Gold v. Secretary of Health, Education and Welfare* 463 F.2d 38 (2d Cir. 1972); *Leggett v. Chater* 67 F.3d 558 (5th Cir. 1995), *Light v. Social Security Administration* 119 F.3d 789 (9th Cir. 1997); *Orteza v. Shalala* 50 F.3d 748 (9th Cir. 1995); *Cavitt v. Schweiker* 704 F.2d 1193 (10th Cir. 1983); *Ragland v. Shalala* 992 F.2d 1056 (10th Cir. 1993); *Mullen v. Gardner* 256 F. Supp. 588 (E.D.N.Y. 1966); *Kelley v. Callahan* 113 F.3d 583 (8th Cir. 1998).

19. For other cases analyzing the use of the "sit and squirm" test, see *Aubeuf v. Schweiker* 649 F.2d 107 (2d Cir. 1981); *Van Horn v. Schweiker* 717 F.2d 871 (3d Cir. 1983); *Jenkins v. Sullivan* 906 F.2d 107 (4th Cir. 1990); *Spencer v. Schweiker* 678 F.2d 42 (5th Cir. 1982); *Weaver v. Secretary of Health and Human Services* 722 F.2d 310 (6th Cir. 1983); *Bishop v. Sullivan* 900 F.2d 1259 (8th Cir. 1990); *Teter v. Heckler* 775 F.2d 1104 (10th Cir. 1985); *Gay v. Sullivan* 986 F.2d 1336 (10th Cir. 1993); *Johns v. Bowen* 821 F.2d 551 (11th Cir. 1987); *Tyler v. Weinberger* 409 F. Supp. 776 (E.D. Va. 1976).

20. The sample sizes shift because only certain cases invoke each rule. For example, in some cases, ALJs did not make a negative credibility determination, denying the claim on other grounds, such as a failure to comply with prescribed treatment. In these cases, the rule was not relevant. In other cases, there were no extramedical factors to substantiate or validate the determination, rendering this aspect of the credibility rules irrelevant.

21. For a sample of relevant Social Security federal court cases, see note 19.

22. Mr. Tommie (89-4093, CA) served in Vietnam, and his alleged impairments stemmed from that military service. Based on my reading of the transcripts, no other service-related impairments were alleged.

23. The preference historically afforded ALJ applicants who are veterans has disproportionately filled the ALJ corps with men who previously served in the military (Verkuil et al. 1992). This factor could have some bearing on the proclivity of some judges to establish whether claimants have a history of military service. If military service influences judges' credibility determinations, there is little doubt that women are disadvantaged by this practice.

Chapter 5

1. The only other studies that have examined these issues are the DHQRP Reviews (SSA 1995, 1997; chap. 3). However, the SSA's findings did not do a detailed text analysis of the hearing and decision-making process. Instead, RJs found, in general terms, that ALJs did or did not protect claimants' rights or did or did not inform claimants of their right to representation.

2. For a sample of relevant cases on this issue, see chapter 4, note 10.

3. Based on my 10 years' experience representing disability claimants before the SSA, judges are reluctant to postpone hearings because of the pressure to process claims quickly. See also GAO 1997; SSA 1995, 1997, for recent discussions on OHA hearing and decision-making practices.

4. This contention is based on informal conversations with several ALJs regarding their objections to claimants who wished to postpone.

5. For a full discussion of this issue see chapter 2, note 6.

6. For other relevant cases on unrepresented applicants, see chapter 4, note 10.

Chapter 6

1. The 1994 amendments to the Social Security Act (P.L. 103–296) place a 36-month cap on disability benefits for people with addictions and require drug testing. The 1996 amendments to the Social Security Act (P.L. 104–121) eliminated benefits to people who allege drug or alcohol addictions unless claimants can prove an underlying or unrelated impairment (Mills and Arjo 1996).

2. Relevant cases on involuntariness and alcohol or drug addiction include *Arroyo v. Secretary of Health and Human Services* 932 F.2d 82 (1st Cir. 1991); *Rutherford v. Schweiker* 685 F.2d 60 (2d Cir. 1982); *Jones v. Sullivan* 954 F.2d 125 (3d Cir. 1991); *Matullo v. Bowen* 926 F.2d 240 (3d Cir. 1990) *King v. Califano* 599 F.2d 597 (4th Cir. 1979); *Neal v. Bowen* 829 F.2d 528 (5th Cir. 1987); *Smith v. Secretary of Health and Human Services* 893 F.2d 106 (6th Cir. 1989); *O'Connor v. Sullivan* 938 F.2d 70 (7th Cir. 1991); *Thompson v. Sullivan* 957 F.2d 611 (8th Cir. 1992); *Hardy v. Chater* 64 F.3d 405 (8th Cir. 1995); *Tylitzki v. Shalala* 999 F.2d 1411 (9th Cir. 1993); *Andrews v. Shalala* 53 F.3d 1035 (9th Cir. 1995); *Saleem v. Chater* 86 F.3d 176 (10th Cir. 1996).

3. See Rice 1992 for a discussion of codependency theory and its ramifications on people's lives.

4. In a similar case, another ALJ felt justified lecturing a claimant on her tobacco use (Moore, 89-6436, IL). Interestingly, at least one circuit court recognized the discrimination smokers encounter and reversed the decision of an ALJ who denied the claimant benefits due to her habit, on the grounds that her problems would not be relieved by quiting smoking (*Kelley v. Callahan* 133 F.3d 583 (8th Cir. 1998)).

5. See Link, Mirotznik, and Cullen 1991; Melton and Garrison 1987 for a discussion of the stigma people with mental disabilities experience and the stereotypical assumptions the larger culture holds. These attitudes are frighteningly consistent with Nagi's (1969) findings on the biases of judges in cases involving mental impairments. That these attitudes persist among judges thirty years later is disturbing.

6. A number of federal court cases recognize that educational levels achieved by claimants do not necessarily reflect their capacity to read and write. Toward this end, ALJs are encouraged to inquire into a claimant's literacy. See, for example, *Albrilton v. Sullivan* 889 F.2d 640 (5th Cir. 1989); *Wilcults v. Apfel* 143 F.3d 1134 (8th Cir. 1998); *Dollar v. Bowen* 821 F.2d 530 (10th Cir. 1987); *Wolfe v. Chater* 86 F.3d 1072 (11th Cir. 1996). For relevant definitions of literacy and related issues, see 20 C.F.R. 404.1564 (b) (1) and *Wolfe v. Chater* 86 F.3d 1072 (11th Cir. 1996).

7. See Schoultz 1986 for a discussion of the discrimination faced by people who are illiterate. The National Center for Education Statistics (1993) reported that adults who demonstrate limited reading skills describe themselves as reading or writing English well. Matthew Adams (1994) of the Student Coalition for Action in Literacy Education, confirmed the view that people who are illiterate will overestimate their ability rather than admit to their limitations.

8. See Mills 1993 for a more elaborate discussion of the issue of gender bias in Social Security decision making. See also U.S. Court of Appeals [Ninth Circuit] (1992, 1993); and chapter 3, notes 1–3, for other insight into the gender bias in the system.

9. For an insightful discussion of the social pressure, particularly on black women, to be attractive, see Collins 1991, chap. 4.

10. See chapter 4, note 19 for relevant case law prohibiting judges from basing their decisions on personal observations alone.

Chapter 7

1. Evidence of this dynamic was detected in the recent study of ALJ decision making (SSA 1995), which revealed that claimant credibility was one of five primary factors affecting ALJ award rates. Implicit in this finding is the assumption that credibility can also have a negative effect on ALJ decision making.

2. SSA could and should add to the DHQRP Data Collection Form explicit questions about the influence of bias on ALJ hearing and decision-making practices. See, for example, Mills 1993.

3. Some of these ideas come from the Justice and Diversity training I designed for OHA with Benchmark Institute, a continuing legal and leadership education training center in San Francisco, Calif.

Table of Claimants' Cases

The cases listed below form the database of hearings and decisions from which the substantive analysis is derived.

Acevedo, Maria. 87-2767, CA.
Alexander, Elwood. 90-1220, CA.
Allen, Bervin. 89-2788, IL.
Alva, Maria Luisa. 84-0617, CA.
Bell, George. 90-5548, IL.
Brown-Blick, Marion. 89-2659, CA.
Burr, Glendine. 87-10636, IL.
Costello, Frank. 88-7350, IL.
Curran, Katherine S. 88-2459, MA.
Davenport, Renee R. 89-1268, MA.
Davidson, Gerald. 88-4892, IL.
DeAlmeida, Jose R. 87-3402, CA.
Degryse, Linda. 88-2082, MA.
DeMeo, A. Louise. 90-10131, MA.
Diaz, Lauro. 86-20473, CA.
Flynn, Lawrence H. 88-9370, IL.
Forsyth, Claire. 99-1887, MA.
Foster, Benjamin. 89-3214, IL.
Galasso, Beatrice. 88-0280, MA.
Garcia, Maria D. 87-5693, CA.
Harner, Ruth. 86-4185, CA.
Harold, Eugene. 89-5168, IL.
Harper, John. 89-4374, IL.
Hereford, James. 90-1115, CA.

References

Adams, M. 1994. Interview by author. 30 March.

Alfieri, A. 1994. The ethics of violence: Necessity, excess, and opposition. *Columbia Law Review* 94:1721–50.

*American Jurisprudence.*1962. 2d ed. Rochester, N.Y.: Lawyers Co-operative Publishing.

American Psychiatric Association. 1994. *Diagnostic and Statistical Manual of Mental Disorders,* 4th ed. Washington, D.C.: American Psychiatric Association.

Apfel, K. 1998. Testimony. *Social Security: Issues Facing the Social Security Commissioner.* Washington, D.C.: House Ways and Means Committee, March 12.

Ayanian, J., and A. Epstein. 1991. Differences in the use of procedures between women and men hospitalized for coronary artery disease. *New England Journal of Medicine* 325:221–25.

Balkin, J. M. 1987. Deconstructive practice and legal theory. *Yale Law Journal* 96:743–86.

Balkus, R. 1998. EEO profile. OHA, ALJ. Faxed Communication. Falls Church, Va.: OHA.

Banks, T. L. 1990. Gender bias in the classroom. *Southern Illinois University Law Journal* 14:527–43.

Becker, M. E. 1989. Obscuring the Struggle: Sex Discrimination, Social Security, and Stone, Seidman, Sunstein & Tushnet's Constitutional Law. *Columbia Law Review* 89:264–88.

Bell, D. 1995. Racial realism. In *Critical Race Theory: The Key Writings That Formed the Movement,* ed. K. Crenshaw, N. Gotanda, G. Peller, and K. Thomas, 302–12. New York: New Press.

Bernoski, R. 1997. Testimony. *Social Security Oversight of the Disability Appeals Process.* Washington, D.C., House Ways and Means Committee, April 24.

Blendon, R. J., A. C. Scheck, K. Donelan, C. A. Hill, M. Smith, D. Beatrice, and D. Altman. 1995. How white and African Americans view their health and social problems. *Journal of American Medical Association* 273 (4): 341–46.

Brennan, W. 1988. Reason, passion, and "the progress of the law." *Cardozo Law Review* 10:3–23.

Burns, R. B., E. P. McCarthy, K. M. Freund, S. L. Marwill, M. Shwartz, A. Ash, and M. A. Moskowitz. 1996. Black women receive less mammography even with similar use of primary care. *Annals of Internal Medicine* 125 (3): 173–81.

Cardozo, B. 1921. *The Nature of the Judicial Process.* New Haven: Yale University Press.

Colameco, S., L. A. Becker, and M. Simpson. 1983. Sex bias in the assessment of patient complaints. *Journal of Family Practice* 16:1117–21.

Collins, P. H. 1991. *Black Feminist Thought: Knowledge, Consciousness and the Politics of Empowerment.* New York: Routledge.

Coughenour, J., P. Hug, M. Patel, T. Bird, and D. Hensler. 1994. The effects of gender in the federal courts; The final report of the ninth circuit gender bias task force. *Southern California Law Review* 67:745–1106.

Cover, R. M. 1986. Violence and the word. *Yale Law Journal* 95:1601–29.

Devine, P. 1989. Stereotypes and prejudice: Their automatic and controlled components. *Journal of Personality and Social Psychology* 56:5–18.

Dixon, R. 1973. *Social Security Disability and Mass Justice: A Problem in Welfare Adjudication.* New York: Praeger.

Dorris, M. 1989. *The Broken Cord.* New York: Harper and Row.

Dresser, R. 1992. Wanted: Single, white male for medical research. *Hastings Center Report* 22 (January–February): 24–29.

Dubin, J. C. 1993. Poverty, pain, and precedent: The Fifth Circuit's Social Security Jurisprudence. *St. Mary's Law Journal* 25:81–141.

Durston, L., and L. Mills. 1996. Toward a new dynamic in poverty client empowerment: The rhetoric, politics, and therapeutics of opening statements in Social Security disability hearings. *Yale Journal of Law and Feminism* 8:119–44.

Eliot, G. 1871/1992. *Middlemarch.* New York: Bantam.

Elliott, K., and D. Coker. 1991. Crack babies: Here they come, ready or not. *Journal of Instructional Psychology* 18:60–64.

Frug, M. J. 1992. *Postmodern Legal Feminism.* New York: Routledge.

GAO [U.S. General Accounting Office]. 1976. *The Social Security Administration Should Provide More Management and Leadership in Determining Who Is Eligible for Disability Benefits.* Washington, D.C.: General Accounting Office.

GAO. 1989. *Denied Applicants' Health and Financial Status Compared with Beneficiaries'.* Washington, D.C.: General Accounting Office.

GAO. 1992. *Racial Difference in Disability Decisions Warrants Further Investigation.* Washington, D.C.: General Accounting Office.

GAO. 1994. *Most of Gender Difference Explained.* Washington, D.C.: General Accounting Office.

GAO. 1997. *Social Security Disability: SSA Must Hold Itself Accountable for Continued Improvement in Decision-Making.* Washington, D.C.: General Accounting Office.

Golin, E. 1995. Solving the problem of gender and racial bias in administrative adjudication. *Columbia Law Review* 95:1532–67.

Goodrich, P. 1986. *Reading the Law: A Critical Introduction to Legal Method and Techniques.* Oxford: Blackwell.

Greene, L. 1997. Tokens, role models, and pedagogical politics: Lamentations of an African American Female Law Professor. In *Critical Race Feminism: A Reader,* ed. A. K. Wing, 88–95. New York: New York University Press.

Guinier, L., M. Fine, and J. Balin. 1997. *Becoming Gentlemen: Women, Law School, and Institutional Change.* Boston: Beacon.

Harrison, P., N. Hoffman, and G. Edwall. 1989. Sexual abuse correlates: Similarities between male and female adolescents in chemical dependency treatment. *Journal of Adolescent Research* 4:385–99.

Hulewat, P. 1996. Resettlement: A cultural and psychological crisis. *Social Work* 41 (2): 129–35.

Jackson, T. 1996. Lessons learned from a domestic violence prosecutor. In *Domestic Violence Law: A Comprehensive Overview of Cases and Sources,* by N. Lemon, 561–62. San Francisco: Austin and Winfield.

Jackson, V. C., and S. Deller-Ross. 1996. Report of the special committee on gender to the D.C. circuit task force on gender, race, and ethnic bias. *Georgetown Law Journal* 84:1657–1893.

Johnson, J., E. Whitestone, L. A. Jackson, and L. Gatto. 1995. Justice is still not colorblind: Differential racial effects of exposure to inadmissible evidence. *Personality and Social Psychology Bulletin* 21:893–98.

Jung, C. G. 1966. *The Practice of Psychology: Essays on the Psychology of Transference and Other Subjects.* Trans. R. F. C. Hull. New York: Pantheon.

Kennedy, D. 1992. Legal education as training for hierarchy. In *The Politics of Law,* ed. D. Kairys, 38–58. New York: Pantheon.

Kennedy, D. 1995. A cultural pluralist case for affirmative action in legal academia. In *Critical Race Theory: The Key Writings That Formed the Movement,* ed. K. Crenshaw, N. Gotanda, G. Peller, and K. Thomas, 159–200. New York: New Press.

King, G. 1992. Letter to Lawrence J. Thompson. In *Racial Difference in Disability Decisions Warrants Further Investigation,* by U.S. General Accounting Office. Washington, D.C.: General Accounting Office, 1992.

Kollmann, G. 1997. *Social Security: Recommendations of the 1994–1996 Advisory Council on Social Security.* Bethesda, Md.: Penny Hill Press.

Kozol, J. 1985. *Illiterate America.* Garden City, N.Y.: Anchor Press.

Krauskopf, J. 1994. Touching the elephant: Perceptions of gender issues in nine law schools. *Journal of Legal Education* 44:311–40.

Labaton, S. 1992. Benefits are refused more often to disabled blacks, study finds. *New York Times,* 11 May, A1.

Lahey, K. A. 1991. Reasonable women and the law. In *At the Boundaries of Law: Feminism and Legal Theory,* ed. M. A. Fineman and N. S. Thomadson, 3–21. New York: Routledge.

Lee, P. E., S. Porath, and J. E. Schaffner. 1994. Engendering Social Security disability determinations: The path of a woman claimant. *Tulane Law Review* 68:1477–1526.

Link, B., J. Mirotznik, and F. Cullen. 1991. The effectiveness of stigma coping orientations: Can negative consequences of mental illness labeling be avoided? *Journal of Health and Social Behavior* 32:302–20.

Llewellyn, K. 1962. *Jurisprudence: Realism in Theory and Practice.* Chicago: University of Chicago Press.

Macare, C. N., G. V. Bodenhausen, A. B. Milne, and J. Jetten. 1994. Out of mind but back in sight: Stereotypes on the rebound. *Journal of Personality and Social Psychology* 67:808–17.

Malow, R., J. West, J. Pena, and C. Lott. 1990. Affective and adjustment problems in cocaine and opioid addicts: Second annual symposium of the Society of Psychologists in Addictive Behaviors. *Psychology of Addictive Behaviors* 4:6–11.

Mashaw, J. L. 1983. *Bureaucratic Justice.* New Haven: Yale University Press.

Mashaw, J. L. 1995–1996. Unemployment compensation: Continuity, change, and the prospects for reform. *University of Michigan Journal of Law Reform* 29: 1–24.

Mashaw, J. L. 1996. Panel: The structure of government accountability: Reinventing government and regulatory reform. Studies in the neglect and abuse of administrative law. *University of Pittsburgh Law Review* 57:405–22.

Mashaw, J. L., C. Goetz, F. Goodman, W. Schwartz, P. Verkuil, and M. Carrow. 1978. *Social Security Hearings and Appeals.* Lexington, Mass.: Lexington Books.

Masson, E. M. 1995. Social Security Administration nonacquiescence on the standard for evaluating pain. *William and Mary Law Review* 36:1819–54.

Melton, G., and E. Garrison. 1987. Fear, prejudice, and neglect: Discrimination against mentally disabled persons. *American Psychologist* 42:1007–26.

Mills, L. 1988. The disability benefit applicant. Unpublished manuscript.

Mills, L. 1993. A calculus for bias: How malingering females and dependent housewives fare in the Social Security disability system. *Harvard Women's Law Journal* 16:211–32A.

Mills, L. 1996. On the other side of silence: Affective lawyering for intimate abuse. *Cornell Law Review* 86:1225–63.

Mills, L. 1997. Intuition and insight: A new job description for the battered woman's prosecutor and other more modest proposals. *UCLA Women's Law Journal* 7:183–99.

Mills, L. 1998. *The Heart of Intimate Abuse: New Interventions in Child Welfare, Criminal Justice, and Health Settings.* New York: Springer.

Mills, L., and A. Arjo. 1996. Slipping them a mickey: Disability benefits, substance addictions, and the (un)deserving poor. *Georgetown Journal on Fighting Poverty* 3:125–60.

Minow, M. 1990. *Making All the Difference: Inclusion, Exclusion, and American Law.* Ithaca: Cornell University Press.

Minow, M. 1995. Stripped down like a runner or enriched by experience: Bias and impartiality of judges and jurors. In *Courts and Justice: A Reader,* ed. G. L. Mays and P. R. Gregware, 366–87. Prospect Heights, Ill.: Waveland Press.

Minow, M., and E. Spelman. 1988. Passion for justice. *Cardozo Law Review* 10:37–76.

Mirvis, D. M., R. Burns, L. Gaschen, F. T. Cloar, and M. Graney. 1994. Variation in utilization of cardiac procedures in the Department of Veteran Affairs health care system: Effect of race. *Journal of the American College of Cardiology* 24 (5): 1297–1304.

Naffine, N. 1990. *Law and the Sexes: Explorations in Feminist Jurisprudence.* Sydney: Allen and Unwin.

Nagi, S. 1969. *Disability and Rehabilitation: Legal, Clinical, and Self-Concepts and Measurements.* Columbus: Ohio State University Press.

National Center for Education Statistics. 1993. *Adult Literacy in America.* Washington, D.C.: Educational Testing Service.

NOSSCR (National Organization of Social Security Claimant's Representatives). 1995. *Social Security Forum.* November. Midland Park, N.J.: NOSSCR.

NOSSCR. 1996. *Social Security Forum.* April. Midland Park, N.J.: NOSSCR.

NOSSCR. 1997. *Social Security Forum.* April. Midland Park, N.J.: NOSSCR.

NOSSCR. 1998. *Social Security Forum.* April. Midland Park, N.J.: NOSSCR.

Obiora, L. A. 1996. Neither here nor there: Of the female in American legal education. *Law and Social Inquiry* 21:355–432.

Padilla, A., R. Cervantes, M. Maldonado, and R. Garcia. 1988. Coping responses to psychological stressors among Mexican and Central American immigrants. *Journal of Community Psychology* 16:418–27.

Pear. R. 1997. U.S. challenges courts on disabilities. *New York Times,* 21 April, B9.

Peller, G. 1985. The metaphysics of American law. *California Law Review* 73: 1151–1290.

Redman, S., F. Webb, D. Hennrikus, J. Gordon, and R. Sanson-Fisher. 1991. The effects of gender on diagnosis of psychological disturbance. *Journal of Behavioral Medicine* 14:527–40.

Resnik, J. 1988. On the bias: Feminist reconsiderations of the aspirations for our judges. *Southern California Law Review* 61:1877–1944.

Rice, J. 1992. Discursive formation, life stories, and the emergence of co-dependency: "Power/knowledge" and the search for identity. *Sociological Quarterly* 33:337–64.

Rothblum, E., P. Brand, C. Miller, and H. Oetjen. 1990. The relationship between obesity, employment discrimination, and employment-related victimization. *Journal of Vocational Behavior* 37:251–66.

Saldena, D. H. 1995. Acculturative stress: Minority status and distress. In *Hispanic Psychology: Critical Issues in Theory and Research,* ed. A. M. Padilla, 43–54. Thousand Oaks, Calif.: Sage.

Scales, A. 1986. The emergence of feminist jurisprudence: An essay. *Yale Law Journal* 95:1373–1402.

Schoultz, C. O. 1986. Reading between the lines: The high cost of ignorance. *Training and Development Journal* 40:44–47.

Singer, J. 1988. Legal realism now. *California Law Review* 76:465–544.

Skoler, D. 1994. Fighting racial bias: How one federal agency confronted the problem. *Human Rights* (September): 18–21.

Smart, J. F., and D. W. Smart. 1995. Acculturative stress of Hispanics: Loss and challenge. *Journal of Counseling & Development* 73 (4): 390–96.

Snow, J. T., and M. B. Harris. 1985. Maintenance of weight loss: Demographic, behavioral, and attitudinal correlates. *Journal of Obesity and Weight Regulation* 4:234–55.

SSA (U.S. Social Security Administration). 1981. Office of Research and Statistics. *Consistency of Initial Disability Decisions among and within States.* Washington D.C.: U.S. Department of Health and Human Services, Social Security Administration.

SSA. 1992. Office of Hearings and Appeals. Office of Training. *Hallex: Hearings, Appeal and Litigation Law Manual for ALJs: Administrative Law Judge Hearings.* Vol. 1, div. 2. Baltimore, Md.: U.S. Department of Health and Human Services, Social Security Administration.

SSA. 1993. Office of Hearings and Appeals. *Training materials.*

SSA. 1995. Office of Program and Integrity Reviews. *Findings of the Disability Hearings Quality Review Process.* Washington, D.C.: SSA Pub. No. 30–013.

SSA. 1996–1997 (December 28–March 28). Office of Hearings and Appeals. *Case Control System. Summary of Involvement at Hearings.*

SSA. 1997. Office of Program and Integrity Reviews. *Findings of the Disability Hearings Quality Review Process.* Washington, D.C.: SSA Pub. No. 30–013.

SSA. 1998. Office of Hearings and Appeals. *OHA Case Control System. Profile of Participant Involvement at Hearings Held. Highlights for Fiscal Year 1997.*

Steingart, R., M. Packer, P. Hamm, M. E. Coglianese, and B. Gersh. 1991. Sex differences in the management of coronary artery disease. *New England Journal of Medicine* 325:226–30.

Stone, D. 1984. *The Disabled State.* Philadelphia: Temple University Press.

Swent, J. F. 1996. Gender bias at the heart of justice: An empirical study of state task forces. *Southern California Review of Law and Women's Studies* 6 (1): 1–87.

Taibi, A. 1990. Frontier of legal thought III: Note: Politics and due process: The rhetoric of social security disability law. *Duke Law Journal,* 913–66.

Thomas, T. N. 1995. Acculturative stress in the adjustment of immigrant families. *Journal of Social Distress and the Homeless* 4 (2): 131–42.

Tolchin, M. 1989. Judges who decide Social Security claims say agency goads them to deny benefits. *New York Times,* 8 January, I, 16.

Trope, Y., and E. Thompson. 1997. Looking for truth in all the wrong places? Asymmetric search for individuating information about stereotyped group members. *Journal of Personality and Social Psychology* 73:229–41.

Unger, R. 1983. *The Critical Legal Studies Movement.* Cambridge, Mass.: Harvard University Press.

Unger, R., and M. Crawford. 1992. *Women and Gender: A Feminist Psychology.* New York: McGraw-Hill.

U.S. Court of Appeals [Ninth Circuit]. 1992. *The Preliminary Report of the Ninth Circuit Gender Bias Task Force.* Seattle, Wash.: U.S. Ninth Circuit Court.

U.S. Court of Appeals [Ninth Circuit]. 1993. *The Effects of Gender in the Federal Courts: The Final Report of the Ninth Circuit Gender Bias Task Force.* Seattle, Wash.: U.S. Ninth Circuit Court.

U.S. House. 1994. Committee on Ways and Means. *Green Book: Background*

Material and Data on Programs within the Jurisdiction of the Committee on Ways and Means. Washington, D.C.: Committee on Ways and Means.

U.S. Senate. 1978. Committee on Ways and Means. Subcommittee on Social Security. *Disability Adjudication Structure.* Washington, D.C.: U.S. Government Printing Office.

U.S. Senate. 1982. Committee on Finance. *Staff Data and Materials Related to the Social Security Disability Insurance Program.* Washington, D.C.: U.S. Government Printing Office.

U.S. Senate. 1992. Select Committee on Aging. *Insurmountable Barriers: Lack of Bilingual Services at Social Security Administration Offices.* Washington, D.C.: U.S. Government Printing Office.

Verkuil, P., D. Gifford, C. Koch, R. Pierce, and J. Lubbers. 1992. *The Federal Administrative Judiciary.* Washington, D.C.: Administrative Conference of the United States.

von Hippel, W., D. Sekaquaptewa, and P. Vargas. 1995. On the role of encoding processes in stereotype maintenance. In *Advances in Experimental Social Psychology,* ed. M. P. Zanna, 177–254. New York: Academic Press.

Wadden, T., and A. Stunkard. 1987. Psychopathology and obesity. *Annals of the New York Academy of Sciences* 499:55–65.

Whittle, J., J. Conigliaro, C. B. Good, and R. Lofgren. 1993. Racial differences in the use of invasive cardiovascular procedures in the Department of Veterans' Affairs medical system. *New England Journal of Medicine* 329:621–27.

Williams, P. 1995. *The Rooster's Egg: On the Persistence of Prejudice.* Cambridge, Mass.: Harvard University Press.

Wills, D. 1997. Domestic violence: The case for aggressive prosecution. *UCLA Women's Law Journal* 7:173–82.

Zelenske, E., and D. Udell. 1994. Defining and addressing ALJ bias and unfitness in the Social Security system. *Clearinghouse Review* (April): 1460–1468. Los Angeles: National Senior Citizens Law Center.

Zipursky, B. 1990. Deshaney and the jurisprudence of compassion. *New York Law Review* 65:1101–47.

Table of Codes, Regulations, Rulings, and Rules

Table of Cases

Index